RISING FROM
HISTORY

U.S. CATHOLIC THEOLOGY
LOOKS TO THE FUTURE

RISING FROM
HISTORY

U.S. CATHOLIC THEOLOGY
LOOKS TO THE FUTURE

Edited by Robert J. Daly

The Annual Publication of the
College Theology Society
1984

Volume 30

UNIVERSITY
PRESS OF
AMERICA

LANHAM • NEW YORK • LONDON

Annual Publication • 30

Copyright © 1987 by

The College Theology Society

University Press of America,® Inc.

4720 Boston Way
Lanham, MD 20706

3 Henrietta Street
London WC2E 8LU England

Printed in the United States of America

Co-published by arrangement with
The College Theology Society

Typeset at Saint Joseph's University Press, Philadelphia

Library of Congress Cataloging-in-Publication Data

Rising from history.

   (The Annual publication of the College Theology
Society ; v. 30 (1984))
   Includes bibliographies and index.
   1. Catholic Church—Doctrines—History—Congresses.
2. Catholic Church—United States—Doctrines—History—
Congresses. I. Daly, Robert J., 1933-   . II. Series:
Annual publication of the College Theology Society ;
v. 30.
BX1747.R57   1987   230'.273   87-2011
ISBN 0-8191-6155-1 (alk. paper)
ISBN 0-8191-6156-X (pbk. : alk. paper)

All University Press of America books are produced on acid-free
paper which exceeds the minimum standards set by the National
Historical Publication and Records Commission.

TABLE OF CONTENTS

IV. NEW VISIONS AND CHALLENGES

PREFACE

This collection of essays, representing a selection of the papers presented at the 1984 national convention of the College Theology Society held at Cardinal Stritch College in Milwaukee, continues the work of reflection on foundational theological issues which has characterized the recent meetings and publications of this Society.

Organizing this volume around the convention's theme, "The Future," presented some special challenges. (1) Would it be possible to bring order and coherence to a theme so vast and open-ended? (2) Could a coherent unity be found among the rich variety of papers submitted to the editor? In the end, attention focused on the second question when, aided by the recommendations of the various section coveners of the convention, the editor was able to detect a unifying theme: history. Theoretically, this should not surprise; within a *Weltanschauung* which is linear rather than cyclical, creational/incarnational rather than radically spiritualized, the future is never very far from the past and the present.

That this collecion answers the second rather than the first question means, however, that the house our key opens is not a complete, perfectly proportioned mansion. But it does have a structure and a unity. *Rising from History* describes the kind of house it is, and *U.S. Catholic Theology Looks to the Future* are apt words to inscribe over its portal. They who choose to enter will be able to find their way comfortably, will find it a good place in which to dwell for a while.

Part One, RISING FROM HISTORY, has two essays, one general and one particular. In the first, Nathan Kollar's "The End and the Future," locating its reflections in the context of the contemporary resurgence of religious apocalyptic thinking and feeling, systematically surveys and interrelates the various attitudes toward the end and the future which have characterized the great religions of the world.

Then David O'Brien's "Choosing Our Future: American Catholicism's Precarious Prospects" focuses our attention on the particular situation of the U.S. Catholic church as it rises from its multi-faceted past, struggles with a complex present, and gropes with uncertain tread towards an unpredictable future. If there is a unifying thread (and with that, an implicit program) coursing through the myriad of events, persons, movements and projects detailed by O'Brien, then it is the challenge--always present in the church's history but now especially strong since Vatican II's Constitution on the Church in the Modern World--not to evade the tensions inherent in the relationship of church and world.

Part Two, AMERICANISM: THE PAST AND THE FUTURE gathers the reflections of four scholars who, for considerably more than a decade, have been reflecting on that episode of American Catholic history (1884-1899) known as Americanism. William Portier in "The Future of Americanism," introduces the episode as "a case study in the relationship between Catholicism and American culture." He then goes on in "Two Generations of American Catholic Expansionism in Europe: Isaac Hecker and John J. Keane," to provide a nuanced study of the relationship between Hecker, founder of the Paulists, and Archbishop John J.Keane. It may be too much to call them "Americanist prototype and disciple," but neither is Hecker's profound influence on Keane to be minimized.

Thomas Wangler's "Myth, Worldviews and Late Nineteenth Century American Catholic Expansionism" studies Americanism "as a reform movement seeking to impose upon the European Catholic church an Americanized catholicism." In doing so, Wangler gives special attention to the worldviews of Hecker and the three major Americanist advocates: Archbishop John Ireland of St. Paul, Bishop John Keane, founding rector of the Catholic University of America, and Msgr. Denis O'Connell, rector of the North American College in Rome.

Robert Ayers in "The Americanist Attack on Europe in 1897 and 1898" then traces the activities of the major Americanist advocates in the last two years before Leo XIII's fateful condemnation.

In response to Portier, Wangler and Ayers, Margaret Reher calls poignant attention to the Americanists' failure to read judiciously the "signs of the times," to their somewhat naive attempt to "catholicize" the American dream and export it to Europe, and points out the striking parallels between that situation and the one currently facing the American Catholic church

Part Three, WHAT HAS BEEN AND WILL BE, contains five essays, each of which takes up a different aspect of Christian theology and life. Joseph Merkt's "The Discovery of the Genetic Development of Thomas Aquinas' Theology of Hope and Its Relevance for a Theology of the Future" shows that Aquinas' theology of hope is far more complex, far richer than Moltmann's criticism assumed, and that it possesses broad ramifications for political theology, liberation theology, and even developmental psychology.

In "Re-Conceiving the Trinity as Mystery of Salvation," Catherine LaCugna pursues the Rahnerian axiom of the identity between the 'economic' trinity and the 'immanent' trintiy in an attempt to restore trinitarian faith to the center of Christian doctrine and spirituality.

The transcendental thinking of recent theologians such as Lonergan and Rahner provides Denise Lardner Carmody in her "Feminist Spirituality as Self-Transcendence" with a base from which to sketch out a spirituality which is faithfully Christian, does not evade the pervasive negative experience of sexism, and still looks ahead to the future with optimism.

The presidential address of Rodger Van Allen, "The Chicago Declaration and the Call to Holy Worldliness" reviews the rich discussion that followed upon that December 1977 statement. It is a particular instance of the U.S. church's attempt to be faithful to the tension between church and world. The question of the role of the laity in the church is Van Allen's point of entry; the answer, he suggests, is a far more adequate appropriation of the New Testament doctrine of universal priesthood.

The final article in this section, "Becoming Peacemakers: Moral Perspectives for Dwelling in Peace" by J. Milburn Thompson suggests four particular "moral movements" which should characterize our efforts towards a peaceful transformation of ourselves and our society: "from macho-militarism to feminist humanism, from deceit to truth, from American justice to biblical justice, and from indifference to transforming initiatives."

Part Four, NEW VISIONS AND CHALLENGES moves from spirituality to feminism to computer ethics. James Bacik's "A Spirituality for the Future: Situational and Systematic" draws upon his own experience as a spiritual director as well as the analytical perspectives of Karl Rahner in order to outline two quite different paths, the one situational and free-flowing, the other systematic and structured, which different persons, depending on their circumstances, may need to follow in order to achieve self-transcending union with God and neighbor.

Frances Leap's "Feminist Movement: The Ethics of Revolution" is the most visionary piece in this collection. Consciously choosing to speak of religious feminism prescriptively (i.e., what it ideally is and should be) rather than descriptively, she goes on to speak of feminism as essentially movement, indeed cosmic movement, in which all creation, all persons, are struggling for freedom and fullness.

The final essay of the section, Edward Stevens' "Computer Ethics: Types of Issues being Raised" outlines some of the technological situations which will ever more pervasively control the concrete ways in which we and our society will move toward the future.

ACKNOWLEDGEMENTS

The College Theology Society is proud to issue *Rising From History*, the 30th number in its **ANNUAL PUBLICATION SERIES**. The contents of the volume took life at the Society's Annual Meeting which was held from May 31 to June 3, 1984 at Cardinal Stritch College in Milwaukee, WI. On behalf of the officers and national board members, I express our sincere gratitude to all those who contributed to this highly successful meeting. In particular, we appreciated the Franciscan hospitality extended by Sister Camille Kliebhan, O.S.F., the college's president.

We also express heartfelt thanks to Mary L. Schneider of Michigan State University for her work as the convention coordinator and to Lucille Walsh of Cardinal Stritch College, who served as the local chairperson.

Robert Daly, of Boston College, has done a fine job in editing this important book. The chairperson of the committee of research and publication, Robert Masson of Marquette University, and the committee's managing editor, Joseph Gower of Saint Joseph's University, deserve thanks for their work in overcoming obstacles in bringing this book to completion. This is the first of the **ANNUAL PUBLICATION SERIES** to be co-published with University Press of America. Along with **CTS RESOURCES IN RELIGION**, **CTS STUDIES IN RELIGION**, and **CTS REPRINTS IN RELIGION**, this brings all our series under the imprint of a single press. Special acknowledgement is made of the services rendered by Molly Carroll and Carmen Croce of Saint Joseph's University Press and by Terri Boddorff and Jed Lyons of University Press of America.

Rodger Van Allen, President
College Theology Society
Villanova University

I.
RISING FROM HISTORY

THE END AND THE FUTURE

Nathan R. Kollar

THE END: NO FUTURE?

Today's world includes many who have no future. Many who have abandoned hope for any future for themselves or the world they live in. The reason for this abandonment of the future is the absolute conviction that the world will end. No matter what one's religion, there are many who look at "the bomb" in hopeless terror; at over-population in frigid fear; at pollution with agonizing indecision. For these people there is no future and the end is near.

Secular apocalyptic horsemen daily ride the air waves proclaiming with voices of doom that the end is near. The message of these T.V. horror shows gains even further support from members of the academic and scientific community who in best-sellers and weighty tomes proclaim: "No more. All of this, no more!"

The secular world ultimatized in many contemporary religions finds its echo in a large number of fundamentalist groups whether Christian, Islamic, or Jewish. From their perspective these promised secular disasters are the hand of God bringing to an end a disastrous and sinful era.

But what of these ends? Whether in secular or supernatural terms, is there any way for us to understand these people rather than respond to them solely out of base fear? This essay provides a way of understanding all these promised catastrophies.

The ability to imagine, to abstract, to work purposefully is our human blessing and curse: our blessing, because these abilities enable us to produce the works of art and technology which dot our landscape; our curse, because these same abilities force us to recognize the fact that everything we do will end; everything we have done will disappear. The technological age participates in the blessing and curse. Some see this age as producing a new world limited only by our creative imagination. Others see the technological age as the last age of earth, when life itself will be annihilated. In either of these cases technology is a symbol of both beginning and end: an end to this world and a beginning of another. Technology may be a new symbol but expectations of radical change in the world order are not new. People have lived with these expectations since the beginning of the world: individuals have expected the world to end and lived in the light of that expectation. We have much to learn from those who have lived and labored with the realization that all they do will disappear. In this paper I will briefly describe modern technology as symbolic of the end, examine the myths and stories of the end in the major world

4

religions in order to understand their common themes, and finally suggest a common element in all descriptions of the end which is necessary for understanding those prophets of technological disaster and the end of the world.[1]

Technology: Symbol of the End: Apocalypse and/or Utopia

Human technology is subject to the radical diversity of good and evil found in human nature. Of itself it is neutral. As a human instrument it can produce both good and evil. To "enhance life" in this the technological age, we must look to the vision of those humans who deal with the various technologies. Do they/we forsee modern technolgy as enhancing the present life? What qualities will it enhance? Are these desirable qualities? Are they/we optimistic or pessimistic about the end of the human race? The most basic question is that of our end or goals. What is our end? Can we achieve it by ourselves? Must we be aided by a force or cause beyond ourself? A God? Nature? History? Does our end or goal occur suddenly in an apocalypse? Perhaps it occurs gradually, in a utopian manner? What should we expect? Strive for? What is best for us and the world: to continue as we are, to end it all, to develop a new better life? Will modern technology and the age it initiated bring utopia or apocalypse? Unless we ask the question of apocalypse or utopia we speak of the quality of life without looking at goals. The result of not inquiring into our goals is to deepen that professional instrumentalism which looks to *how* to change life without a concept of *why* we should change. The result of such professionalism is a type of psychic numbing which finds people going about their daily tasks unaware of what is or will happen to them. Lacking the imagination to forsee a "why" or goal for life, they are afraid to wake up. If they do awaken they will see six possible scenarios for modern technology.

Modern technology if succesful, can bring about:[2]
1) Apocalypse with utopia. The world will be destroyed during the technological age but the world which rises from the rubble will be the best possible one.
2) Apocalypse with dystopia. The world will be destroyed during the technological age and a world more evil than the present will rise from the rubble.
3) Utopia without an apocalypse. The new, perfect life comes about as a consequence of the technological age without the destruction of the material world that we know. Instead there is a radical shift in the relationship between humanity and nature such that a perfect world results.
4) Dystopia without an apocalypse. Without the destruction of the world as we know it, humanity deepens the present evil during the technological age to

produce the deepest chaos possible and still retain human life.
5) Total annihilation of all materiality.
6) The technological age gives way to another age which assumes modern technology and its consequent mentality into itself.

Technology easily becomes a symbol in which we see mirrored our individual and communal values. In describing the technological age and imagining its end, we sketch our understanding of the present difficulties of both individual and society. In speaking about the age of technolgy, we speak, through our fears and hopes, of an idealized world -- one where the traumatic choices of this age need not be made and people live a better life. A symbol always manifests something of itself and ourself. Symbols such as our car, our mode of dress, our language, our interaction rituals, our very body exemplify this manifestation. The technological age is symbolic as these items just mentioned are symbolic. Yet it is a new symbol that is difficult to grasp in its complexity. If we look at the way other ages and the literature they produced symbolized the end, we may be able to learn something of ourselves and what is required in our age.

Other Symbols of the End and their Basic Themes

Many people abandon hope for the future when faced with their own death -- the end of their individual life, the "I". The technological age, as a symbol of the end, forces us to examine the end of communal life, the "we". Actually the individualism of personal survival is a late development in human history. This "we" question has a longer history than the "I" question.[3] The historical development of the idea of individual after-life demonstrates a time when people began to ask the question, "Will I survive?" rather than "Will we survive?" The response to the question was "yes." Within the last four hundred years, however, the survival of the individual after biological death has been questioned by the majority of thinkers. As the "scientific" methodology came to dominate all ways of searching for the truth, the question of individual other-worldly immortality was increasingly answered, "no" or "we do not know." Implicit in these responses was a reference to other types of this-worldly survival listed by Lifton,[4] for instance, as immortality in family, work or nature. This kind of immortality presupposes the continuance of a world where our work or family can exist. The advent of modern technology, and in particular nuclear technology, threatens these types of this-worldly communal immortality with the same response as was formerly given to individual survival: "No, we will not survive," or "We do not know if we will." The modern person faces complete annihilation of both the individual and the world.

The response to these questions of annihilation can be found among the world's religions. Various story writers and theologians of these religions have thought and imagined about the end for thousands of years. Their answers are varied, yet an examination of their views presents the same six options of the end which we discerned in the technological age. By looking at the visions of life inherent among religionists perhaps we can gain a glimpse of our own vision for at least what is needed in this the age of technology.

The variety and descriptions of this world's end are limited only by human imagination. A total categorization of them is impossible yet there are some categories common to all visions of the end: time, event, cause and consequences. To understand these categories we must first understand the vocabulary and literature they are derived from.

Basic Literature and Vocabulary of the End

The consideration of the end in religious literature is described as eschatological.[5] Eschatology is concerned with the last things, the end, of the individual person (personal eschatology) or of the whole race (collective eschatology). We are concerned with collective eschatology. The eschatological description may be historical, i.e. this is actually what happened and what can be expected to happen within a perspective of time which had a beginning and will have an end; cyclical, i.e. this is a description of the rhythms of the universe which have a meaning beyond themselves but will continue to undulate forever. We are interested in historical and cyclic eschatology.

The end may be expected at any moment in this the last-stage apocalyptic eschatology; or the end may be difficult to discern because it is the result of a slow evolutionary process resulting in a good life for all (utopian eschatology) or an evil life for all, a dystopian eschatology. We are interested especially in apocalyptic and utopian eschatology because these two types of literature were common ways of describing the end and are the descriptions we must depend upon for our understanding of how the human race has faced its possible extinction in previous ages.

Apocalypse is a species of eschatology in which there is not only a general consciousness of living in the last stage of history but that this last stage itself is going to end shortly. This type of writing either interprets current events to move people to act or gives validity to the present by placing the present in the role of bringing about the end. Apocalyptic writing avoids univocal meanings, the appeal of apocalyptic stories is the conviction that time is related to eternity; that history has a discernable structure and meaning in relation to its end and that the end is a product not of change but of divine plan. Apocalyptic literature in the technological age gives this security to those who see it as an authentic description of present and future life.

Apocalyptic texts from various religious backgrounds and ages display family resemblances[6] in key areas that include: first, a sense of the unity and structure of history conceived as a divinely predetermined totality; second, pessimism about the present and conviction of its imminent crisis; and third, belief in the proximate judgment of evil and triumph of the good, the element of vindication for the author's beliefs. This vindication can take many forms: this worldly or otherworldly, individual or collective, temporary or definitive or a combination of some or all of these elements.

There are a few famous types of eschatology which are constantly in the news. They are, for the most part, associated with fundamentalist Christian groups.

These are the millenarian eschatologies of premillenarianism, postmillenarianism and amillenarianism. Millenarianism or chiliasm is the belief among some Christians that Jesus will establish a kingdom on earth for a thousand year period. Premillenialists believe that Jesus will return suddenly upon the fullfilment of certain conditions. These conditions vary a great deal amongst believers. A post millenarist believes that Christ will come and then the thousand year period will begin. Amillenarists do not take the thousand year idea literally and believe that we are in the millenium now but Christ will come at the end of it. All millenarianists agree that Jesus will come personally, visibly and with great glory. They disagree as to when, how and how many times he will come.[7]

Utopian literature[8] also reflects a specific meaning and common themes. There are various meanings of the term itself: it is a literary genre, a constitution for a perfectly scientific foundation for a universal republic. But at the heart of all of these lies the myth of a heaven on earth which is utopia.

The foundational images and types of Utopia were nutured by two fonts: (1) the Judaeo-Christian which looked forward to a paradise created with the world and destined to endure beyond it; (2) the Hellenic, an ideal beautiful city built by human beings without the assistance, and often in defiance, of the gods. We see both of these traditions come together in More's Utopia and in those developments since then which find Utopia as more than an island but a program of life.

These understandings of the end, both Christian and non-Christian can be better understood by looking at their concepts of time, the event itself, and the cause of the end and the consequences upon the world and humans on the end of the world.

Time

When we speak of the end of the world we are faced with the basic question of existence and non-existence, what the theologian Paul Tillich called metaphysical shock.[9] *We* are; is it possible that *We* cannot be? Few religions would suggest that the annihilation of this world would be such that there would be *nothing*. Philosophers, following the intuition of religious myth, suggest that to even imagine "nothing" we must make it "something". Essentially non-being, not being, is just that, a negation of being, a taking away of all existence. This is beyond experience and imagination. We cannot imagine "nothing". We experience individual cessation of being in death, but there is still evident to the senses the corpse, and perhaps to faith, a resurrection, immortality, nirvana, or re-incarnation.

Gnosticism is the only religion which comes close to imagining the end as non-being when it claims all materiality will disappear to leave the spirit alone existing. Aside from Gnosticism all other religions are optimistic as to the continuation of the material world, even though some may see materiality as the source of evil and suffering.[10]

The Western religions of Judaism, Christianity, and Islam, have a positive view of materiality and a linear concept of time. Whether the end will be sudden, so there will be an evident moment of complete change or whether it will be gradual, so we cannot be sure when the new life has begun -- Western religions acknowledge that the world is going toward an end and once it ends there will be a new, happier world. The technological age could be a symbol of the advent of a new life either through total destruction of this world or through the gradual creation of a new one. The technological age could symbolize apocalypse or utopia to the Western religions.

This is quite different from another view of time and of the end. Eastern religions such as Hinduism and Buddhism conceive of the end of the world as never occuring. Time is circular, the end of one cycle is actually the beginning of another. Thus contemporary technology may be seen as a symbol of the end in as much as it destroys this world, which has become as evil as possible, to begin another cycle with a world of primitive goodness which, in turn, would also end in worldwide evil and destruction.

In Buddhism and Hinduism imaginative chronological systems have been worked out comprising periods of 12,000 years (mahayugas), each year of which represents 360 human years. In turn 100 mahayugas make up one kalpa, or one day in the life of Brahma, and span the duration of a world from its creation to its destruction. After a period of quiescence, the world would be re-created by Brahma for another kalpa.

The views of time as either a straight, purposeful line or as a circular, repetitious, wheel are two distinct views of the end which have become part of the sacred world of the classical religions as well as the secular world of humanistic religion. Both views seem well founded in human experience of time itself either as a part of the rhythms of life or as something beyond our control, advancing no matter what we do or attempt. These views of time in the religions as well as in experience affect our expectations and descriptions of the end.

The influence of these views can be seen in an oft expressed scenario of the end of the age of technology. Our inability to handle the instruments of our imagination results in our destruction of the world. The world is destroyed either totally or in part. In either case humanity as we know it would have to begin over again. Whether those remnant humans would be happy or not would be left to the norms of happiness implicit in the value system of the apocalyptic writer describing the end of this age. Many readers of this volume are writing their own apocalypse as they describe the future.

Futurologists in the West also look forward many times to linear change. In perhaps a utopian manner, they use their research, statistics and purposeful planning to forsee a new life in continuity with this one. Again, this new life must be evaluated through an instrumentality beyond statistics and research. Their good life must be examined for its quality, not its mere existence beyond the various threats provided by technology. The quality of life demands an (e)valuation. A schema of many of the religious views which does this would be the following.

THE END: RELIGIONS AND TEMPORALITY: VISIONS OF THIS END-TIME[11]

Eastern Religions	General Meaning of the Present Age		
Little emphasis upon time.	**Hinduism** A symbol of human's general illusion arising from ignorance.	**Hinayana Buddhism** The same as Hinduism.	**Mahayana Buddhism** It is illusory yet the events of this age provide us with an opportunity to show compassion.
World & Humanity: eternal uncreated			
	Taoism Part of the ever changing process in which the harmony & unity of the Tao is present.	**Confucianism** An opportunity to restore the basic harmony of the universe which existed of old.	**Shinto** Another expression of the kami - the spiritual force in all things.
Western Religions Great emphasis upon time.	**Judaism** The creation of God which, if it is part of God's purpose, will be the last days of earth.	**Christianity** The same.	**Islam** The same
World & Humanity: Possibly eternal in a new form. Created			

Humanistic Religions
Great emphasis
upon time.
World & Humanity:
  relative and fragile
Utopian or Dystopian

Event: The Languages

The description of the end must use highly imaginative language. Those describing the total cessation of life are faced with the task of conveying an unexperienced reality: total change. We all know the difficulties in describing what occurs upon the death of an individual. We easily describe what occurs to the material dimension of the person while searching for an appropriate image to convey what has happened to the total person. In describing the end of the world, we have little to base our prognosticating upon except present knowledge. If the end has occurred it is not within our written memory. Thus we must stretch our present language to fit future possibilities. Upon examining the various eschatologies we realize there are two significant layers of language used to describe the end. One which denies the present, e.g. the sun will fall to the earth, starvation will destroy all, parents will hate their children and the children their parents; and, another language which compares the end with the present by extrapolating from the present in the description of the future, e.g. a war between Russia and the United States will engage the whole world in nuclear war such that all plant life and humans will be destroyed. This same usage of language will be found in describing the time after the end: negative usage is found in such statements as "there will be no more death, hate, hunger, and war"; comparison language is found in descriptions of the time-after as a wedding celebration or the time when the lion and the lamb will be able to live together in peace.

Event: The Meaning

These levels of usage reflect the difficulty in forseeing the future. At the same time they do offer, when prognosticating a new life, a strand of hope tied to the present. These stories reflect that in the present are the seeds of a new world. As Ernst Bloch has said so well:[12] Western descriptions of the end neither deny the world as it exists nor simplistically place faith in progess, but rather, these eschatological statements are calls for freedom in the midst of lostness and alienation.

In the East, however, the language, while using the same techniques, emphasize, instead how the unenlightened soul is doomed to suffer an infinite series of incarnations, with all of their attendant pain of successive births and deaths. Reference to the end of the world is of little consequence to the principle thrust and essential vision of Eastern religion.

These meanings of eschatological literature in East and West emphasized the fundamental vision of these two cultures wherein the East emphasized the self's true destiny and the illusory nature of the world, whereas the West looks forward to a new just earth and paradise.

Cause

The end is brought about by our actively engaging in those activities which will produce it or by passively waiting while fate/the inherent Karma of the world/God effects the end. An adaptation of the categories of Bryan Wilson, a sociologist of religion, can be helpful in describing the conditions under which various religions and religionists see the creation of a new world for themselves alone or for the entire earth. They describe the method by which the "new" comes in many ways. The following are typical categories of description.[13]

1) The conversionist: sees this age as corrupt because people are corrupt. If people can be changed then the world will be changed. A complete change in the world is seen not as available through contingent agencies outside the person but only by a profoundly felt, supernaturally wrought, transformation of the self. The "objective" world will not change but the acquistition of a new subjective orientation to it will itself be the cause of the apocalyptic or utopian end.

2) Revolutionist: the age we live in is evil because the human and natural world are evil. All must be destroyed in order to have a better world. The breaking down and building up is beyond human powers. We can destroy the world but certainly we cannot re-create it. We can, however, participate in the process of overturning the world but in doing so we know that we are merely putting a shoulder to the already turning wheel.

3) Introversionist: the age we live in is irredeemably evil and one can only hope to withdraw from the sources of evil that cause it. The world will not change suddenly. We alone can change. As individuals we must end our old life and renounce the world by leaving it. Only those who belong to the "enlightened" "the saved" will attain true happiness. What happens to the evil world does not matter.

4) Manipulationist: this age is the advent of a new world in which we will attain total happiness. It is possible to have Utopia now; evil will be overcome if we learn the right means, improved techniques, to deal with our problems. Apocalypse can be easily avoided if we learn the proper techniques. What we have is good, we can make it better with the right means and technologies.

5) Thaumaturgical: we are living in Utopia. The technological age is the best world possible. We can relieve ourselves of present and specific ills by special dispensations. We can change individuals and make them happy. We should not look to some ideal future for all. Miracles and oracles charge us not to look to the new principles about life we have discovered for the future, and future change is to come about only if we discover the good in our midst.

6)Reformist: the world is evil. It can be dealt with according to supernaturally given insights about the ways in which social organization should be amended. We will save ourself with the help of supernatural agencies. We gradually change the world if we act in accord with these agencies.

The following schema summarizes these general thoughts by applying these ideal constructs to the Western vision in which there is present a personal God.

A WESTERN MODEL OF THE CAUSATION AND EFFECT OF THE AGE OF TECHNOLOGY

Classification		Agent/Cause	After Effect
Revolutionist:	God will overturn the world.	God	Apoc./Utopia
Conversionist:	God will change us.	God	Utopia
Thaumaturgist:	God will grant particular dispensations and work miracles now	God	Utopia
Manipulationist:	God wishes to change our perception of the world.	God/Us	Utopia
Introversionist:	God calls us to abandon	Us	Life as usual for the world
Reformist:	God calls us to amend the world.	Us	Utopia

Many times there is a significant person who is seen as responsible for bringing to an end this age and initiating the next. The term "messiah" has been applied to such a person. Three types of messiah are significant to our discussion: the apocalyptic type of messiah who predicts a cosmic catastrophe and subsequent deeds of salvation in accord with his/her vision of life and foreseeing a radically different world; the utopian type who exhorts his/her followers to qualify for salvation by adhering to strict codes of belief and behavior; the returning savior messiah who comes to restore the pristine perfection of the world.

We see, then, the ways the end may come about and at the same time how we, or one significant person, can play a part in that coming. The exact description of the cause is found in the various myths/stories of the religion.

After the End, What?

The description of the language of the end, the temporality of the end, and the cause of the end have supplied us with the background for understanding the consequences of the end upon the world and humankind. There is only one major aspect left to consider: who will participate in the new beginning?

There are a number of options all of which are found in religious literature.

1) Everyone will be renewed and live a life of happiness as a consequence of the end.

2) Everyone will be damned to a life of chaotic hell as a consequence of the end.

3) Only those who share the true vision of the end, and prepared for it will live in the new world. Those who did not share this vision of life and death will cease to exist or spend the rest of the new time in a kind of hell.

4) Everyone will continue to live in the new cycle of existence as they have lived in the past because the consequences of their past lives influence their present living. They can escape the cycles of the world or of life only by realizing what is truly permanent and beyond change.

All four of these options may be found in one religious organization, especially in the West, while option four is common to most Eastern religions.

VISIONS OF THE NEW AGE[14]

Classic Visions of the New Age

Hinduism: The realization that we are eternal spirit (Atman is Brahman)
Buddhism: Enlightenment for each person.
Taoism: The individual is one with the Tao through mystical union.
Confucianism: The old way is restored. The cosmic order is present.
Judaism: A New Earth. Yahweh is recognized. His will followed by all.
Christianity: A New Earth. Humanity and nature is freed of its divisions through participating in Jesus' love.
Islam: Paradise. all those who obeyed Allah live on eternally.

Humanitiarian Visions
- An integrated life is achieved through creative interaction.
- Social and economic justice is achieved for all.
- Biological immortality, physical comfort and security are achieved with an infinite increase of technological aid

The End

To believe that this world will come to an end is a claim to describe the future as well as a challenge to engage it. There are many groups of individuals who upon looking to possible futures decide to stop some of them from coming. People have banned together to ban the bomb, be dead rather than Red, stop pollution, plan the world's parenthood, and stop the doomsday clock from ticking. These and many other movements look to a certain end and proclaim: no more. They plot strategies for influencing the outcome of the present set of tensions and possible end of our world. Yet their imagination seems to stop at the end.

A common theme in all the religious scenarios we have examined is a description not only of the end but of what comes after. Many modern apocalyptic visionaries seem to lose their vision once the end occurs. But this is the exact time we need vision. One function of the apocalyptic stories was to provide hope for those being overcome by the threatening evil. We need visions of hope in our present apocalyptic visions. Without visions of hope, the courage to continue diminishes. Indeed the end must be seen to include a future.

THE END: A FUTURE

NOTES

1. The material which follows is dependent upon all the cited references but also upon a paper "Four Possible Futures" given at the CTS annual meeting as well as an article of mine in *Death Education* 7 (Spring, 1983) 9-24.

2. For an interpretation of the themes presented here cf. B. McGinn, *Visions of the End* (New York: Columbia U., 1979) and F.E. Manuel and Manuel, F.P., Utopian Thought in the Western World (Cambridge, MA: Belknap,1979).

3. J. Hick, *Death and Eternal Life* (San Francisco: Harper and Row, 1976).

4. R.J. Lifton, *The Broken Connection: On Death and the Continuity of Life* (New York: Simon and Shuster, 1979).

5. R.H. Charles, *Eschatology: The Doctrine of a Future Life...* (New York: Schocken, 1963; originally published in 1899). H.H. Rowley, *The Relevance of Apocalyptic* (London: Oxford, 1944). N. Cohen, *The Pursuit of the Millennium* (2nd ed.; New York: Oxford U., 1979), M. Eliade, *Cosmos and History: The Myth of the Eternal Return* (San Francisco: Harper and Row, 1959).

6. Cf. McGinn, op. cit.

7. Cf. W. Griffin, *Endtime: The Doomsday Catalog* (New York: Macmillan, 1979).

8. N. Cohen, op. cit.

9. P. Tillich, *Systematic Theology* (Chicago: U. of Chicago, 1951) vol. 1.

10. Cf. H. Jonas, *The Gnostic Religion* (2nd ed.; Boston: Beacon, 1963). R.M. Grant, *Gnosticism* (San Francisco: Harper and Row, 1961).

11. The chart is dependent upon R. Monk et al., *Exploring Religious Meaning* (Englewood Cliffs, N.J.: Prentice Hall, 1973) and R.J. Streng et al., Ways of Being Religious (Englewood Cliffs, N.J.: Prentice Hall, 1973).

12. E. Bloch, *Das Prinzip Hoffnung* (Berlin: Aufbau, 1954) 1-59

13. B. Wilson, *Magic and the Millennium* (San Francisco: Harper and Row, 1973).

14. This chart has been adapted from Monk, op. cit.

CHOOSING OUR FUTURE: AMERICAN CATHOLICISM'S PRECARIOUS PROSPECTS[1]

David J. O'Brien

Reading the signs of the times and looking far ahead, as Pope John XXIII would have us do, makes most of us very nervous. For some reason or other, as this paper will try to suggest, we are inclined to look to the future with considerable pessimism. In this we are unlike our American Catholic predecessors like Isaac Hecker, who noted in his diary shortly after his conversion in 1844:

> Ah thou eternal, ever blooming virgin, the Future, shall I embrace thee?. . .Shall I see next year this time that my hopes have been fulfilled? My past hopes have been more than fulfilled . . . . Faith is the great magic power. This is the great miracle worker. Whatsoever thou believest with all thy might is thine already.[2]

I suspect, too, that we are unlike many of our academic colleagues, who place far more trust in the historical process than do those of us who dabble in religion. They may regard Daniel Bell as the best guide to the human future; we are more apt to rely on the visions of Edgar Cayce, to nod our heads knowlingly when told that Harold Lindsay's *The Late Great Planet Earth* was America's biggest of best sellers in the 70s or, at the very least, to bring to the shore with us this summer Daniel Berrigan's meditation on the Book of Revelation, *The Nightmare of God.* Reasonable men and women that we are, we mediate such reading through the filters of our training and expertise, to say nothing of our vacations at the beach. Catholic as most of us are, our nervousness probably expresses itself in laughter more than prayer. American as we are, our anxiety may focus on one or another scenario of the human future, but the real problem that shakes our consciousness is less our guess about what is to come than the agonizing awareness that we must choose. If, like our social science counterparts, we really trusted the historical process, it would not be so bad. Or if, like Cayce and Lindsay, we really trusted in the ultimate beneficence of the Lord of History, or at least His kindness to us, His friends, it would not be so bad either. But we are, for better or worse, people of the modern temper, aware of our own awareness, conscious of our own consciousness, given to analyzing and scrutinizing that most interesting sign of the times, ourselves, so we are simply not sure of anything but our own immediate existence and the knowledge that we will choose, today, tomorrow, till the end, and the choice seems sometimes more than we can handle. In Mary Gordon's *Final Payments* the heroine exclaims, after the death of her father, "I would have to invent a life for myself." After the death of so many of our fathers, and mothers, so must we all.[3]

History has become in our time a self-consicous human project. This is the most important single fact about our contemporary historical situation. All of us are familiar with the daily reality of persons, perhaps ourselves, wrestling with the problem of deciding what to do; the adolescent confronting an incredible array of choices regarding education, work, sex, drink, drugs and religion; the married couple contemplating separation or divorce; the depressed person in middle life, even persons in religious vows, considering a change of careers; people of all ages experiencing the need to make clear decisions about their relationship with Christ and His church. At the other end of the spectrum, all of us are conscious today of the nuclear reality: we have the power to end history. Our own bishops write, in their recent pastoral, "The Challenge of Peace":

> We live today, therefore, in the midst of a cosmic drama; we possess a power which should never be used, but which might be used if we do not reverse our direction. We live with nuclear weapons knowing we cannot afford to make one serious mistake. This fact dramatizes the precariousness of our position, politically, morally and spiritually.[4]

Our American and Catholic experience of this perilous new freedom results from the convergence of three streams of historical change in our lifetime, each of which eroded social institutions and cultural symbols that once provided a degree of security, legitimacy, taken for grantedness. First there was the gradual collapse of the American Catholic subculture, made up of families, neighborhoods, parishes and ethnic groups, all sustained by a common sense of being a religious minority. At the very same time, the world wide Catholic subculture which was the product of the nineteenth century resistance to modernity also unravelled at Vatican II. If all that were not enough, yet a third pattern of change converged with these others as the United States itself underwent massive cultural upheaval in the sixties. Whether it was the advent of a new religious pluralism, the collapse of various denominational subcultures, the sexual revolution, the racial crisis or the war in Vietnam, something happened. Self-conscious choice became the norm, traditional and communal discipline seemed to break down and people where thrown on their own resources.[5]

For the American Catholic church the heart of all this was voluntarism: a new experience of freedom. We see this new voluntarism, and the self consicousness from which it springs, throughout the church, in renewal programs focused on small groups sharing personal responses to scripture; in prayer, growing from the heart of one's own expereince of God; in sacramental programs encouraging those involved to reflect on their lives and ask what, if anything, this experience means; in the widespread popularity of the new Rite of Christian Initiation of Adults, in which both catechumen and community become clear and self-conscious about the conversion to which all are called. In the gaps between church teaching and popular practice on birth control, in the widely perceived inability to be prescriptive about matters of justice and peace, in the proliferation of new forms of ministry and ministry training, and in evangelization efforts of all sorts we see the reality of voluntarism, we affirm its basis in the dignity of the human person and we refine our view of the church as a community of free men and women. One result has been the emergence of that word, ministry, unknown among Catholics a few years ago. Standing in some tension with hierarchical, clerical church organization, ministry brings with it themes of community, mutuality, and equality, a theology of gifts, even participatory democracy, if you will.[6]

In the historical literature we are told that this new situation arises from a long delayed process of Americanization. Years ago, John Tracy Ellis and Andrew Greeley offered the long conventional picture of a church which had become fully American and wrestled with the consequences of that change.[7] Philip Gleason more systematically argued that the process of assimilation, speeded up after World War II, forced the church to accomodate to changes in its clientele. The future required simply the delicate adjustment of the differing but not conflicting claims of religious and secular, private and public life.[8] Now we have a new history by James Hennesey, filled with information, confirming this basic Americanization hypothesis. The American church stands at the climax of assimilation, at "a revolutionary moment," Hennesey believes. Because Catholics, finally at home in America, still retain "a special sense of themselves," Hennesey is confident that "the community will approach those challenges out of its own tradition, its own social memory, its own special understanding of reality."[9] Greeley remains similarly optimistic, despite the failure of church leaders to catch up with the Americanization of the Catholic people. For Greeley the process of Americanization can be documented in terms of income and status and finds its premiere expression in the "communal Catholics", now quite at home in their American world. Theirs is a selective Catholicism, to be sure, for they have discovered what was long self evident to European Catholics: "as long as you define yourself as Catholic, no one is going to throw you out of the church or refuse the sacraments to you, regardless of what you do in your bedroom or what reservations you may have on doctrinal matters such as papal infallibility." Like Hennesey, Greeley believes Catholics retain, more than most, suspect elements of a Catholic style, a "special sense of themselves", which Greeley defines as an analogical imagination, sacramental experience, comic story and organic community, all described in a forthcoming book modestly entitled *How to Save the Catholic Church.* Greeley sums up the confusing variety of this "do-it-yourself" Catholicism with his characteristic combination of irritation, affection and optimism:

> A Rembrandt landscape after a storm: ineffective, confused and conflicted, if sincere, church leaders; poor religious education; disheartened priests; unenlightened preaching; angry women; a vigorously independent laity; a moribund sexual ethic; economic success; cultural resurgence; distinguished theologians; increased religious devotion; shortages of priests; democratization of local institutions; fads; conflict; shouting; anger; hope, and a new religious sensibility among the young--thus American Catholicism 20 years after Pope John XXIII's breeze became a whirlwind after crossing the Atlantic.

> There is no reason to think that the storm will stop blowing for the next two decades, though there may well be a re-evaluation of some apsects of the heritage--Gregorian chant for example--which were thrown out along with the bath water. The American Catholic Church will continue to be a noisy, contentious, disorderly place.

> No one will mistake it for a mausoleum. [10]

Greeley's optimism rests in part on his generally benign view of American society and culture. Indeed in his insistence that the church's problems arise from this incompetent handling of religion, an argument based on his assessment of the persistence of faith, piety and distinctive Catholic imagination, he is not far from Michael Novak, whose most recent book protests against church intrusion into secular matters and overuse of secular disciplines and criteria in theology and demands a return to the common faith of the Creed. [11] Novak and Greeley are more than comfortable with a dualism of church and society in which careful adjustments of secular and religious claims should be adequate to sustain Hennesey's "special sense" of Catholic identity. Other observers are not so sure. Philip Murnion, for example, after working for three years with successful parishes in the United States, noted that they were strong on community, prayer, fellowship and participation. Still he worried about their tendency toward exclusive membership, poor preaching, the loss of priestly identity, the decline in church attendance and the lack of compelling sacredness in sacramental celebration. The problem of sacraments, like the separation of faith and daily life, is primarily a matter of meaning, Murnion argues. Failure to renew the liturgy and to develop an adequate approach to political life, according to Murnion, both express a "crisis of sacramentality" in which "nothing less than the Catholic style of Christianity is at stake." [12] In a similar vein, sociologist Robert Bellah has noted the dominance in American society of a bureaucratic individualism which finds its expression in a sense of radical personal autonomy and a quest for self-fulfillment. So profound and all embracing is this individualism that we cannot even comprehend the older notion of the church as the body of Christ, the idea that it is in and through the church that the believer comes to be what he or she is. Formation of small groups and base communities may help, but alone they may also encourage rather than oppose the privatization and depoliticization of religion. As Bellah sees it, "the Church as the body of Christ can remind us that we will survive only insofar as we care for one another." For Bellah, "nothing else today is of greater importance" than making the church in this sense viable and effective.[13]

Hennesey and Greeley may trust the historic process to sustain a special sense of Catholicity, but Murnion and Bellah argue that two of the basic elements of what is commonly called Catholic, sacramentality and Church, are becoming increasingly problematic. Perhaps this is to be expected, for the voluntary principle, now understood as a matter of personal reponsibility to decide for oneself not only the religion with which one will affiliate but to define the terms of the affiliation, "do it yourself" Christianity, has moved the American church beyond the self-conscious construction of a subculture to a pluralism marked by the experience of the autonomous self exemplified in Mary Gordon's exclamation about inventing a life. From this experience flows an evangelical style, with emphasis on personal decisions, interior spirituality, reliance on scripture, a democratic hermeneutic, free church approaches to local community life and benevolence and goodwill as vehicles for Christian insertion into public life.[14] These items characterize Christian response to freedom and pluralism, and always have; people, churches and communities regularly try to limit their impact through the construction of more or less coherent subcultures in which personal, family and communal values can be expressed, supported and transmitted across the generations. Americanization is not a process that began with John Carroll and was shortcircuited by the old world conservatism of immigrants and the traditionalism of the organized Catholicism of the twentieth century, but an ongoing process of interaction between individual and group values and the changing social and cultural landscape of the United States.

Support for such an argument is found in the work of historian Timothy L. Smith, who had gone furthest in challenging the assumptions of the Americanization Model. Concentrating on the experience of later immigrants from southern and eastern Europe, Smith argues convincingly that parishes often owed their origin to lay initiative and that the lay persons who built the churches were for the most part optimistic, hopeful and ambitious, determined to take advantage of the new opportunities America afforded. At the same time they saw no reason why they should not hold on to the values, traditions and religious faith they had brought with them. For Smith, the ethnic group was a corridor through which people passed, not a room that walled them off; it was a nursery of two patriotisms, the American one providing symbols and ideals to legitimate continuing concern for the liberation and progress of the homeland. In the ethnic community, men enjoyed new opportunities for education, self improvment and leadership while women enjoyed new status, sharing responsibility for family income and household management. For the children of such settled families, who dominated churches and ethnic organizations, the group provided identity, affirmation and a ground for active, assertive engagement with the amoral but not necessarily hostile world beyond the group.

Smith directly challenges those who have held that "the religious and ethnic sentiments of immigrant minorities are anachronisms that must give way to the processes of assimilation and modernization." Instead he argues that ethnicity, a sense of peoplehood, arose from the self-conscious efforts of a bewildering variety of groups to "protect or advance the economic, cultural and religious interests of persons who, by reason of some combination of actual or supposed common origin, language or faith, believe they constitute one people." Ethnic interests and identities "gave both to faith and to the sense of peoplehood a fluid and instrumental quality that was more future oriented than backward looking." Ethnicity, then is not nationality but peoplehood, and it has in modern history been invariably linked to religious symbols and images. Like the ancient Hebrews, ethnic groups usually adhered to "systems of religious thought" which not only served to legitimate social arrangements "but, through prophetic proclamation in a time of crisis (could) help break the chains of custom by making new and revolutionary demands, dissolving myths, and declaring a transcendant ethic not identifiable with any existing society or social institution." Consciously rejecting metaphors of melting pots and mosaics in favor of "kaleidoscopic change", Smith suggests a fluid, undogmatic and compassionate understanding of social dynamics which would, by implication, find the contemporary Catholic search for group identity and a sense of mission, a definition of both separateness and universality, as a long standing, perhaps permanent feature of an always mysterious and changing church, now enmeshed in the precarious setting of pluralism.[15]

The suggestion of this interpretation of U.S. Catholic history would be that the superficial unity of the American Catholic community in the post war years, a unity which gave the changes of the sixties that peculiar sense of disintegration, was a temporary and quite uncharacteristic moment in a history dominated by complex interaction of religion and society expressed in particular communities and personal lives.[16] The dream of Christendom lives on in the isolation of a sectarian Catholicism which claimed to be *the* Church and the custodian of true culture set over against an American world which it loved all too much. This was the Catholicism which could in the the 1920s and 1950s decry the selfishness, materialism and secularism of its American world while taking pride in numbers of communicants, the size and splendor of its buildings, the worldy success of its members and the victories of its football teams. That particular Catholic and very American subculture is gone, because its people, its self-definition, and its cultural setting have all changed.

This suggests that there is no interpretation of American Catholic history that will fully encompass the complexity of the historical experience or give rise to a single direction for the American church. There will be room enough in the American Catholic church for a wide variety of theologies, forms of community life and mission. The role of bishops, of traditional statements of orthodoxy, and of massive mobilization for action have all become problematic. Whether looked at from the point of view of theology, politics, stages of development, or effective evangelization there appears to be a bewildering variety, and there will continue to be!

Once again this internal pluralism seems less surprising when set in the context of American Protestantism's long experience with freedom, pluralism, and the rise and decline of particular Protestant subcultures, from Puritan and federalist New England to those southern counties where everyone was poor and Baptist. In the classic studies of American Protestantism by H. Richard Niebuhr, we find models of interpretation which seem increasingly relevant to Catholics. On the one hand, Niebuhr found in the sociological structure of American churches a tendency toward class differentiation, with congregations ranging from the enthusiastic churches of the disinherited through the piety of middle class Methodists to the security and respectability of Episcopalians. But this tendency toward conformity and cooptation was regularly challenged by the common scriptures and the regular reappearance of the demands of the Kingdom of God in America embodied in movements for revival, mission or moral reform, pulling believers out of their comfortable pews. More broadly Niebuhr found the existence of classic models of Christ and culture, each expressing authentic responses to faith in the midst of life, none exhausting the full range of Christian possibilities. In summary, Niebuhr argued that Christianity and American democracy interacted with one another in ways which produced a dialectical model of religious life, with tendencies toward "order and movement", towards the istitutionalization of religious experience in settled forms of theology, church organization, parish life and education, and towards the expression of belief in the radical demands of the Gospel in revivals seeking deeper faith, movements for reform aimed at making the church conform more closely to the Kingdom of which it was witness and movements for social reform aimed at insuring that God's will is done on earth as well as in heaven.

24

Movements challenged settled discontent. Orders regularly accomodated new demands and movements waned, only to appear in new guises in another generation. This sense of order and movement across a variety of settings increasingly corresponds with the experience of an evangelically oriented Catholicism. It is unsettling and suggests a world whose patterns are never fixed, but perhaps that is as it should be.[17]

My teacher Hayden V. White once suggested that modern historiography crippled itself by clinging to notions of Darwinian science and Victorian literatures despite the radical transformation of twentieth century understanding of art and science. Could the same thing be said of our understanding of American Catholicism and American religion? If Catholics are now Christians first, if they prefer religious experience to organized ritual practice and Scriptures to catechisms; if Catholics believe the dignity of the human person means freedom for believers as well as non-believers, and if they doubt that their nation or world will become Catholic in the near future, then the neat patterns that once grounded distinct identity will not be recaptured, save at the price of isolation and irresponsibility. Pluralism is the product of freedom; the power to "choose a future", like it or not, brings with it "precarious prospects", for churches, for communities and for people. We Catholics have arrived, to be sure; arrived not as Americans, because we always were, but arrived into the center of that America which, like the ancient holy of holies, turns out to be empty. Spiritually on our own, we are socially and organizationally not in the Kingdom of God, but in the mainline, as the always deflating honesty of Martin Marty gently reminds us:

Catholicism, then tomorrow will continue to be typed as 'mainline', with all the rights, privileges and liabilities attendant thereto. Hate organizes better than love, fanaticism attracts more than openness, absolutism focuses more than responsibleness. Life in the mainline is difficult in a world that does not want to encourage toleration for ambiguity or empathy for the choice of others. Catholicism will hear voices that call it away form mainlinity and Catholic pluralism-in-unity-in-pluralism. But the Catholicism we see at the edge of tomorrow has so many constituencies, so many clientele interests, so many styles of Christian confession, that it is not likely to be able to move from mainline to margin, from diversity to monolith. That will not make life easy for the leaders of tomorrow's Catholicism, or secure for their followers. But the call of Christ is not only to safe paths in sheltered ghettos but into a world of myriad needs and opportunities.[18]

It is more than understandable that a growing number of Catholic leaders are uncomfortable with this present situation of American Catholicism.

Before the Council Karl Rahner argued that, in what he called "diaspora", where the church sees itself as a more or less permanent minority, there is a natural reaction to deny that such a situation can or should exist. "What, after all, does a person do if he sees the diaspora situation coming and thinks of it as something which simply and absolutely must not be?", Rahner asked. "He makes himself a closed circle, an artificial situation inside which it looks as if the inward and outward diaspora isn't one; he makes a ghetto."[19] At the time this was an interpretation of the sources of the integral Catholicism of the post-modernist church, but it appears a more general phenomenon in situations of pluralism and freedom where the church must always fear seduction by the culture. So rapid and complete has been the collapse of the American Catholic subculture that such attitudes were bound to appear. By the late 1960s, Monsignor Ellis was worried that accomodation had gone too far, for he thought liberal Catholicism was tending toward an alliance with secular humanism. Avery Dulles, one of the more moderate and reasonable American theologians, joined with a number of Protestants and Catholics in signing the Hartford Affirmations, a set of orthodox Christian propositions they felt needed reaffirming in the midst of what they regarded as intemperate secular theologies and social and political radicalism.[20]

Dulles has been among those who have responded to the current situation of the church with a critical reassessment of the whole process of renewal. In his view, Vatican II was "essentially a compromise between the vision of the church as a hierarchical and divine society oriented toward eternal life and the newer vision of the church as a free society called to serve the human community." Unfortunately, the latter overwhelmed the former, endangering the very existence of a distinctive Catholic church and community. One reason was the domination of liberalism, a school of thought whose desire for freedom bordered on the adolescent:

> For reasons that are historically understandable, liberal Catholics of the recent past have been preoccupied with the problem of getting out from under what they see as repressive 'authority'. Liberalism teaches Catholics how to reject, but not how to cherish, their own past, how to embrace, but not how to critique, the secular. Many Catholics, who in adolescence or young adulthood, experienced the shock of Vatican II, have yet to learn how a church that changes can be revered and loved. Having fought the battle against authoritarianism, they will have to ask themselves how, with their new freedom, they can make a distinctively Catholic contribution to America.[21]

Dulles cites the period of the American religious depression as analogous to the present situation among Catholics. American Protestantism fell into decline between 1926 and 1936, in part because it had grown too close to the world; liberal theology baptized all the basic elements of modernity and even reinterpreted Christian doctrine and scriptures in terms of modern ideas. Many Protestants, as a result, could not answer the question "why the church?" H. Richard Niebuhr, Reinhold Niebuhr and others, in an American brand of neo-orthodoxy, insisted on the need to place, "the church against the world", and its corollary, cited by Dulles, the need for "the church to be the church." Rediscovering Christianity's own ground in reaffirmation of basic Christian truths of sin, redemption and grace, they made a "course correction" in liberalism without compromising the social gospel message of the church's public responsibility. this movement restored the vitality of the Protestant churches and carried them to impressive growth during the 1940s and 1950s.

Yet what Harry Emerson Fosdick said of the neo-orthodox leaders could also be said of modern Catholic critics of the last period of American church history:

> What present day critics of liberalism often failed to see is its absolute necessity to multitudes of us who would not have been Christian at all unless we could thus have escaped the bondage of the then reigning orthodoxy. Of course, the results are not the whole answer. Of course, it left out dimensions of Christian faith which would need to be redis-covered. Despite that, however, it offered a generation of earnest youth the only chance they had to be honest while being Christian.[22]

Fosdick had in mind the narrow, pessimistic and long dessicated Calvinism that still formed the religious ethos in which multitudes of middle class Prot-estants grew up. William Hutchinson has demonstrated that significant numbers of liberal theologians and social gospel activists had serious problems of personal faith in their youth.[23] failing to experience conversion or the presence of grace, they nevertheless had no desire to abandon the historic faith of their parents and found in liberalism and/or social action means of affirming their loyalty to their tradition and establishing a ground for their Christian identity while rejecting the coldness, aloofness and indifference to worldly suffering of their religious inheritance. In doing so, they created the ground of reason, scholarship and social responsibility that made the "course correction" of neo-orthodoxy possible.

Similarly, the modern day critics of Catholic renewal almost without excep-tion forget the rigidity, isolation, obscurantism and narrow insistence on loyalty which dominated the Catholic subculture such a short time ago. The identification of American military power with the righteous action of God, the childish innocence of religious education, the force feeding of a dull and isolating scholasticism in college classrooms, the oppression of separated and divorced Catholics, the insistence on loyalty to the Catholic subculture at the expense of racial justice and social reform, the list is endless and constitutes not just a set of intellectual problems but elements of a culture which, however valuable in preserving a sense of Catholic identity and elements of a Catholic imagination, had become stifling to the human spirit.

Why need all this be said? Surely that church had its saints. Almost in spite of itself that church produced Sangnier and Maritain, Mounier and Suhard, Peter Maurin and Dorothy Day, to say nothing of our parents. The Catholic subculture, with the clergy at its center, offered comfort to many of the afflicted; it challenged its young to a kind of heroism in its defense; it upheld some truths the modern world was forgetting; at times it even had a certain nobility. But all at a price.

There was the price of isolation and arrogance, as if only the church had truth, and all outside was chaos arising from failure to acknowledge the church's claims. Recall Hilaire Belloc:

> For what is the Catholic Church? It is that which replies, coordinates, establishes. It is that within which is right order; outside the puerilities and despairs. It is the possession of perspective in the survey of the world. . . . Here alone is promise and here alone a foundation. . . . One thing in the world is different from all others. It has a personality and a force. It is recognized (and when recognized violently loved or hated). It is the Catholic Church. Within that household the human spirit has a roof and a hearth. Outside, it is the Night!

Inside the light, outside the darkness. Insulated from modern tragedies by such righteousness, Catholics were spared as well responsbility for this world and its people. In its popular form this angle of vision was expressed in a ditty remembered by Frank Sheed: "We are the sweet, selected few / The rest of you are damned / There isn't room enough for you / We can't have heaven crammed." [24]

Faced with another historic crossroad at Vatican II, the church chose a different course. In the midst of the cold war and the awakening of native peoples and dormant cultures, Roman Catholicism groped for a new image of itself in history. With John XXIII it came; "Now more than ever, certainly more than in past centuries, our purpose is to serve man as such, and not only Catholics, to defend above all and everywhere the rights of the human person and not only those of the Catholic church." [25] John's words were echoed at the Council, when, almost without knowing it,

28

the world's bishops became modern day pilgrims for God and liberty: "The joys and hopes, the griefs and anxieties of men of this age, especially those who are poor or in any way afflicted, these too are the joys and hopes, the griefs and anxieties of the followers of Christ." [26] Placing itself beside and with the people, the church necessarily identifies most especially with the poor, the afflicted and the oppressed, providing a new standpoint, a new vision, gradually and haltingly, against enormous resistance within and without, a new church. In this generation, then, the great turn has been made. After centuries of preoccupation with its own integrity, unity and survival, the church has taken a new turn toward men and women in the midst of history. No longer standing on a safe mountaintop of its own cosmic self-righteousness, Catholicism chooses to join the human community, to become, in the Council's words "truly and intimately linked with mankind and its history."[27]

But this new option, too, has its price, for it is no longer clear what it means to be Catholic. Karl Rahner argues that the historic significance of Vatican II lies in the transition from a western dominated Catholicism, present in branch plant fashion throughout the world, to a "world church" with authentic new Christian churches emerging from every continent and culture. [28] Faced with this emerging pluralism at the 1974 Synod of Bishops, the church's leaders could not reach agreement on the exact balance to be struck between "indigenization" within diverse cultures and the unity of the church through Rome. Pope Paul VI's "Apostolic Exhortation on Evangelization" which followed that synod argued for the insertion of Christianity into the very heart of world cultures, seemingly affirming the diversification of theology and pastoral practice, while recent events indicate a reaction toward Roman centralization and control. In the United States this worldwide struggle with pluralism blends with the nation's own distinctive culture of individualism and freedom to make Catholic identity ever more problematic and precarious. The problem is real: how can one remain truly Catholic amid a bewildering variety of theologies and styles? How can one be a responsible participant in modern life and a loyal member of a single church?

It is an old American problem. In the early nineteenth century American Protestants struggled with a rapid multiplication of churches, viewed as irrational chaos by European commentators and seen by many Christians as contradicting the will of God. Joseph Smith, the founder of Mormonism, recounts his first visit with the angels: "I asked the personages who stood above me in the light, which of all the sects was right-and which I should join. I was answered I must join none of them, for they were all wrong." Philip Schaff, the first to record the history of this emergent pluralism saw the United States as a "motley sampler of all church history." The nation, he argued, "was destined to be the Phoenix grave of all European Protestantism and Romanism." None of these would ever become dominant, but "out of the mutual conflict of all something new would gradually arise." With Schaff appeared an interpretation of diversity which saw it as less than what the Lord expected but in itself evidence of the persistence and vitality of the Holy Spirit. The sect, in contrast, as Sidney Mead comments,

> Is a group that does claim to be 'the church' of Christ on earth, basing its exclusivistic claim on those particularities of emphasis in doctrine and practice which distinguish it from all the other groups its absolutizes and universalizes its peculiar mode of apprehending, articulating and applying the Gospel. A sectarian exhibits, as one Evangelical said, the tendency of each individual 'at least in thought, to hold that Christendom to be one must be drawn within the circle of belief in which he dwells, and which he thinks to be the very citadel of the truth of God'. A denominationalist, on the other hand, curbs this natural tendency with the acute suppostion that perhaps 'God can see a Christian where we can not' and affiliates with one of the denominations 'on the maxim-Preference, not exclusion.'"[29]

As Schaff put it in 1879, sectarianism, in the American sense, was "nothing more than extended selfishness, which crops out of human nature everywhere and in all ages and conditions of the church."[30]

It is almost too much, the argument that the search for a distinctive and exlusive sense of Catholicity may be nothing more than "extended selfishness." Yet, among protestants of Schaff's time and Catholics of our own, there are understandable dynamics which seem to give rise to this American brand of sectarianism. The tendency toward such sectarianism arises from a felt need to affirm the distinctiveness and significance of one's own church and to do so in ways which establish both its superiority to other churches and to competing organizations and institutions. Immigrant pastors did this instinctively, building church membership and morale by emphasizing the distinct and superior claim of the church to represent communal traditions and values and to meet needs ignored or even created by the larger secular society, and to do all this in ways which placed no unnecessary barriers in the way of their people's desire for personal freedom, economic success and social acceptance. Today, once again, church leaders, men and women who have given their lives and devotion to the church in a time of rapid change when that commitment has been challenged and therefore became self-conscious, are tempted to make their own resolution normative for the community, as David O'Rourke has pointed out.[31] The need for professional and personal identity combines with the church's need for a unique and distinctive ground for its claims to give rise to a new sectarianism, complete with an "extended selfishness." The church is not just *a* church, but *the* church; it stands in isolation from and judgment upon secular society. The language and the context have changed, but the message remains the same: the church, this church is the center and end of human history.

Discontent with the mainline, and with the compromise and ambiguity it requires, spreads across the ideological spectrum of American Catholicism. The larger Catholic church, the broad Christian ecumenical community, even most members of the churches, seem too comfortablly accomodated to a world which stands once again in polar opposition to the Gospel and the demands of Christian faith. In Daniel Berrigan's prophetic reading of the book of Revelation, for example, history is running out of control:

> The powers of this world, inflated beyond bearing, move to bring an end to history; just as they had presumed to set history in motion, to move it along, a mighty current, the empery of the Great powers, their diplomacy, their city trading, their colonies and 'spheres of influence', their wars, their (truly) gross production. But in their view, even this was not enough. Power, such power, moves inevitably, inexorably, toward Armaggedon; it must have things clear, tidy, final, on its own terms. Things indeed shall be made clear. But on entirely different terms. This is God's promise; we are to abide by it.[32]

Berrigan's couragious and faith-filled public witness against war, along with his consistent willingness to dialogue with others, indicates that he retains more hope than his writings suggest that both church and world can be redeemed, but his language suggests a pessimism and need for prophetic renuciation of the world which, in identifying with those whose prophecy is unself-conscious, would create a new center of history, a church of the poor, which would indeed be *the* church.

Berrigan is not alone in this sometimes romantic sense that the church is to be found where men and women, out of oppression, form authentic Christian community without that agonizing modern necessity of choice. Thus in speaking of base communities and liberation theologies in the third world, especially in Latin America, it is rarely those who have made a decision to devote their lives to the oppressed, the middle class activists and intellectuals who forged a new pastoral practice by choosing to minister among the poor, who are the subjects of church renewal, but the poor themselves who are assisted to discover that they are the chosen ones of God, the new people, among whom new communities and a new church will be born. Here there is none of the ambiguity of the American immigrant experience, the chastened understanding that the poor, if given the chance, might choose to be like the middle class, that women, if given the chance, might choose to be not too unlike men, that minorities, if given the chance, might make many of the choices common among the majority. Rather there is a romantic belief that somehow, through the presence of the spirit, without the intervention of human instruments, the dream of liberation will produce a pure liberation, a new church and a new society, a new man, unlike the old. After all, in worldly terms, we can do nothing but trust in the liberating presence of the spirit. One is reminded of the vision of Morris West in *The Clowns of God* as the returned Lord gathers his people to begin again and announces to one small group:

> You are not the only community thus brought together. There are many others, all over the world. . .they are all the same because they have followed the same beckoning finger, and bonded themselves by the same love. They did not do this of themselves (but were) chosen to keep the small flame of love alight, to nurture the seeds of goodness in a small place, until the day when the Spirit sends you out to light other candles in a dark land and plant new seeds in a blackened earth.[33]

If the images of light and darkness outside recall Hilaire Belloc, perhaps the association is no accident. Once again the world outside is seen as the realm of power and death; the world inside, inside a new church, is the one source of hope and possibility. The closer to that new church, the farther removed from the world, the more one is what one should be.

Such images, extreme as they may sound, dominate much of the discussion of church mission in contemporary American Catholicism. Education and action for justice and peace spring less from the careful, nuanced and highly rational messages of the Popes and the Council, than from an evangelical encounter of scripture with modern society: what would Jesus do? Small groups of highly committed Chrisitians, offering a social and political education which combines personalist action with reflection on the Gospel, generate movements powerful in their criticism of the modern world and challenging in their witness to an alternative way of life. Like the traditionalism of the pre-conciliar Catholic church, which identified with pre-modern, even medieval forms, the new social gospel by its disassociation from the modern world, offers a continuing prophetic judgement upon its practices and, to the extent it embodies that judgement in community, a witness to alternative ways of living. The future to be chosen, at least in North America, is a future in which the church recovers its scriptural inheritance, detaches itself from modernity, risks the loss of members and the isolation of tiny groups, and awaits a future that is in the end beyond its control and even its responsibility.

This vision informs the consistent judgement of so many that the peace pastoral is an interim document of a church on the way from just war to pacifism, a judgement affirmed in a passage in that letter which stands in remarkable contrast to the overall tone of the bishops' discussion of war and peace:

> It is clear today, perhaps more than in previous generations, that convinced Christians are a minority in nearly every country of the world - including nominally Christian and Catholic nations. . . As believers we can identify rather easily with the early church as a company of witnesses engaged in a difficult mission . . .To obey the call of Jesus means separating ourselves from all attachment and affiliation that could prevent us from hearing and following our authentic vocation . . . . This means, of course, that we must regard as normal even the path of persecution and the possibility of martyrdom. We readily recognize that we live in a world that is becoming increasingly estranged from Christian values. In order to remain a Christian, one must take a resolute stand against many commonly accepted axioms of the world. To become true disciples, we must undergo a demanding course of induction into the adult Christian community. We must continually equip ourselves to profess the full faith of the church in an increasingly secularized society.[34]

A prophetic church of this type would, at least, be *the* Church as Avery Dulles had hoped. That concern to make *our* church once again *the* church informs as well the approach of many who at first glance have little in common with Berrigan or the peace bishops. Charismatic Ralph Martin, for example, calls believers to action, to stand up for the truth in and out of the church, to draw the line, even at the price of "division in our own hearts; the sword of the spirit will divide true from false, the unclean from the clean; the same will happen in our families, our parishes, our dioceses, our ecumenical relationships." In this struggle, "what had been wrongly united will be separated and those who have rallied to the banner of Christ will be more certain about who they are and what they are working for; so perhaps will those who have rallied to the banner of Satan."[35]

Members of Catholics United for the Faith and readers of *The Wanderer* dislike Charismatic "enthusiasm", but they share a similar view of the church and prescription for the future. James Hitchcock, probably the most impressive representative of the Catholic right, like Dulles, believes the compromise moderation of the Council was upset by the headlong rush to "relevance" of the post conciliar elites. Instead of holding to the necessary tension between the church and the world, liberals simply surrendered. The chapters of his book outline what has happened to American Catholicism: "The Loss of History", "The Imperial Self", "The Sensation of Movement", "The Illusion of Pluralism", "The Triumph of Bureaucracy", "The Road to Utopia", "The Kingdom of Politics" and "The Coming World Religion." He hopes to see in the future the dissipation of such liberalism, leaving in its stead only three representatives of authentic Christianity: evangelical Protestantism, Orthodoxy, and a restored Roman Catholicism marked by a sacral liturgy, orthodox catechetics, moral firmness and confident self-definition, a church which combines sincere human kindness, genuine personal openness and warmth with firm conviction and a willingness to teach and, if necessary, rebuke. Hitchcock is more insistent on the upholding of truth, that Catholicism once again claim to be *the* Church, than the definition of its content, more convinced of the need for institutions and communities which are distinctively Catholic than alert to the problem of defining that distinctiveness in ways which meet any test other than documentary definitions of doctrine.[36]

If the prophetic radicals would renounce all of Christian history since Constantine in order to restore primitive simplicity and purity of witness, Hitchcock and his allies, and, one suspects, the Roman Cardinals and bureaucrats presently working to contain American renewal, would erect the products of that long history, the particularities of western Catholicism from Trent to Vatican II, into absolutes and universals which themselves constitute the continuing presence of Christ and his spirit in the midst of history. In more mundane form, they erect a specifically Catholic political and cultural agenda, composed of those problems and issues which most clearly distinguish Catholic concerns from those of their neighbors. The subcultural roots of this type of conservatism are evident in J. Brian Benestadt's critique of the bishops' social teaching. In addition to criticizing their lack of a coherent political philosophy, Benestadt argues that the bishops and their staffs have taken up an agenda of social and political problems established by "secular trends", presumably social justice and world peace. Worse, they ignore problems more "appropriate" to their concern as bishops, such as "the decline of serious religious belief . . . . the spread of individualism and materialism; the breakdown of community and fraternity . . . hedonism, moral permissiveness and pornography", suicide, drug abuse, "violence and low academic achievement".[37]

Once upon a time, the conservative position sustained the unity and coherence of a massive American Catholic population. So strong is the desire to recapture a Catholic ground which will combine the particular identity needs of a people with claims to universality, that the conservative are as willing, perhaps even eager, to confine true faith and church to small groups set off against an evil world as are their justice and peace counterparts. Indeed, this common desire for smaller, more intensely committed communities defined in opposition to the world unites left and right. Again, Avery Dulles reflects wider impulses in contemporary Catholicism. Like the renewal leader in the parish who wishes to make every event an occasion for the clarification of commitment to the church, Dulles argues that church now requires "committed individuals who are personally strong enough to stand up against the prevalent assumptions of the civilization in which they find themselves." That civilization, presumably the modern world in general and American society in particular, is not a fit habitation for a real Christian:

> In the prevailing paganism of the near future (a future already in some-ways upon us) Christians who wish to retain any firm beliefs or adhere to any moral norms will have to distance themselves from the dominant culture. They will probably be unable to form a new religious subculture of their own. They will have to be fiercely loyal to the Gospel, concerned with specifically religious values, and somewhat withdrawn from the secular culture, which will go its own way without being greatly influenced by the Church.[36]

What distinguishes all these position, I believe, is their common lament of worldliness and their call for Catholic separatism. The church and its members have become at home in their world, Americanized, if you will; Greeley, Novak, and their friends want that event sanctioned; most theologians, pastoral reformers, and social activists want it reversed. The boundaries between the church and the world have become all but invisible, as the world has broken through into the church and swallowed up its loyal, disciplined Catholic people. Almost without exception these comentators place the church at the center of their vision. Lay persons at home in the world have surrendered to the siren call of modern materialism; bishops who take on a public role without reference to a specific Catholic agenda have surrendered to "secular trends." Whether that world is seen as dominated by a logic and calculus of death, as with Daniel Berrigan or under the sway of Satan, as with Martin, or as permeated by projects set by liberal, atheistic enemies, as with Hitchcock, it is an arena at best indifferent, at worst positively hostile to authentic Christian life. Dulles, to describe the situation of Christians, cites a second century letter to Diognetus: "They reside in their repective countries, but only as aliens; they take part in everything as citizens and put up with everything as foreigners; every foreign land is their home, and every home a foreign land." In the twentieth century the story is told of a West Virginian mining strike in which radical agitator Mother Jones held out against a settlement which ended a rash of violence and allowed starving miners to return to work. Asked about Mother Jones' opposition to the settlement, a miner responded: "Mother Jones don't live here; in fact Mother Jones don't live anywhere." Amid the precarious problems of the world and the church, the answer seems clear: Christians do not live anywhere except, possibly, in church.

Is the choice of sectarian, perhaps prophetic, church justified by a reading of the signs of the times in light of Christian faith? After all, how can the follower of Jesus live comfortably, indeed perhaps even live at all, in a world marked by injustice, poverty, political oppression and a drift toward man-made Armageddon? Can any reason be given to support the effort of Joseph Cardinal Bernardin to promote an energetic Catholic effort to influence American public life toward a "seamless garment" of pro-life values which would embrace abortion, capital punishment, nuclear arms and poverty, an effort that implies an activist engagement in worldly activities? Can there be any religious, theological, ecclesial value placed upon the specifically political work of a Mario Cuomo? And how can a real Catholic, loyal to that tradition, sustained by the heroic sacrifices of our predecessors, be at home in a world of abortions, drug abuse, sexual kinkiness and "low academic achievement"? One answer, perhaps too simple to be true, is that it is, for better or for worse, our world. We might argue that, as immigrants and outsiders, we never really had any constructive role in American society and therefore do not bear re-sponsibility for its problems. Most of us need only reflect on our own family histories to know that is not entirely true. This is, in the end, our world; we have helped to make it what it is and by our choices we will help determine what it will become.

Thomas Merton found at the heart of the central modern problem of war and violence a pervasive lack of responsibility. Alert to the fatalistic irra-tionality which lay behind the language of nuclear strategists who justified preparation for war as the only means to peace, he was equally sensitive to the widespread tendency, amid the confusion and fear spawned by such mad-ness, to withdraw altogether from public life. The lover of justice, the good person, was tempted, Merton said, quoting Plato, "to remain quietly at his own work, like a traveller caught in a storm who retreats behind a wall to shelter from the driving gusts of dust and hail. Seeing the rest of the world full of iniquity, he will be content to keep his own life on earth untainted with wick-edness and impious actions, so that he may leave this world with a fair hope of the next, at peace with himself and God." Even pacifists, Merton noted, often betray such a "world denying and individualistic asceticism" which sees war as both inevitable and intolerable, as intolerable as the corrupt society which it embodies and which must be renounced. "It is perhaps true that sometimes individuals may be forced into this position, but to view it as nor-mal and to accept it as preferable to the risks and conflicts of public life is an admission of defeat, an abdication of responsibility", Merton argued. "This secession into individualistic concern with one's own salvation alone may in fact leave the way all the more open for unscrupulous men and groups to gain and wield unjust power." Merton did not want to move the monastary to the prophetic edge of the church and the world, but to their center, there to engage in the midst of pluralism with the central issues of public life:

> We must judge and decide not only as individuals, preserving for our-
> selves the luxury of a clean conscience, but also as members of society
> taking a common burden and responsibility. It is all too easy to retire
> into an ivory tower of private spirituality and let the world blow itself to
> pieces. Such a decision would be immoral, an admission of defeat. It
> would imply a secret complicity in the overt destructive fury of the
> fanatics.[39]

The real choice then, is not between a faithful church and a pagan world, but between responsibility and irresponsibility, between acknowledgement that people are worthwhile, that there is a goal to human history and a mean- ing to human existence, and the always demonic suggestion that the only meaning and value that exists lies in religion, the church, our church. For those who choose to accept responsibility, there can be no escape to an island of self righteousness, a location of ourselves based on the illusion that we can be responsible by avoiding responsibility, even if that location be a church. It is this realization of responsibility which informs the effort of some bishops to participate in reshaping a public dialogue in the United States. Led by Car- dinal Bernardin (and more recently also by Archbishop Weakland and the drafters of the economics pastoral), the bishops are attempting to recognize the diversity of the Catholic community, to affirm the prophetic impulse pre- sent within the church, and yet to remain within this world, accepting respon- sibility for its current life and precarious prospects. As Bernardin put it in describing the overall thrust of "The Challenge of Peace":

> Historically, the moral issues of war and peace have spilled over into
> ecclesiology; today the cosmic dimensions of the nuclear question have
> moved many to say that the Christian posture can only be one of
> separation--personally, vocationally and ecclesially--from the societal
> enterprise of possessing nuclear weapons. Despite the radical moral
> skepticism of the pastoral letter about ever containing the use of nuclear
> weapons within justifiable limits, the bishops were not persuaded that
> this judgement should lead to an ecclesial posture of withdrawal from
> dialogue or participation in the public life of the nation. Rather, in
> accord with the traditional Catholic conception, they affirmed a posture
> of dialogue with the pluralistic secular world. I am the first to say--after
> the past three years--that it is a precarious posture, but one I find more
> adequate than either total silence within society or absolute separation
> from society.[40]

While by no means resolving the church's internal problems, Bernardin and his associates are clearly trying to draw Catholics into civic life to help define principles which will structure the public debate on matters of common concern. Bernardin's speeches outlining a "seamless garment" of pro-life principles carry this project further, disturbing all those who wish to see a more specifically Christian or Catholic position set forth on specific issues, be it war or abortion.

The bishops fully and explicitly recognize the problem posed by Dulles and so many others: how can the church be the church, with its own distinct identity, and at the same time undertake with full seriousness its mission to society, to humanization and justice and peace? As Elisabeth Schüssler Fiorenza has shown, prevailing arguments on behalf of the church's social and political ministries all fall short in one way or another. Religious identity should not be defined "precisely in its specific difference from the ethical, social or political" dimensions of human life, she writes. When that is done, political theology is only critical; "the mission of the Church is defined precisely and exclusively in its specific difference from other groups; what is shared in common is overlooked." The first task is rather "to uncover the latent value and symbols that undergird a particular society", confronting these with the values and symbols of Christianity.

> The church is acting properly as Church when its proclamation confronts the operative values and visions of a society. The danger for the church's political ministry is not that it will be too confrontative; the danger is that, as a member of society, the Church itself might lose sight of the applicability of its very own vision. Hence the need for a self reflective and reconstructive political theology.[41]

But Fiorenza's dialectical approach can be turned around. Just as there is a danger that political society may tend to absolutize particular national beliefs, values and symbols, so there is the danger that a particular church may so absolutize its particularities as to render itself the center of human history and make loyalty to itself the basic ground of its members presence in the world. It may do this in the form of premature and apocalyptic prophecy or in the simpler terms of making every teaching a prescription for church-related activity, devaluing in the process public life and thus weakening the prospects for the improvement, renewal and transformation required by the commitment to human dignity, justice and peace. It is one thing to insist upon the independence of the church, its right to be the church; it is quite another to make of that church the sole or dominant center of value in any particular culture. For in any particular culture, be it Poland, Chile or the United States, the church is at one and the same time a community of faith and a constituent element of its

38

particular world; it is responsible for its own fidelity and integrity, but also for the moral well-being of that society in which it is a participant.

Always we must remember that in discussions of church integrity and responsibility, church and world are not two entities, separate and apart from one another. Here and now there is no church without a world, no world without churches. In Joseph Komonchak's suggestive description:

> the world is not that which lies outside the Church; the world includes the Church, and without the Church, the world would not be what it is. Christian believing, hoping and loving are political acts, moments in the realization of the world. If this is the case, then there is not some first moment in which the Church becomes the Church and a second moment in which the Church considers its relation to the world. The Church's self-constitution is itself an act within and with reference to the world.[42]

It is precisely here, I think, that prevailing interpretations of American Catholicism's precarious prospects are most at fault. Theology, pastoral practice and social action all converge around a felt need to establish the autonomous existence of the church, and thus validate the roles and lives of its most dedicated members. In the specific context of modern culture, it seems to me, the natural tendency is to seek that specific, unique set of ideas which set the church off against other institutions and communities in the society. Christians don't live, after all, anywhere. In the end, this process confirms the claims of those who would confine the church to religious matters, exclude it from public and political questions, and allow things to go on as they are. Religion, like peace, is a quite acceptable "option for individuals"; secular matters, like economics and politics, are the realm of the laity. If the separation of church and world is allowed, then it is proper to conclude that priests and bishops should stay out of politics and lay ministry should be confined to the church. But such a stance would reflect an "ecclesiastical narcissism" and "trivialization of the laity."[43] As Archbishop Rembert Weakland put it, in responding to criticism of the forthcoming pastoral on the economy, to divide the world "into two areas, worldly or secular on the one hand, and religious on the other" implies "that somehow the laity are not the church, but some unusual secular branch of it."[44]

Catholics, after all, do not stand on the margins of society in the United States. Most American Catholics, and certainly most bishops, priests, religious and theologians, while perhaps "concerned" about one or another aspect of American society, are quite at home in it. They do not live in monasteries, they are not poor, they are not and do not want to be members of an isolated sect or a revolutionary front. At their best they recognize that for them, unlike their poor or alienated brothers and sisters, no question of social morality or public policy is a matter of Catholic outsiders and non-Catholic insiders, us and them. This American world is already in us, shaping and informing even our supposedly religious symbols and language, while the church and all of us are simultaneously in the world, a world which we, with others, have made. We reject a sectarian, non-political Christianity not as Catholics or Americans, but as both, for it does not adequately express our experience or our responsibility as people who are church members and citizens all at once. We similarly reject an amoral realism on both Christian and American grounds. As decent human beings we recognize the justice of granting exemptions to persons of eccentric belief, but our dissent is not like that, to be satisfied by provision in a manual, alternative service, or refusal of work. We claim that our position is the proper American position and it cannot be marginalized by toleration. If we remain in the midst of life and do not join that monastery or revolution, it is not because we have made a second best choice but because we have been called and believe it is right for us to be there. We want no exemption, but policies, goals, strategies to which we can give our wholehearted support, to which we can devote our lives.

The enduring temptation of the church in a society such as ours is to measure its success or failure by its own standards. Recognizing the intimate relationship between private life and religion, and told by others that religion has no role in public life, churches are apt to regard their only task as personal and communal, to measure vitality and strength by numbers and activities, by the purity of doctrine, the integrity of moral life, the strength of organization. Liberals and conservatives alike measure society by the standards of the church; moral majorities and social actionists alike find the world wrong and attempt to change it in accord with the values of their private worlds. In the process the church becomes a tribe, or an interest group, or a contestant in various public contests; public life is reduced to a colosseum where representatives of private worlds contend for power and recognition. And then, in reflective moments, all wonder what happened to the public interest, why common values are not translated into public policy, why power alone seems to matter and nice people do horrible things. The Mafia chieftain who loves his family, prays to the Virgin and funds the parish building drive, the machine boss who never misses mass, the executive who serves on the local United Way Board but closes his plant because wages are lower in Taiwan, the loving Christian who plots nuclear strategy are products of the same culture which produces the radical christian who confuses prophecy with disengagement from a corrupt society, the spiritual director who directs souls deeper into themselves and never turns them back toward the world in which they live, the bishop or pastor who thinks things will be alright as soon as everyone has had a conversion experience.

To be sure, both theological self-understanding and sociological imperatives require close attention to the construction of forms of associational life which will provide the experience of community. There is no escaping that. But radicals and conservatives often seem at one in focusing exclusive attention on the private dimension; the one regards the public as all but lost, the other as beyond the appropriate reach of the church. Yet, what the church committed to justice and a world badly in need of it both require are new types of persons who integrate community and society, men and women of faith, deeply committed to their community, and at one and the same time men and women of their age, competent in their professions and disciplines, engaged in other organizations, intelligently active in public affairs. To be sure, we need the church and its self-conscious project, so we need ministers. But they are ministers to the ministers, servants of those who do God's work in the world, in family, community, profession, politics, culture. For all the strength of our renewal since Vatican II, we have yet to learn that lesson.

A Catholicism which embraces both church and world in a critical and constructive spirit grounded in Christian love was the dream of liberal Catholicism. Evidence of the decline of such liberalism abounds. It can be seen in the weakness of the national episcopal conference, which remains unsure of its role and speaks generally with a very weak voice in the councils of the universal church, despite its recent courage on nuclear weapons. Internally there is a states rights church, with each diocese dominated by the personality of the local ordinary, with no national center for reflection or action. Most national organizations and movements remain dull and uncreative, providing few real resources for the local churches and exerting only slight impact on the national conference of bishops. Most national organizations now have great difficulty interesting able persons in assuming positions of leadership. This weakness of national organization reflects the erosion of the liberal dream of a truly American Catholicism, engaged with the life of the nation and energizing local churches to come out of their parochial preoccupations to assume responsibility for the mission of the church within the national community. John Coleman, whose essays provide the best current commentary on American Catholicism, has noted that the mission of the church to defend and promote the dignity of the human person is a "worldly vocation" which should center upon the laity who have access to the means by which culture and politics are shaped, but "almost *nothing* like this pastoral strategy is currently available in the American church."[45] Similarly, the professed desire to influence public policy on matters of social justice and world peace implies a sense of civic responsibility, but even now the church lacks an adequate theory of citizenship, and few scholars are trying to provide one. Finally, despite much talk of collegiality and shared responsibility, there remain too many glaring examples of arbitrary action. In the absence of effective commitment to church reform involving an authentic sharing of responsibility, including at the national level, Rome will continue to divide and conquer, and thus to disrupt pastoral work and serious renewal. More positively, the construction of forums for dialogue and decision, comparable to those modelled in the mid 70s by the Call to Action, can keep alive the possibility of mutual correction and cooperation, multiply opportunities for effective public witness and enhance the possibility of American participation in the broader dialogue of the world church, itself an indispensible element of positive action for peace, justice and human rights.

The liberalism of American Catholicism at the time of the Council was undoubtedly naive in its understanding of the nation and its people; surely it needs a "course correction", a more chastened appreciation of the demonic potential of power and deeper concern for the personal, spiritual and organizational dimensions of church life and ministry. But the answer to the Americanist problem is not withdrawal to some mountaintop of biblical prophecy and self righteous desertion of the public arena. Nor is it a new conservatism of Catholic power and doctrinal orthodoxy. Rather it requires recovery of a sense of mission, inspired by contemporary church teaching and rendered operative by close attention to the specifically American character of our own situation. It means probing the depths of the American experience, including the American experience of our own people, to develop a body of ideas which can give meaning to ministry and work and faith in the day-to-day life of American Catholics. It means a bottom up strategy of pastoral development based upon the experience and the responsibility of the people of the church. It means a theology of mission which gives a central place to the laity, to politics, to work, to neighborhood life, and an approach to pastoral planning which is participatory and democratic. It means a social theology and strategy which adds to themes of criticism and witness a sense of constructive responsibility; if things have to be changed, how are we to change them?

Social change begins with social consciousness, but that is consciousness not only of how bad things are measured by the Gospel, but consciousness of how we already are participants in this culture, this world, and not another, awareness of how deeply and inescapably American we already are. Like it or not, there are no mountaintops to which we can withdraw to be Christian, not American. The missionary in Africa, the Black writer on the left bank, the ambitious Bostonian in the papal court, all discover, in the end, that they are Americans. Some days we would like to be wholly Catholic or wholly Christian, uncontaminated by time and place and culture. But history isn't like that. When we loved America too much, sending our sons to die for it and comparing their sacrifice to Christ's, when we hated America too much, calling it murderous and welcoming its anger, we were equally its children. We are not the first generation to experience exile, internal or external, to be spiritual refugees in the heart of our country, and to mistake our exile community for the saving remnant of the Lord. Most of us will eventually feel called home again.

Our Americanness is the concrete, fleshy human context of our call to be Catholic Christians. Like all contexts, it is in as well as out, shaping not just the conditions of our public life but our very feelings about God and one another. Let us unpack our Americanness, probe the spiritual meaning of our American adventure, find the words, the symbols, the language that will lead us back to this people, our people, and with them to the people of the world. Authentic prophecy takes place within and on behalf of a specific people; do we think that people is only Catholics, as if we alone are chosen, for God's sake and our own? Authentic church is in and for the world, not the abstract world of humankind or "the poor" or "women", but the real world around us, open to all, speaking on behalf of all, inviting all to the full realization of their humanity, sacramentalizing the rich human experience around us, liberating all persons from the slavery of poverty and tyranny, sin and death. We desperately need an American standpoint, sufficiently Christian to understand and illuminate human experience in this our land, yet not so super- or pseudo-Christian as to claim to be judge and contradiction of all that America means. It is one thing to be a stranger and an alien through imposition, as the faithful and patriotic Pole or Chilean must be under regimes that exclude such persons from an active role in national life. It is quite another to choose exile, especially when one is the heir to the sacrifices of generations of poor people who struggled precisely that we might have the freedom to choose which is now the central theme of our experience. No more than you do I know the precise character of our relationship with our country, but I do believe that we will discover new meaning in our Catholicity and begin to really believe in the hopes we so often express for a more just and peaceful world when we make our decision to accept and struggle with the fact, however painful, that this is our land and these are our people. It is America, as much as Catholicism, which has made us who we are; we will not resolve our problems by making new ghettos but by caring deeply for this new world we have once again entered.

NOTES

1. This paper, in much longer form, was delivered to the College Theology Society's convention on June 2, 1984. It has been sharply reduced in length at the request of the editor. A longer version will be printed in pamphlet format by the National Catholic Reporter.

2. Isaac Hecker, Diary, December 18, 1844 in Hecker papers, Paulist Fathers Archives, New York.

3. Mary Gordon, *Final Payments* (New York: Random House, 1978) 3.

4. "The Challenge of Peace: God's Promise and Our Response," no. 124

5. I have examined the tripartite sources of change in the American church in "Some Reflections on the Catholic Experience in the United States" in Irene Woodward, Ed., *The Catholic Church: The United States Experience* (New York: Paulist, 1979) 5-42. See also Sidney Ahlstrom, "National Trauma and Changing Religious Values," *Daedalus* 78 (1978) 13-29.

6. John Coleman, S.J., "The Future of Ministry," *America* 144 (March 28, 1981) 243-249.

7. John Tracy Ellis, *American Catholicism* (rev. ed.; Chicago: U. of Chicago, 1969); Andrew Greeley, *The Catholic Experience* (Garden City, N.Y.: Doubleday, 1967).

8. Philip Gleason, "The Crisis of Americanization" in Gleason, ed., *Contemporary Catholicism in the United States* (Notre Dame: U. of Notre Dame, 1969) 3-32.

9. James Hennesey, S.J., *American Catholics* (New York: Oxford U., 1982) 331.

10. Greeley, "Going Their Own Way" *New York Times Magazine,* (October 10, 1982) 28-29. See also Andrew Greeley, *American Catholics: A Social Portrait* (New York: Basic Books, 1977); *The Communal Catholic* (New York: Seabury, 1976); *Crisis in the Church* (Chicago: Thomas More, 1979).

11. Michael Novak, *Confession of a Catholic* (San Francisco: Harper and Row, 1983).

12. Philip Murnion, "A Sacramental Church," *America* 148 (March 26, 1983) 226-228

13. Robert Bellah, "Religion and Power in America today," *Commonweal* 109 (December 3, 1982) 650-655.

14. See David J. O'Brien, "Literacy, Faith, Church: An American Religious Perspective," in John V. Apczynski, editor, *Foundations of Religious Literacy,* Proceedings of the College Theology Society , 1982 (Scholars Press, Chico, CA: 1983) 3-30

15. Timothy L. Smith, "Religion and Ethnicity in America," *American Historical Review* 83 (1978 1155-1185. See also Timothy L. Smith, "Lay Initiative in the Religious Life of American Immigrants, 1880-1950" in Tamara Harevan, ed., *Anonymous Americas* (Englewood Cliffs, N.J.: Prentice Hall, 1971) 214-249; Smith, "Immigrant Social Aspirations and American Education; 1880-1930," *American Quarterly* 21 (Fall, 1969) 534-536.

16. Philip Gleason, "In Search of Unity: American Catholic Thought, 1920-1960," *Catholic Historical Review* 65 (1979) 225.

17. H. Richard Niebuhr, *The Social Sources of Denominationalism* (New York: Meridian, 1957); *The Kingdom of God in America* (New York: Harper, 1937); *Christ and Culture* (New York: Harper, 1951); "The Protestant Movement and Democracy in the United States," in James W. Smith, ed., *The Shaping of American Religion* I (Princeton: Princeton U., 1961) 20-71

18. Martin Marty, "Protestant and Jewish Relations" in Edward C. Herr, *Tomorrow's Church: What's Ahead for American Catholics?* (Chicago: Thomas More, 1982) 226.

19. Karl Rahner, *The Christian Commitment (New York: Sheed and Ward, 1963) 29.*

20. *Peter L. Berger and Richard John Neuhaus, editors, Against the World, For the World* (New York: Seabury, 1976); Avery Dulles, *The Resilient church* (Garden City, N.Y.: Doubleday, 1977)

21 Avery Dulles, S.J., "Thinking it Over," *The Wilson Quarterly (Autumn, 1981) 131.*

22 *Harry Emerson Fosdick, The Living of These Days* (New York: Harper, 1956) 53.

23. William R. Hutchinson, "Cultural Strain and Protestant liberalism," *American Historical Review* 76 (1971) 386-411.

24. Hilaire Belloc, quoted in William Halsey, *The Survival of American Innocence (Notre Dame: U. of Notre Dame, 1980) 14; Frank Sheed, The Church and I* (Garden City, N.Y.: Doubleday, 1974).

25. John XXIII, quoted in Giancarlo Zizola, *The Utopia of Pope John* (Maryknoll, NY: Orbis, 1974) 246.

26. "The Pastoral constitution on the Church and the Modern World," in Walter Abbott, editor *Documents of Vatican II* (New York: America, 1966) 199-200.

27. *Ibid.,* 307

28. Karl Rahner, "Towards a Fundamental Theological Interpretation of Vatican II," *Theological Studies* 42 (1981) 716-727.

29. Sidney E. Mead, "Prospects for the Church in America," in Philip J. Hefner, editor, *The Future of the American Church* (Philadelphia: Fortress, 1968) 1-29

30. Quoted in *Ibid.,* 18.

31. David O'Rourke, "Revolution and Alienation in the American Church," *Commonweal* 110 (February 11, 1983) 76-79.

32. Daniel Berrigan, *The Nightmare of God* (Portland, Oregon: Sunburst, 1983) 128-129.

33. Morris West, *The Clowns of God* (New York: Bantam, 1981) 395.

34. "The Challenge of Peace," par. 276-277. In the first two drafts the bishop used the phrase "neo-pagan" society.

35. Ralph Martin, *A Crisis of Truth* (Ann Arbor: Servant, 1982) 223.

36. James Hitchcock, *Catholicism and Modernity: Confrontation or Capitulation?* (New York: Seabury, 1979).

37. J. Brian Benestadt, *The Pursuit of a Just Social Order* (Washington: Ethics and Public Policy, 1982).

38. Avery Dulles, "The Situation of the Church, 1965-1975," Unpublished paper. Similar ideas are contained in *The Resilient Church.*

39. Thomas Merton, The Nonviolent Alternative; ed. by Gordon C. Zahn (New York; Farrar, Straus and Giroux, 1980) 29, 33, 117, 209.

40. Joseph Cardinal Bernardin, "Church Impact on Public Policy," *Origins,* 13 (February, 1984) 567.

41. Elisabeth Schüssler Fiorenza, "The Church's Religious Identity and its Social and Political Mission," *Theological Studies* 43 (1982), 197-225.

42. Joseph Komonchak, "Clergy, Laity and the Church's Mission to the World," *The Jurist* 41 (1981) 425-447.

43. *Ibid.* 445.

44. Archbishop Rembert Weakland, "Where Does the Economics Pastoral Stand?," *Origins* 13 (April 26, 1984) 758.

45. John Coleman, S.J., *An American Strategic Theology* (New York/Ramsey: Paulist, 1982) 51.

II.
AMERICANISM:
THE PAST AND THE FUTURE

THE FUTURE OF "AMERICANISM"

William L. Portier

The Americanism episode (1884-1899) stands like a great divide in the middle of both the institutional and intellectual histories of Catholicism in the United States. 1984 was the centennial year of the third plenary council of Baltimore. Twenty-seven years ago, in 1957, the late Thomas T. McAvoy published his now standard study on Americanism. He introduced it with a chapter on the third plenary council of Baltimore in 1884. As we mark the centennial year of this council it is fitting that we look back and do some future-oriented remembering about Americanism.

Surveying the beginnings of the Americanist episode from the vantage point of one hundred years, it appears as a case study in the relationship between Catholicism and American culture. The question which agitated Catholics in the United States at the turn of the century is still a live one: Is American culture fundamentally benign or hostile to Catholicism? In the nineteenth century, the question about whether one could simultaneously be a good Catholic and a good "American" was posed from the outside. Now that we have "made it," we pose the question from the inside.

As Americanism was about a vision of where the world was going and the place the United States had in that movement, so, at the end of the "American century," Catholics in the United States must have a vision of history to guide their actions with respect to their nation and with respect to what Karl Rahner called the emerging "world Church."

As we mark the centennial of the Americanism episode's beginning, Catholics in the United States are faced with at least three possible visions of where history is going, three myths which relate Catholicism to the "American" experience. I use the term *myth* in a broad sense to mean a basic narrative structure whose symbols help religious people make sense out of historical events. The first comes very close to the apocalyptic and sectarian. In this myth of the Catholic left, the nation "America" is the evil empire whose demonic power must be resisted at every turn by those who are true Christians. The president becomes a Herod, the pentagon a house of death to be drenched with innocent human blood. All the biblical symbols of sin and death are called down upon the nation. At its best, this vision of history voices a powerful Christian protest against all that is idolatrous in American nationalism. This idolatry reaches its climax in the "nuclearism" which stands ready to sacrifice any value, including that of innocent life, in exchange for the phantom security of the deterrent. At its worst, the myth of the Catholic left betrays the inclusivenenss of the gospel and the Kingdom in the name of prophetic witness and a call to national repentance which is often more stylized than real. History is reduced to a religious dualism in which the faithful resistance community stands steadfast and alone against the evil nation.

The second myth would drape the nation in the messianic symbols of the scriptures. It is part of the long American tradition going back to John Winthrop and the seventeenth-century Puritans, and of which the Catholic Americanists of the nineteenth century were also a part. Because they came at it from the outside, we can perhaps understand their excesses. It is more difffficult to understand the recent revival of the worst aspects of nineteenth-century Catholic Americanism in someone like Michael Novak and those for whom he speaks. The nineteenth-century racial mythology of Latin and Saxon come to life again as Novak pronounces upon the ethnic experience in the United States (the ethnic Catholic as the best American) and upon the North-South relationship in terms of "democratic capitalism." Finally, in the tortured reasoning he uses to defend the deterrent, Novak comes perilously close to erecting the obvious goods of the form of government of the United States into some form of religious absolute which we can use any means to defend. At its best, this myth affirms and celebrates the more than two hundred year history of political freedom in the United States. Ambiguous as they are, our political symbols have shown themselves resilient enough to require the inclusion of those who have been excluded from this history. At its worst, this myth too betrays the inclusiveness of its own symbols by reducing history to another dualism in which the righteous empire, America, is set in mortal combat against the atheistic forces of Soviet communism.

Rather than to the righteous empire, city on the hill, strand of American tradition, the third myth appeals to the symbols of Enlightenment faith in reasoned public discourse as it comes to us from the founding fathers. Rather than the apocalyptic dualism of the two previous visions of history, this myth offers a more pluralistic view of history's movement. It is inclusive. History's board has more than two pieces. This is in the best sense of the term a *liberal* myth, mediated through the symbols of law and marketplace and the public debate which both imply. The great temptation of the children of righteous empire is to invest the political process with religious symbols for ultimate good and evil. This turns political disagreements into cosmic battles. We see this in the Catholic Americanists as they bought into the story of the city on the hill. They might have learned from the founding fathers' attempt, largely for practical reasons, to secularize the political process. Catholic thinkers in the United States from Orestes Brownson and Isaac Hecker to John Courtney Murray have argued for the compatibility of this secularizing strand with Catholic thought in general and with the natural law tradition in particular. But we see also in Brownson and Hecker the tension between the American ideal of secularizing the political process and the obvious intent of the scriptures to speak in terms of God's sovereignty over history. This tension suggests that the liberal myth alone is not sufficient as a Christian world-view.

The bibilical doctrine of sin warns us that what is put forth as reasoned discourse may not always be so. In addition, therefore, to the celebration of "America," public life must always have room for the prophetic witness who calls the nation to true repentence. Only the liberal myth on the other hand is complex enough to do justice to the inclusiveness of the symbols of both Kingdom and nation. Only some form of the liberal myth allows the prophet to warn that this is not true peace, this is not true freedom, without setting him or her at mortal odds with history. If we want truly inclusive justice and truly inclusive peace, the liberal myth bids us go into the market place and argue for them in terms of law and reason and the other symbols of this story. This will engender political conflicts rather than cosmic battles.

Biblical faith assures us that the lions of the day will be sufficient thereto. God will raise up the prophets to warn us that our reasoned discourse has become irrational, a sinful cover for our own self-interest. From the symbol of the messianic Kingdom which the Americanists invoked in such a one-sided way, we can take the critical principle necessary to correct the Pelagian tendencies of the liberal myth. Because of the sin of which we are called to repent, worldy empires are rarely righteous and rarely reasonable. On the other hand, if the doctrine of creation (the *imago Dei*), the natural law tradition which is meant to express it, and the Council of Trent on justification mean anything, neither are worldy empires wholly demonic. If there is one certitude in all of this, it is that a Christian view of history, especially in Catholic form, cannot end in dualism.

TWO GENERATIONS OF
AMERICAN CATHOLIC EXPANSIONISM IN EUROPE:
ISAAC HECKER AND JOHN J. KEANE

William L. Portier

With its victory in the Spanish-American War at the turn of this century, the nation "America" began its rise to the status of a global power. Carried by the momentum of "Manifest Destiny", prominent American bishops mounted a campaign, complete with code names and press leaks, to export American Catholicism to Europe. In the terms of the American arrangement of separation of church and state, they prescribed a trans-Atlantic cure for the religious and political ills of Old Europe.

One cannot survey the vast literature on this episode in American Catholic history without coming upon the name of Isaac Hecker (1819-1888).[1] Yet in that literature, the question of the Paulist founder's relationship to the Americanist movement and to the figures involved in it remains a controversial one. Was Hecker the prototypical Americanist or merely a pawn in the Machiavellian intrigues of the Americanist bishops?[2] The present essay will contribute to the resolution of this question by arguing two related points.

First, at crucial junctures in his life, Isaac Hecker proposed the establishment of Paulist Houses in Europe. They would serve as agents of renewal in the Church and as agents of reconciliation between church and age. Insofar as they exemplify a kind of American messianism with respect to the European Church, these various proposals for establishing the Paulists in Europe anticipate the Americanist expansionism of the 1890's. In a very general sense, then, Hecker is indeed an Americanist prototype. Second, during the last decade of Hecker's life, he and Archbishop John J. Keane (1839-1918) were close friends. Hecker's influence on Keane was considerable. Specifically, Hecker influenced Keane in his public espousal of Americanist ideas. In the person of Archbishop Keane, therefore, we come closest to finding a link between the two generations of American Catholic expansionists.

I. Paulist Expansion into Europe

Hecker first proposed the idea of sending Paulists to Europe in his Vatican I notebook. After that the idea passed through a number of phases. During his sojourn in Europe from 1873 to 1875, Hecker went so far as to consider seriously the possibility of separating himself from the American Paulists in order to form a similar association in Europe. When events dictated his return to the United States, the idea underwent further modification. He still hoped to found a new association in Europe but one that might somehow retain its connection to the original Paulists in New York. When it was proposed for the final time in 1885, Hecker had returned to his Vatican I conception. He saw the European venture as something which would be undertaken by the American group. We will consider the 1870, 1875 and 1885 phases of this proposal in turn.[3]

His experience at the first Vatican Council in 1870 convinced Hecker that the Church had, with the definition of papal infallibility, embarked on a course antagonistic to the democratic tendency of the age.[4] He came to believe that the European Church was incapable of renewing itself. "The mission of the United States in the order of Divine Providence," he wrote to his brother, "is to solve in advance the problems of Europe."[5] As these letters make clear, the providential arrangement of separation of church and state would specifiy the American contribution to the religious and political problems of the European Church.

The Paulists figured in Hecker's 1870 discussion of America's messianic mission to Europe from the beginning. He spoke of the need for an order of spiritual zouaves with a new perspective which would transcend the traditional partisan divisions of the Old World.[6] Since he envisioned them as the religious embodiment of American ideals, Hecker conceived for the Paulists in Europe a role which corresponded to the larger mission of American civilization in regard to the continent.[7] When he returned home from the Council his fellow Paulists were understandably cool toward a proposal which would stretch their already limited manpower in an unrealistic if not quixotic attempt at European expansion.

Hecker would return to Europe in the Spring of 1873. He travelled widely there in hopes of restoring his health until the Fall of 1875. His providential interpretations of events there convinced him that Church and age had been placed on collision course.[8] He came to believe that he as an American had been called by God to help resolve this European crisis. 'It is in this work of the Church in Europe at the present moment [that] I am conscious with an overwhelming conviction [that] Divine Providence calls me [to] labour."[9] This conviction about a personal calling to a European mission was a major turning point in his life which he likened to the events of 1857-58. As his belief that Providence was calling him to convert America had issued in the founding of the Paulists in 1858, so this new sense of calling eventually gave birth to the notion of a new association of Paulists for the reconversion of Europe. "The past was for the United States, the future for the world," he declared.[10]

Hecker's "An Exposition of the Church in View of Recent Difficulties and Controversies and the Present Needs of the Age" (1875) gave voice to this new sense of mission as an "international Catholic."[11] By April of 1875, he was asking about the possibility of "a movement similar, but not the same, as the Paulists in the United States," which would help to meet the needs of the

European Church.[12] This proposal was the "Exposition's" natural completion. The old Paulist ideal would take on a new European form.[13] This new movement would provide the means, lacking in the "Exposition's text, to put its goal of Church renewal into practice. It would also be separate from the Paulists in New York and involve Hecker's own separation from those he now referred to as his "former companions."[14] These thoughts on a new "form" to the "Paulist idea" were interrupted by the receipt of a cable from Augustine Hewit, informing him of the community's decision that he return home by November 1, 1875.

When Hecker returned to the United States, he spoke with Hewit about the possibility of a European foundation. Although Hewit said that he would not make any opposition to such a proposal, Hecker did not raise the matter again for nearly a decade.[15] In 1885, only three years before his death, Hecker revived the 1870 version of his proposal for a Paulist foundation in Europe.

> I formerly thought that we should not make new foundations because our Fathers were divided on some points, and for other reasons. But when I considered how others in our circumstances had made ventures in past ages of the Church, relying on God, then I began to think differently. And if you should ask me where we should make the new foudnations, I should say Dublin and London, and then France and Rome, and in Germany, having regard to the races. And if it be said that a new foundation taking five or six men would badly cripple us. I answer that God would supply the want; we rely blindly on God.[16]

Most significantly for present purposes Hecker revived his European expansion proposal in concert with his close friend and disciple in the spiritual life, the soon to be Americanist, Bishop Keane. This last attempt at realizing the dream of European expansion took the form of a correspondence with the Cardinal Archbishop of Westminster, Henry Edward Manning. The association of Hecker's proposal with the names of Keane and Manning, as well as its expression in terms of American messianism, allow us to see in it an anticipation of the Americanists' later messianic gestures toward the continent.

II. Hecker and Keane

Our knowledge of the Hecker-Keane relationship is based primarily on sixteen letters which Keane wrote to Hecker during the decade prior to the latter's death. In addition there are a number of Keane's letters to the Paulist, Walter Elliott, author of the *Life of Father Hecker* (1891). These hitherto unpublished letters of Keane's are preserved in the Paulist Archives. Since Keane is thought to have destroyed his correspondence, we will never have the Hecker half of the Hecker-Keane correspondence.[17]

The following treatment of the Hecker-Keane relationship will be divided into four parts: (1) Keane's 1872 attempt to join the Paulists, (2) Keane's 1881 summer at Lake George, (3) Keane's correspondence with Manning regarding a Paulist foundation at London in 1885, (4) Keane's encouragement of Walter Elliott.

1. Keane's 1872 Attempt to Join the Paulists

After Keane's ordination to the priesthood in 1866, he was sent as an assistant to St. Patrick's Church in Washington, D.C. His friendship with Hecker dates back to that time, as the latter's travels brought him frequently to St. Patrick's[18] Hecker gave the young Keane a copy of one of his favorite spiritual books, *The Spiritual Doctrine of Louis Lallement* (d. 1635) which, according to Denis O'Connell, Keane "read and assimilated perfectly." O'Connell attributed his close friend's "ever deepening devotion to the Holy Ghost as the immediate guide for the soul in all its spiritual consciousness" to the influence of Hecker.[19]

By 1872 Keane had decided to become a Paulist and asked his archbishop, James Roosevelt Bayley of Baltimore, for the necessary permission.[20] At this time Hecker's health had begun to fail and he wrote to Archbishop Bayley explaining that if Keane became a Paulist, he hoped to entrust him with the editorship of the *Catholic World*.[21] While acknowledging that Keane would have made an excellent Paulist, Bayley refused his permission on the grounds that Keane was also an excellent diocesan priest and would probably some day be a bishop.[22] It is clear from this episode that at this time Hecker looked upon the younger Keane as a protege. In 1878 Keane did indeed become a bishop as Bayley had predicted. In the letter which invited Hecker to his consecration as Bishop of Richmond, Virginia, Keane expressed his hope that in his future work as a bishop "you and your associates may yet be my greatest auxiliaries."[23] On the occasion of Keane's death in 1918, Walter Elliott wrote of him:

> When he came to New York he always lodged with us, both before and after Father Hecker's death. With both Fathers and novices he was as one absolutely at home--as if he were in fact, as he was at heart, a Paulist.[24]

2. Keane's 1881 Summer at Lake George

One of the most significant contacts between Hecker and Keane occurred during the summer of 1881 when Keane spent two months with Hecker at the Paulist summer retreat at Lake George, New York. Suffering from a "serious impairment of his sight," the bishop had been advised by his doctors to take a few months rest.[25] This time of rest was spent in the company of Hecker at Lake George and Keane spoke warmly of the benefits he derived from it.[26] In addition, however, there is also some evidence that during the summer of 1881 Hecker exercised considerable influence on Keane's thinking about America's providential mission and gave him the needed support to express these ideas publicly. On October 16, 1881, Keane preached at a mass of thanksgiving to commemorate the centennial of the colonial victory at the Battle of Yorktown.[27]

The burden of Keane's discourse dealt with the providential destiny of the American nation. Keane shared Hecker's concern for the interpretation of concrete historical events. With Hecker he affirmed that historical events must be viewed in the light of God's overruling providence. In this light, the victory at Yorktown, the turning point of the American revolution, "ranks among the foremost of the great events that have shaped the destinies of the world."[28] Like Hecker, Keane interpreted the emergence of the republican form of government on American soil as the result of centuries of education of the human race by Providence. But the United States did not present to the world the democratic form of government "in its grandest proportions" simply for its own sake. Keane dramatically affirmed that this gift had been bestowed by Providence so that the United States could function as "a teacher, through whose lips and in whose life He was to solve all the social problems of the Old World."[29]

While the Catholic Americanism in Keane's discourse at Yorktown is clearly similar to Hecker's, the similarity in itself is not sufficient to warrant the conclusion that Keane received these ideas through the influence of Hecker. That is why the following letter, in which Keane explicitly acknowledges Hecker's influence on the ideas in the Yorktown address, is so important. Keane wrote:

> I trust you recognized how its best points were of your inspiring, and that I endeavored to profit by every idea and hint you offered me. I am sorry that, in trying to clothe the thoughts attractively, I should have made them obscure. I hope, however, the ideas will be sufficiently grasped by all readers to produce the impression intended.[30]

He described his utterances as "in a certain sense an experiment" which he was sure would attract criticism. Nevertheless he affirmed them as "the honest convictions of my heart," and expressed his willingness to stand by what he had said "before any tribunal." He continued:

If our summer at Lake George is so pleasant a memory to you, think what it must be to me. You were only giving out of the abundance of your heart; -- the profit was all mine. I shall ever look back to it, not only with pleasure, but with deep thankfulness to God for it has done me more good than you can know.[31]

While Keane was in Europe making his *ad limina* visit to Rome, he again wrote of Lake George as the scene "of some of the greatest spiritual graces ever bestowed on me."[32] Testimonies like these, particularly the letter of October 22, 1881 which specifically refers to the *ideas* in the discourse, have an important bearing on the controversial question of Hecker's influence on the Americanist movement of the 1890's. Thomas Wangler has remarked on the noteworthiness of the fact that prior to their trip to Europe in 1886, "both Ireland and Keane had accepted the standard American view of the United States as the 'New World'."[33] The work of Keane's which he cites in support of this assertion is the Yorktown address of 1881. Wangler also points to the likelihood that Cardinal Manning and Pope Leo XIII were not the first to introduce Keane to the Americanist ideology.[34] If Keane's Yorktown address represents, as it appears to do, his first public espousal of the Americanist myth or program of ideas, then his letter to Hecker of October 22, 1881 is highly significant. It identifies Hecker as the source of these ideas. On the basis of Keane's own testimony, therefore, we must conclude that during the summer of 1881 Hecker's influence led Keane to adopt as his own and publicly espouse the body of ideas which eventually became the Americanist ideology of the 1890's. As we have seen above, Hecker himself has held these ideas at least since the time of the first Vatican Council.

3. Keane's correspondence with Manning in 1885 regarding a Paulist foundation in England

In 1885 Hecker was sixty-six years old and suffering from a chronic illness which had debilitating effects. Despite his weakened condition, however, he had not given up on the dream of opening Paulist houses in the chief cities of Europe as agents of renewal and regeneration. Efforts to this end were renewed in the summer of 1885 through the good offices of Keane. At Hecker's request, the bishop wrote a letter to Cardinal Manning asking, in Hecker's name, for permission to establish a Paulist house in London. Manning and Keane were acquainted as the result of a visit the latter had made to Manning on his way home from Rome in 1883.[35] At this time they had discussed, among other things, their common interest in promoting devotion to the Holy Ghost and Manning's desire to renew the spirit of his clergy and people. In this connection, Keane wrote as the Paulists' "agent and advocate," and as what he hoped would be "the instrument of divine Providence" in proposing the Paulist foundation to the Cardinal. He saw this proposal as related to the great work they had discussed two years earlier. The work Keane described to Manning was "missions, preaching, giving retreats, etc." Keane did not hesitate to recommend the Paulists to Manning in highly complimentary tones. He described the Paulists in terms of what Hecker hoped would be their distinctive relationship to the age. He spoke of them as priests who aimed to be:

> like their holy patron, truly Apostolic men, appreciating the Providence of the age, understanding its needs, entering into its mind and heart, and laboring, in the truly Catholic and Apostolic spirit of the Apostle to the gentiles, to turn it to God.[36]

Keane's letter to Manning is dated August 1, 1885. Instead of mailing the letter, however, he placed it in Hecker's hands to send at his discretion. By September 9, Hecker still had the letter. His notes for this date reveal him as decidedly in favor of European expansion. He described the proposed London house as "wholly missionary, without any public church or oratory." He added his desire that the Paulists in London would not cause any financial burden to the local church and concluded: "I am in favor of extension into Europe, and I say, emphatically, I cannot help it."[37]

The other Paulists, however, did not share their founder's enthusiasm for the European venture. On September 15, 1885, Keane wrote in response to a letter from Hecker:

> I was not exactly surprised to learn that the letter had not been sent to Cardinal Manning--for it was but natural that views should differ about the project, or even your own views, perhaps, be modified in regard to it, or to the way of setting it in motion. And yet I cannot help feeling sorry that the venture should not be made, even as proposed.[38]

Keane closed this letter by referring the matter to Providence.

Cardinal John McCloskey of New York, Hecker's first confessor upon his conversion, had died on October 10, 1885. Keane came to New York for the funeral. It was at this time that he and Hecker had their final consultation about the letter to Manning. This letter was apparently mailed around mid-October 1885. This date is based on the testimony of Elliott. On October 16, 1885, Elliott wrote Hecker from Baltimore that he had just seen Bishop Keane "fresh from you." At this time Keane had suggested to Elliott that he begin to ask Hecker questions and keep a record of his answers. Thus began Elliott's memoranda which would provide source material for his controversial biography of Hecker.[39] In one such memorandum, dated November 2, 1885, Elliott recorded Hecker's statement that he and Keane had consulted about the letter to Manning while the bishop was in New York for Cardinal McCloskey's funeral. At this time Keane did not change the wording of the letter, "but added that since its date, Father Hecker had been thinking and praying over the matter, and this was the final conclusion."[40]

On November 23, 1885, Keane wrote Hecker that he had heard "not a word as yet from across the water." "You took some months to think over my letter before sending it, -- and he may take as long before answering it; -- but God will make no mistake."[41]

A few days after Christmas, Keane wrote to inform Hecker that he had received a negative reply from Manning on the proposed Paulist house in London. Keane enclosed Manning's letter and added the following comments:

> The enclosed from Cardinal Manning has reached me this moment. Though I can well guess how you will see and adore the will of God, still I will not acknowledge this letter till I hear from you. If you think of anything to say in the way of following up the proposition made, I am quite ready to put it before him. This looks like the ending of the matter as far as he is concerned; but if any different light comes to you, speak and your servant heareth.[42]

Hecker responded quickly. On January 15, 1886, Keane wrote to say that "after mature deliberation" he had written to Manning again, "giving him the substance of your letter in your very words."[43] Keane concluded the letter with a statement of his intention to be with Hecker in New York by "next Friday evening." Hecker had engaged the bishop to preach at St. Paul's church on the feast of the conversion of St. Paul on January 25.[44] During the weekend of January 23-25, therefore, Hecker and Keane were together in New York. Keane was again in New York in February in connection with his tour of the Northeast in order to raise money for the proposed Catholic University of America.[45]

On June 4, 1886, he wrote to Hecker regarding his preoccupation with the "matter of our conversations when I was last with you." This is perhaps a reference to one of the occasions of Keane's winter visits to New York mentioned above. The letter encouraged Hecker in his attitude of abandonment to God's will and prayed that the Holy Spirit would be to him a Comforter.[46] Hecker must have replied with an invitation for Keane to spend another summer at Lake George. The bishop, already busy with the task of raising money for the Catholic University, declined the invitation in his next letter, dated June 17, 1886. He reported that Manning had yet to answer his second letter and mentioned the possibility of discussing the topic of Paulist expansion into

Europe with Archbishop Walsh of Dublin.[47] After this Keane's letters make no further mention of the proposed Paulist house at London. Manning probably never answered the second letter.

4. Keane's encouragement of Walter Elliott

In December of 1885, Elliott announced his intention to return to New York in order to remain with Hecker. He hoped to make a contribution to the latter's happiness "and to the success of your providential mission."[48] Keane had encouraged Elliott in this direction. By June he was expressing his delight that Hecker was "making such good use of Father Elliott's pen." He encouraged Hecker to: "stir him up and push him on and bring out all that's in him for the glory of God and the good of our country."[49] Thus at Keane's own urgings, Walter Elliott was becoming the protege and editor of the *Catholic World* that Hecker had originally sought in Keane.

By the Fall of 1888, Elliott had taken over the editorship of the *Catholic World,* a position that Hecker had earmarked for Keane back in 1872. Keane himself was touring the United States fund-raising for the new Catholic University, whose approval he had secured at Rome during the previous winter. Regarding his efforts at establishing the new university on a solid basis, Keane wrote from Notre Dame: "I hope your spirit has been and will be my inspiration and guide throughout. Hurrah for Hecker! Treat him well, old boss, and may God grant him abundant peace and blessings."[50] This is Keane's last letter to Hecker, who died on December 22, 1888.

From Keane's correspondence with both Hecker and Walter Elliott, it is clear that Keane regarded Elliott as Hecker's successor. He dubbed Elliott the "Eliseus" to Hecker's "Elias," and promised to be his companion in the task of promoting Hecker's prophetic vision:

I fear Dr. Begen was right in saying that poor dear Father Hecker's brain power was about exhausted, and that he could not be expected to do much brain work anymore. I think his time of planting seed is about over. God will make it fructify, and other hands must reap. Among them, your own will have to be a great power. You are his Eliseus, -- and you and I will work together on the lines which he has pointed out as a prophet. I think your great present work is to help him prepare to meet God, with a heart full of loving trust in Our Lord Jesus Christ.[51]

News of Hecker's demise reached Keane at Rome where he had gone to seek approval for the university's statutes.[52] He wrote to Elliott, expressing his intention to write a memorial article on Hecker:

I don't need to tell you how the news of our dear old Father's departure went to the very depths of my heart and soul. Thank God, we know that Providence can make no mistake--and he *was,* if ever man was, an instrument and servant of Divine Providence. May the will of the dear master be done--and may the dear, noble leader still guide and aide us from on high.[53]

Keane added: "while I would fain keep silence, I feel that I *ought* to pen a few lines on Father Hecker." Keane's remark about keeping silent should most likely be interpreted in light of difficulties he was then experiencing with the Holy Office at Rome.[54] The "few lines" eventually became Keane's memorial article which led off the *Catholic World* for April 1889. It was entitled simply "Father Hecker."[55] As he had in his letter to Elliot, Keane's memorial described Hecker in terms of Providence as a "vessel of election for the good of his generation."[56] As he recounted the highlights of Hecker's career, Keane waxed most enthusiastically when he came to describe Hecker's confidence in America's "providential mission among the nations and peoples of the earth."[57] He dwelt upon Hecker's personal magnetism and portrayed him as a prophetic seer characterized by uncommon insight into the meaning and direction of historical events.[58]

After 1875 Hecker never returned to Europe again, nor did he live to see the Paulists expand into Europe as providential agents of Americanization. After his death, however, Hecker and his ideas did return to Europe and excite considerable reaction there through the medium of Elliott's biography, translated and adapted for the French audience. Although he had often encouraged Elliott to continue Hecker's prophetic work, Keane's connection with the actual production of the biography and its exportation to Europe is not clear. As he drew to the end of his memorial portrait of Hecker, Keane exclaimed:

May some one be yet inspired to do for Father Hecker what Father Chocarne had done for Lacordiare! His inner life, so little known, perhaps so little imagined, has many a wonderful and beautiful lesson that the world stands in need of. The peeps into it that were my privilege will be blessings to me as long as I live.[59]

Whether or not he had Hecker's Eliseus in mind as the author, Keane was very early on record in favor of the need for an inspirational biography of Hecker which concentrated on his interior life. While Keane returned from Rome to the United States and began his work as rector of the new Catholic University, Elliott plunged into the task of writing the kind of biography Keane had described. Whether Keane suggested the task to Elliott and encouraged him during its completion is not known. Nor do we have a written estimate of

Elliott's biography from the pen of Keane. Keane did present a copy of the *Life* to Pope Leo XIII in 1897, but it was the French translation and adaptation. He also urged Elliott to prepare a shorter biography which would be accessible to more people and which he hoped would be translated into Italian.[60]

III. Conclusion

From the above considerations of (I) Hecker's various proposals for Paulist expansion into Europe, and (II) Hecker's relationship with Archbishop Keane, a number of conclusions can be drawn. First, at least from 1875, Hecker had come to hold as firm convictions the complex of ideas which Thomas Wangler has identified as the "Americanist ideology" or the Americanist "myth."[61] (I say 1875, rather than 1870 because it was at the time of his European travel that Hecker's talk of America's mission to Europe took on the near apocalyptic urgency which I associate with the Americanists.) Hecker expressed these convictions in his diary (Notes) during his European sojourn and in his published writings on conditions in Europe after his final return to the United States in 1875. His Americanism was presented as an analysis of historical events, a reading of the signs of the times in light of history's goal, the Church's future triumph. Second, Hecker's reading of the European situation included the belief that European Catholicism lacked the resources to regenerate itself. The torch had been passed across the Atlantic. As a practical response to this complex of beliefs, therefore, and to help the European Church deal successfully with the new democratic age, Hecker proposed to expand the Paulists into Europe. If, as Wangler has argued, Americanism is best understood as an international movement for church reform, a religious manifestation of American expansionsim with respect to Europe, Hecker's proposals for European Paulists as agents of Americanization can be seen as an anticipation of that later Americanism. This is especially so in view of Keane's personal association with Hecker's proposal. Third, the extent of Hecker's influence on the Americanist bishops has been a matter of dispute among scholars. Keane's letters to Hecker testify to the fact that Hecker's influence, at least in the case of Keane, was significant. This lends credibility to Denis O'Connell's later statements about Hecker's relationship to Keane as "his father in the spiritual life."[62] More importantly, the letters show conclusively that Hecker's influence not only touched Keane's spiritual life, but extended to his acceptance and public expression of Americanist ideas. Thus Keane emerges as the most plausible link between Hecker and the Americanist bishops of the 1890's

In spite of this connection between the generations, Emmett Curran's designation of Hecker as a "pawn" in episcopal hands seems quite apt in the cases of Ireland and O'Connell, the other members, along with Keane, in the

Americanist "triple alliance." One cannot fail to be struck by the contrast between the two generations in the pursuit of their "expansionist" goals. Hecker waited on Providence, reluctant to force the hand of God, even when as superior general of the Paulists, he was in a position to do so. The Americanist bishops, on the other hand, and here we must include Keane, were truly Machiavellian in their attempts to help the flow of history along in the direction they wanted it to go.

Although it is justified by the historical record, the designation of Hecker and Keane as "Americanist prototype and disciple" must therefore be qualified. As Wangler has pointed out, we are in need of a more thorough reconstruction of Keane's own thought.[63] On the other hand, the early influence of Hecker on Keane should not be unduly minimized. From 1885 until 1887 when Americanism as a conscious reform movement began at Rome, Keane pursued the goal of European expansion through Hecker and the Paulists. While the figures of Cardinal Manning and Pope Leo XIII may have loomed larger on Keane's horizon after 1887, it cannot be ignored that Hecker was instrumental in introducing Keane to Americanist ideas and that together they attempted to export them to Europe through the Paulists.

NOTES

1. For a good introduction to Hecker's life and thought and a guide to the literature about him, see John Farina, *An American Experience of God* (New York: Ramsey: Paulist, 1981).

2. Among scholars of Americanism, Margaret M. Reher has the most generous estimate of Hecker's impact on the movement. The first chapter of her doctoral dissertation treats Hecker and Keane as Americanist "prototype and disciple." Ireland and O'Connell appear in the second chapter as Americanist "exporters." See "The Church and the Kingdom of God in America: the Ecclesiology of the Americanists" (New York: unpublished Ph.D. dissertation, Fordham University, 1972), pp. 7-91; 92-174. She numbers Hecker among the Americanists out of the conviction that "his thought undergirded the entire development." M.M. Reher, "Pope Leo XIII and 'Americanism'," *Theological Studies* 34 (1973) 690. In a more recent article, Reher states her thesis about the relationship of Hecker to Ireland and O'Connell in more modest form. See "'Americanizing' the Catholic Church," *Dialog* 14 (1975) 290. In his numerous publications on Americanism, Thomas Wangler has tended to deemphasize Hecker's role in the Americanism episode in favor of a more pluralistic view of the Americanists. Varying intellectual convictions led them to embrace the shared reform perspective during the winter of 1887. Because he sees Americanism primarily as the reform movement itself (and he argues that this is the way the Americanist bishops saw it), Wangler does not number Hecker among the Americanists, nor does he consider Hecker's influence to be the primary factor which led any of the three chief Americanists to commit themselves to the movement in 1887. This is true even in the case of Keane. In Wangler's account, Hecker joins the "new apologetic," Cardinal Henry Edward Manning of Westminster and Pope Leo XIII himself as factors leading the Americanists to their shared program of reform. See, for example, "Emergence of John J. Keane as a Liberal Catholic and Americanist (1878-1887)," *American Ecclesiastical Review* 166 (1972) 457-78. More recently Emmett Curran has echoed Wangler's deemphasis of Hecker's role in the Americanism episode. "Isaac Hecker dead would become a much larger threat to conservatives than he had ever been alive, exasperating as he might have occasionally been to Thomas Preston and others of his bent in authority. But Burtsell, McGlynn, and Hecker themselves came in the 1890's to be largely pawns of a new movement toward liberalism that has its bases at Catholic University and the American College and drew its leadership from the hierarchy itself." R. Emmett Curran, *Michael Augustine Corrigan and the Shaping of Conservative Catholicism in America, 1878-1902* (New York: Arno, 1978) 316.

3. Hecker's Notes and correspondence in the Paulist Archives provide the basis for this brief treatment of his proposals for establishing the Paulists in Europe. For a more detailed discussion of these sources, see William L. Portier, "Providential Nation: An Historical-Theological Study of Isaac Hecker's Americanism" (Toronto: Unpublished Ph.D. dissertation, University of St. Michael's College, 1980), chaps 6, 7, 8. For general discussion of the Paulist "idea", see John Farina's essay, "Isaac Hecker's Vision for the Paulists: Hopes and Realities," in Farina, ed., *Hecker Studies* (New York/Ramsey: Paulist, 1983) 182-220. Farina mentions the 1870 and 1875 proposals in passing but does not advert to the 1885 proposal in concert with Keane. See *ibid.* 202-03, 209.

4. See Hecker to Brownson, Rome, January 30, 1870 in Joseph F. Gower and Richard M. Leliaert, eds., *The Brownson-Hecker Correspondence* (Notre Dame: U. of Notre Dame, 1979) 278-83 and the undated draft which follows. This is an extremely important letter for understanding the nature of Hecker's Americanism.

5. Hecker to George Hecker, Rome, January 27, 1870. See also Hecker to same, February 24, 1870, Paulist Archives.

6. Notes, January 20, 1870, Paulist Archives.

7. Hecker to George Hecker, January 27, 1870. To his fellow Paulist, Augustine Hewit, Hecker wrote: "The work that Divine Providence has called us to do in our own country, were its spirit extended throughout Europe, would be the focus and element of regeneration. Our country has a providential position in our century in view of Europe, and our baptizing and efforts to Catholicize and sanctify it gives it an importance in a religious aspect of a most interesting and significant character." Hecker to Hewit, February 23, 1870.

8. Notes, August 1, 1875.

9. Notes, May 31, 1875; cf. Notes, November 10 & 17, 1874.

10. Notes, November 17, 1874.

11. For the text of the "Exposition," see Hecker, *The Church and the Age* (New York: H.J. Hewit, 1887) chap. 1.

12. Notes, April 5, 1875.

13. Notes, May 1, 1875; cf. Hecker to George Hecker, August 4, 1875.

14. The reference to his "former companions" occurs in Notes, November 10, 1874; cf. notes, May 1, 1874.

15. Notes, August 26, 1876.

16. Notes, June, 1885. This quotation also appears in "Father Hecker's Vocation" (for the exclusive use of members of the Paulist community and their novices), no date, p. 61.

17. Keane's biographer, Patrick H. Ahern, records the "tradition" that Keane destroyed his correspondence. See *The Life of John J. Keane, Educator and Archbishop, 1839-1918* (Milwaukee: Bruce, 1955) 367. My own investigations in the Archives of the Diocese of Richmond and of the Catholic University of America have failed to turn up any of Hecker's letters to Keane. See Ahern's comment on the Archives at Dubuque in *ibid.*

18. Walter Elliott, "Personal Reminisces of Archbishop Keane," *Catholic World* 107 (August, 1918), 641 and *Ahern, Life of Keane* 28.

19. O'Connell's funeral oration for Keane is cited by Elliott in "Personal Reminisces . . .," 641. On Keane's efforts to spread devotion to the Holy Ghost among the American clergy, see Joseph Clifford Fenton, "Devotion to the Holy Ghost and its American Advocates," *American Ecclesiastical Review*, 121 (1949) 492-98. Fenton cites at length from Keane's October 8, 1879 pastoral letter on devotion to the Holy Ghost and from the introduction which he wrote in July of 1888 to Otto Zardetti's *Devotion to the Holy Ghost: I, Special Devotion to the Holy Ghost. A Manual for the Use of Seminarians, Priests, Religious and the Christian People* (Milwaukee: Hoffman Brothers, 1888).

20. Ahern, *Life of Keane* 28.

21. "In addition, I have a personal reason for your consent to his trying his vocation with us. My strength for some time has not been what it was, and I am compelled to divide up my cases and duties among companions. To some extent I have already done so. But there is a place for which I find no one in the Community, that is the editing of the *Catholic World.* It is one of the mightiest of my responsibilities and most taking of my cares. Father Keane has a good pen, a literary taste and turn of mind, and many other qualifications which make him suitable for such a position. He has written for the *Catholic World.* With little training and supervision he can relieve me in a great measure of this tax on my energies." Hecker to Bayley, October 22, 1872.

22. Bayley to Hecker, November 6, 1872.

23. Keane to Hecker, August 3, 1878; cf. Ahern, *Life of Keane,* Chap. 3. In December of 1880, Walter Elliott and a group of Paulists gave a mission for Bishop Keane at Richmond. See Keane to Hecker, December 15, 1880.

•24. Elliott, "Personal Reminisces . . .," 643.

25. Ahern, *Life of Keane* 58.

26. Keane to Hecker, October 22, 1881.

27. John J. Keane, "The Yorktown Centennial Celebration," *Catholic World,* 34 (November, 1881) 274-84.

28. *Ibid.* 275.

29. *Ibid.* 279-80

30. Keane to Hecker, October 22, 1881.

31. *Ibid.*

32. Keane to Hecker, Paris, August 7, 1883; cf. Keane to Hecker, July 1883. On the purpose of Keane's visit to Rome, see Ahern, *Life of Keane* 55ff.

33. Thomas Wangler, "The Birth of Americanism: 'Westward the Apocalyptic Candlestick'." *Harvard Theological Review* 65 (July, 1972) 418.

34. *Ibid.* 435.

35. See Ahern, *Life of Keane* 57. In the dispute over the Knights of Labor, Manning would provide indispensable aid in helping the Americanists win a favorable decision at Rome. *Ibid.* 73ff and Wangler, "The Birth of Americanism . . .," 424ff. Keane's letters to Manning are on microfilm in the Archives of the Catholic University of America.

36. Keane to Manning, August 1, 1885 from the microfilm of Manning's correspondence from the American bishops in the Archives of the Catholic University of America. Most of the body of the letter appears in Joseph McSorley, *Isaac Hecker and His Friends* (rev. ed.; New York: Paulist, 1972) 188-89.

37. Notes, September 9, 1885 as cited in "'Father Hecker's Vocation," p. 61. This entry also establishes that Keane wrote the letter at Hecker's request.

38. Keane to Hecker, September 15, 1885.

39. Elliott to Hecker, October 16, 1885.

40. Elliott's "Memorandum," November 2, 1885, as cited in "Father Hecker's Vocation," p. 62.

41. Keane to Hecker, November 23, 1885.

42. Keane to Hecker, December 29, 1885, as cited in "Father Hecker's Vocation," p. 62.

43. "I felt it due to the object in view, that the further word should be said, and it could not be better said than you had put it in your letter to me. So it is gone on its errand, and may God guide all." Keane to Hecker, January 15, 1886, as cited in *ibid.* My efforts to locate the three letters mentioned above have at this writing been unsuccessful. The three letters are: 1) Manning's negative reply to Keane which is mentioned in Keane to Hecker, December 29, 1885, 2) Hecker's reply to Keane upon receipt of #1, 3) Keane's second letter to Manning. The last two are mentioned in the letter cited in this note. In a letter to me on September 13, 1979, Rev. A. Chapeau, acting Archivist for the Oblates of St. Charles, Bayswater, London, described Manning's archives as "scattered and practically destroyed."

44. See Hecker to Archbishop Michael A. Corrigan, December 10, 1885. In asking Corrigan to be the celebrant, he mentioned that Keane had already agreed to preach.

45. Ahern, *Life of Keane* 63, citing a letter from Keane to Gibbons, dated February 11, 1886 and written from New York.

46. Keane to Hecker, June 4, 1886.

47. Keane to Hecker, June 17, 1886. Regarding Archbishop Walsh, Keane wrote: "There is *(entre nous)* some chance of my seeing him within a year, and then I can *talk* it all out to him, and surely will."

48. Elliott to Hecker, December 6, 1885.

49. Keane to Hecker, June 17, 1886.

50. Keane to Hecker, September 3, 1888.

51. Keane to Elliott, September 21, 1888.

52. Ahern, *Life of Keane* 92-3, 97.

53. Keane to Elliott, Rome, January 16, 1889.

54. While he was in Rome, Keane had been questioned by the Prefect of the Holy Office regarding some of the statements in a lecture he had delivered a year earlier on December 18, 1887. The lecture, entitled "The Providential Mission of Leo XIII," had been delivered in Washington, D.C.

and published in pamphlet form by J. Murphy & Co. of Baltimore. Someone in New York had sent an annotated copy to Rome. See Ahern, *Life of Keane* 93-98. Hecker himself had commented at length on this lecture in a lead article for the *Catholic World,* October 1888. See Hecker, "The Mission of Leo XIII," *Catholic World* 48 (October, 1888) 1-13.

55. *Catholic World* 49 (April, 1889) 1-9.

56. *Ibid.* 1.

57. *Ibid.* 7.

58. "When he considered the Providence of God leading up, through all history and through all the vicissitudes of nations, to this wonderful new departure of human society, and pointing out its pathway and its work, his whole being seemed to thrill with an enthusiasm that was electrical in its effects upon its hearers. Who that has had the fortune to behold it can ever forget the picture presented by that colossal man, that worthy annointed of the Lord, standing thus as if on a hill-top of prophetic vision, seeing what to minds of smaller stature and lower standing ground was still invisible, proclaiming the great things that God was surely to work in this land of benediction and the blessings which from it would flow back upon the old world, forcing conviction on unbiased minds by the obvious moral of past and contemporaneous history, and pouring enthusiasm into generous hearts by his picture of the great things that might be done for helping on the kingdom of the Lord." *Ibid.*

59. *Ibid.* 6. Chocarne had written a biography of Lacordaire entitled *The Inner Life of the Very Reverend Pere Lacordaire* (trans. A.T. Drane; Dublin, 1868).

60. Ahern, *Life of Keane* 252. Vincent Holden claims that after reading Elliott's *Life,* Keane remarked: "That is Elliott's Hecker, not Hecker's Hecker." Holden provides no source for the quotation. See Vincent Holden, "A Myth in 'L'Americanisme'." *Catholic Historical Review* 31 (1945) 154.

61. Wangler, "The Birth of Americanism . . .," 421.

62. See O'Connell's letters to Klein and Elliott as cited in Ahern, *Life of Keane* 251.

63. Wangler, "A bibliography of the Writings of Archbishop John J. Keane," *Records of the American Catholic Historical Society of Philadelphia 89 (March-Dec., 1978) 61.*

MYTH, WORLDVIEWS AND LATE NINETEENTH CENTURY AMERICAN CATHOLIC EXPANSIONISM

Thomas E. Wangler

In his classic study of the evangelical Protestant tradition in the United States, *The Kingdom of God in America,* H. Richard Niebuhr pointed to the centrality of eschatology in American religious history. The "future" was variously conceived with the passage of time, but the hoped for "kingdom" was an ever present challenge in each era.[1] The American quest for the millennium, inspired especially by the Second Great Awakening, predated the large Catholic migrations of the mid to late nineteenth century, but each new wave of immigrants, inspired by the widespread European conviction that America was "the future ," the "New" world, reinforced and deepened that more radical, original hope.[2]

As a general rule Catholics did not share with their Protestant fellow-citizens the radical hope of a millennium. Popular Catholic eschatology, as reflected in the liturgy, some of the catechisms, sermons, and even tombstone engravings, was rather focused on joining a celestial community of saints after death.[3] Such traditional eschatology found itself competing with alternatives by the late nineteenth century, one of which will be examined in this essay. The following will thus attempt to recreate the mythic assumptions and operative worldviews of a dynamic religious movement within the American Catholic church of the late nineteenth century, generally known as Americanism. This movement was designed, in the words of one of its advocates, to make "the future into the present."[4] It represented an extension of a civic religiosity developed as part of a broader, romantically inspired devotional/civil religious revival of mid-century.[5] The leading Americanist advocates were Archbishop John Ireland of St. Paul, Minnesota, Bishop John Keane, founding rector of the Catholic University of America, and Msgr. Denis O'Connell, rector of the North American College in Rome. These men, with Ireland as their public leader, created a movement to impose upon the universal church, on the wings of late nineteenth century American expansionism, their vision of an Americanized Catholicism.

I. THE MYTH OF AMERICANISM

The word "myth" has been used in the context of Roman Catholic Americanism since its papal condemnation in 1899 and the subsequent denial that anyone held or taught the reprobated doctrines. In this sense "myth" meant a nonexistent or "phantom" heresy. But if one uses the term in its more modern and scientific sense, i.e. as the narration of and participation in divine activity originating and imposing an order upon the world, one requiring a new form of individual and group thought, behaviour and identity, then there was indeed a "myth" of Roman Catholic Americanism.

This "myth" existed "along-side-of" the orthodoxy of the late nineteenth century American Catholic faith which was clearly focused on the "mythic" narration of the life, death and resurrection of Christ. The catechism and prayer book, for example, authorized by the 1884 Third Plenary Council of Baltimore, the official liturgy of the church, the decoration of the newly introduced neo-Gothic, urban churches, tombstone engravings, hymns, sermons, and the like, reflected a powerful attachment to the passover mystery of the faith.[6] Unlike their Protestant fellow-citizens, however, Catholic commentary on the faith, whether in the formal theology manuals or in sermons and discourses, tended to reflect a certain indifference to time and place, and proceeded in a mostly deductive manner from abstract doctrine or policy. If there is any surprising feature of the Americanist movement it is that its promoters succeeded, without any explicit knowledge of Horace Bushnell or liberal Protestantism,[7] in formulating a fresh set of affirmations relative to the divine activity, and these assertations existed "along-side-of" the Catholic orthodoxy of the period.

By 1886-1887 Ireland, Keane, O'Connell, and the many others who came to be associated with them, had accepted a version of the nation's origin myth, as reconstructed by Robert Bellah,[8] which affirmed in its original form a new and dramatic intervention of the Christian God in bringing the Puritans across the Atlantic in a new exodus. Reading the radical nature of the puritan conversion experience into the geography of the Atlantic, the first settlers of New England affirmed the fruit of this historic, divine intervention as a "new" world, standing in sharp contrast to the "old" world of Europe. As events unfolded, such as the first Great Awakening or the American Revolution, the divine motive for the original intervention was expounded to take into account these new developments.

One can find individual American Catholics affirming elements of the Puritan origin myth of the nation almost as soon as there was a nation. And in spite of their ties to the European papacy, it was natural for American Catholics to interpret themselves as living in the "new" world. But few took the term "new" seriously, at least as far as their religious convictions were concerned. Archbishop Ireland and Bishop Keane had themselves mentioned the "mission of America" prior to 1887, but without the powerful conviction and sense of participation in such a mission which characterized their opinions after that date.[9] They returned from a European trip in the spring of 1887 and began a missionary-like crusade affirming a new manifestation of divine power. God was re-arranging the world, determining the decline of Europe and the emergence of the United States as the "new" world, the "future," destined, as in the puritan dream, to shed its influence around the world. Such was the mythic content of their preaching. Corresponding to this divinely initiated broad cultural shift from east to west, was a parallel ecclesiastical realignment. It was believed by the Americanists that the universal Catholic church would have to adjust to the cultural transition everywhere evident in order to survive, and that the American Catholic church, already acculturated to the "future," would have to assume "responsibility" for guiding the universal church through this crisis. Their European trip had changed their talk about the nation from standard expressions concerning its mission and the like to powerful convictions which required their participation in and responsibility for a world-transforming, divinely initiated process. In other words the "myth " of Americanism had been born.[10]

THE AMERICANIST MOVEMENT

Accepting their providentially bestowed responsibility to lead the universal church into the new age, the Americanists, as they came to be called, initiated a movement to Americanize the universal church. By 1890 they were recognized as a distinct, liberal and reforming group, with an equally clear opposition centered in the person of the Archbishop of New York, Michael Corrigan.

The means devised by the Americanists to further their "cause," or "the movement" as they called their activities in this regard, were primarily focused on forming favorable public opinion relative to themselves and their reform proposals. They had learned while in Rome in 1886-1887 how important, and really how easy, it was to form public opinion in Rome and throughout the Catholic world by manipulating the international flow of news. Using primarily the French-language, semi-official Vatican newspaper, *Moniteur de Rome,* the Americanists planted news stories, discourses, and articles in support of their program. By early 1891 these same men had succeeded in gaining access to the international cable lines crossing the Atlantic, from which newspaper news was derived, and they could literally mold public opinion around the world, instantly and at will. Cables put on the wires in Rome, but datelined Berlin and elsewhere, manufactured a climate throughout the Western world which they hoped would lead to Catholic acceptance of their reform program. The details of this story have been told elsewhere, and need not be repeated.[11]

III. WORLDVIEWS

The major problem connected with the historical reconstruction of Roman Catholic Americanism has been determining just what it was that the Americanists were advocating on such a grand scale. Based on an exhaustive analysis of all the literature that has survived from Ireland, Keane and O'Connell, the following will attempt to re-construct the operative worldviews of each individual. Their Americanist proposals will then be set in those frameworks. Since O'Connell wrote so little only his Americanist proposals can be reproduced. I have also included a short introductory section on the structure of the thought of Isaac Hecker. Although not based on an exhaustive analysis in his case, it was judged necessary to include him in the panorama which follows in order to demonstrate the uniqueness of each of these men and their committments, however much they all shared in common the Catholic faith and the Americanist myth. The focus on worldviews in what follows is an attempt to break out of the pattern which has developed among historians of tracing individual ideas or doctrines within a narrowly conceived American Catholic tradition. Such an approach ignores the cultural context, and the origin and nature of the frameworks, within which such ideas were expressed, or their relative importance and relationships within any given framework.

A. Isaac Hecker

The starting point of Hecker's thought was the human subject, and in this regard he reflected his early contacts with New England transcendentalism. An extremely sensitive, passionate religious seeker, Hecker inquired seriously into the meaning and destiny of human life, studied attentively the needs of the human spirit, human yearnings, aspirations and longings, and discovered, like so many others in New England, the infinite within himself. A life-long committment to a certain subjectivism followed, although he significantly altered this early focus in the context of his conversion to Catholicism in 1844. Hecker and his friend Orestes Brownson studied Kant and German Idealism and finally rejected their exclusive focus on the subjective conditions for knowing. As Hecker later recalled their path:

> Are these subjective yearnings, aspirations, unappeased desires, or religious feelings. . .--are they genuine, real, corresponding to and arising from the reality of certain objects external to the soul? [12]

It was their affirmative answer to this question which led Brownson and Hecker into the Catholic church via what the latter called the "philosophical route." Although both men carried their early transcendentalism with them into the church, each did so in his own way. Brownson moved in the direction of a modified ontologism [13] and Hecker created a possibly unique, certainly very personal, dialectic in which the human subject is viewed as existing in dialectical tension with external reality, i.e. God, Christ, and most concretely the church. In the wake of his conversion Hecker considered the Catholic church as *the* external object which met the deepest needs of the human spirit. A dialectic between subject and object thus became the post-conversion structure of Hecker's thought. While maintaining a strong transcendental point of departure he nonetheless gloried in his liberation from the subjectivism of Ralph Waldo

Emerson and his old Boston Transcendentalist friends. The result was what might best be called a "realistic transcendentalism." His dual committment to realism and transcendentalism, and the resulting dialectic, is very clear in his first two books. Their titles reflect his starting point: *Questions of the Soul* (1855), and *Aspirations of Nature* (1857).[14] The first of these takes one through the author's conversion experience from questions about the human subject to answers found in the church as object. The second dismisses the modern problem of having to decide between "sovereign church or the free soul, authority or personality, God in us or God in our masters," and does so by employing his subject-object dialectic, in which one can affirm all of these things as true, blending them in romatic unity. The title of Hecker's final book, the *Church and the Age* (1887), suggests a less personal and subjective thrust, possibly a historical dialectic, but this is not the case. He still argued that "all things are to be viewed as they bear on the destiny of man."[15] The point of the discussions of such "social" topics as the Church and the age was to encourage Catholics to be more subjective. If Hecker has found his old transcendentalist friends to be too subjective, he found his new Catholic ones not enough so. Statements made by Hecker in urging Catholics to be more modern in this way and open to the inner promptings of the spirit, if not placed by him or his critics in the context of his dialectic, were destined to give rise to misunderstanding, and did, as we know, elicit a papal condemnation. It must be said, however, that Hecker was not simply a subjective transcendentalist or a liberal Protestant. It was this which he left behind in his conversion. His thought was rather "dialectic" in structure, a structure which was not easily understood by the non-dialectic, neo-scholastic frame of mind which controlled the papacy during the reign of Leo XIII. Hecker represented an early and amateurish form of what will be known a century later as a transcendental Thomism.[16]

B. Archbishop John Keane

At least two serious attempts have been made to portray Keane as an intellectual descendent of Hecker. Personal friendship between the two, Keane's desire to enter the Paulists, a certain spirituality, and talk about the Holy Spirit early in Keane's career,[17] made this plausible. Both men were products of Romanticism, tended to interpret things in a dialectical manner, hypothesized groups and nations, and spoke a great deal about "unity" (except when referring to the relations of church and state). In spite of this however the metaphysical committments of the two men were different. Unlike Hecker's subject-object dialectic, Keane interpreted the world through a Hegelian-like dialectic of conflicting social forces

Keane used a modified form of traditionalism to project an original revelation to primitive mankind, thus creating a "golden age" in which an "undivided treasury of primitive truth" was the "basis of all truth and all philosophy." This primordial state of human unity was destroyed when men began to "wander" from the central home of the human family, thus leading to three general human families, only one of which, the Semitic, kept the original unity of mankind. Christ came to re-unite all men, and the church continued this function.[18] But Satan has kept the church from an easy victory. The struggle between the forces of light and those of darkness ensued: "The conflict has never ceased, and the combatants have never been the same"--Providence and Satan, light and darkness, redemption and the fall, Christ and heathenism.[19] By the 1880's one can notice a shift in Keane's understanding of the content of this battle, as it became less general and theological and more political. This political struggle was still, of course, the struggle of God and Satan. The real Christians were represented by those who believed in and respected the God-given, inalienable rights of man; the sons of Satan taught and practiced the principle of might over right.[20] The Roman Empire epitomized the latter, but Christianity finally overcame it. The hoped-for Christian civilization was never fully realized, however, because Christ's teachings about the rights of man "must logically lead up . . . to popular institutions and representative governments." but this was prevented by the European kings who resisted the efforts of the church to assert "the civil and religious liberty which Christ brought into the world."[21] The Reformation only added new, religious divisions to those already existing, with the result that European social life was characterized by "mutual hostility," it's political life was a "perpetual contest between irreconcilable extremes" and its post-Reformation religious life was one in which people hated each other for the "love of god."[22] What was God's reaction to the chaos and conflict of European life? God intervened in a powerful new way, inaugurating a "providential Revolution," and founded the United States of America, the "New" world, as the antithesis of the "Old" World.[23] the resulting New World-Old World dialectic pitted the universal brotherhood, friendliness, charity, harmonious unity, equalization and unification of American life, on the one hand, against Europe's mean, narrow, jealous, divisive, and hostile life on the other. Keane took the final step and characterized Europe as "Satan's" camp, while viewing America as the hoped-for eschatological home where mankind would be reunited into its original unity.[24]

This religio/political understanding of the nation was then easily extended to the relationships among the churches. Keane's well-known ecumenism was rooted in his hope of reuniting all of the churches into a single body, reflecting the original unity of the human race.

May our beloved America press bravely on in the fulfillment of her glorious mission of bringing into unity the scattered children of God.[25]

Keane's understanding of Americanism was consistent with his historical dialectic. Even before the word "Americanism" was being used widely he had used it for his convictions. In 1896 he called for the advance of Americanism:

The dominant force must be Americanism. It is America that has taught the world that if they loved God not to hate one another. Once the dominant force was wealth and might: in the future it must be right.[26]

Here Keane very explicitly used the term "Americanism" in reference to his convictions about the reunion of Christian churches and their rights theory of John Locke. We have every reason to believe that when Keane told O'Connell in the midst of the Americanist controversy that it was really a "conflict between two civilizations"[27] he understood himself engaged in the eschatologcal and dialectical conflict between God and Satan. It is true that in 1898 Keane made a final attempt to explain Americanism, apparently trying to define things as broadly a possible, and to include the main concerns of Denis O'Connell and John Ireland. He could not have been clearer in his patronizing of Europe. So burdened by division and conflict, Europeans, Keane explained, will never understand the harmony which comes from the separation of church and state, as in the United States, nor could they appreciate the fellowship among differing sects, nor the sympathy of the American church for the modern age.[28]

Keane's way of believing the Catholic faith was clearly problematic. The dialectic of conflicting forces, the complete identification of the Christian side of this dialectic with the political and social life of the United States and with the philosophy of John Locke, and the characterization of Europe as "Satan's camp" would not be easily squared with any orthodox form of the faith. It should not surprise us that Thomist trained Archbishop Francisco Satolli, Leo XIII's apostolic delegate to the United States, was so outraged by a speech delivered by Keane in New Orleans in 1896 that he stood up in the midst of it and left the stage.[29] Also, after the papal condemnation of Americanism, when Leo XIII decided to appoint Keane to be archbishop of Dubuque, Iowa, Leo inserted a personal note in the appointment letter urging Keane to fight the heresy of Americanism in his new diocese. Keane was crushed by the note, as he wrote friends, but then tried to cover it over, in a uncharacteristic show of vanity, by noting in his diocesan record book that unlike most appointments, his came with a personal note from the Pope.[30]

78

C. John Ireland

The structure of Ireland's thought was neither Hecker's subject-object dialectic nor Keane's historical dialectic of opposing forces. Sharing the romantic ideal of unity with his fellow Americanists, he reflected yet another alternative. Ireland's worldview is difficult to label, but of the nineteenth century alternatives the term "Thomist" is perhaps nearest the mark. There are no signs of dialectic, traditionalist original revelations, *a priori* conditions of knowing, ontologist intuitive knowledge of God, and the like. All of his assumptions about knowing reflect Aristotle, and his concern with perfecting "this world" is consistent with such a commitment. Separating possible Enlightenment roots and certain elements of liberal Protestantism from the forms of Thomism which were circulating in the late nineteenth century Catholic community does not seem possible. It is certain that Ireland's theological education in the late 1850's at the Marist Scholasticate at Montbel in southern France included the textbooks of the prominent neo-Thomist of the Roman College, Giovanni Perrone.[31]

Ireland's thought was focused on the need to unite the "supernatural" and "natural" orders. While not a pantheist, the Archbishop, on occasion, used the image of uniting soul and body to express this relationship. This pattern was then vaguely extended to a whole set of other relationships--the church and the world, the church and the age, the American church in relation to the American nation, and so on. Since the supernatural was equated with the church, and the goal was to "unite" the supernatural and the natural orders, there was a strong tendency to foster a kind of "ecclesiastical imperialism." A deep tension lies at the base of Ireland's thought. His espousal of liberal or reformatory causes was regularly justified within church circles as a tactical means of gaining "influence" for the church in important quarters. The critic is not really able to separate out his genuine from tactical commitments. An obsession with how the Catholic church looked in the modern age, its public image, was ever present, and was probably stronger than his genuine sympathy for modernity. In typical romantic fashion, his ultimate hope was the creation of a neo-Christendom centered in Washington. If he could succeed in converting the American nation to the Catholic church, then Catholicism would encircle the globe on the wings of American expansionism.[32]

Like most romantics, Ireland viewed history as little more than "philosophy teaching by example." Thus he read his metaphysics into the past. For him "corrupt nature" reigned until the coming of Christ, and then as the Christian religion spread and produced the Middle Ages, the "supernatural was supreme." But then the Renaissance and Reformation led to human self-assertion, and the need of the present hour was to reassert the "supremacy of the supernatural, and to save the age for the church."[33]

This metaphysical and historical understanding of things gave birth to a specific understanding of Americanism. The unique feature of Ireland's Americanism was his urgent push to involve the church in a new mission to the "natural order." By this he meant a manly engagement in the political, social and economic issues of the day. Ireland regularly sniped at the devotionalism of romantic Catholicism, and had little use for the feminine "pusillanimous and self-satisfied sanctuary religion", as he called it. Such a concern with the "supernatural alone would not achieve the hoped for union of the supernatural and natural orders. By the mid-1880's Ireland had re-interpreted the ecclesiology he had learned from his seminary textbooks, and was preaching a second mission of the church, a mission to the "natural order."[34]

In the wake of the papal condemnation of Americanism Ireland made several attempts to define the word in an orthodox way. Following the convictions of his friends, he affirmed the separation of church and state as acceptable to "Catholics in America." Reflecting his own concerns, however, he urged Catholic involvement on behalf of the temporal welfare of the nation, and encouraged a social ecumenism, whereby Catholics, without sacrificing their faith, were to work with all men of good will in creating a more just world. Finally, Ireland urged the church to be willing to adjust its pastoral methods to the new age, as Leo himself had recognized in the condemnation letter. A "New" world required new relationships to the state, to the civil order, and to fellow-citizens with different religious convictions.[35]

D. Denis O'Connell

The worldview of Denis O'Connell is not able to be reconstructed, as only two or three expressions his thought have survived. His Americanism, however, was forcefully stated in 1897 when he held up as acceptable for "Catholics in America" the separation of church and state, and clearly was committed to the rights theory of John Locke. He also, however, made another proposal, perhaps the most radical of the group, that the canon law of the church be reformed in terms of the common law tradition of the English-speaking nations, with its due process provisions, rather than the Roman law of the past.[36] This proposal was made publicly only once, but is consistent with a general Americanist disdain for papal "condemnations." It reflects O'Connell's Roman contacts with Catholic academics, many later associated with modernism, who forsaw the desirability of some form of "due process" in the church.

80

CONCLUSION

This short article has portrayed Roman Catholic Americanism as a reform movement seeking to impose upon the European Catholic church an Americanized Catholicism. What has been called herein the "myth" of Americanism, namely the affirmation of a new intervention of God in favor of the American nation, provided the justification for this reformatory activity, and united the various people engaged in this effort. While some of the reform proposals advocated by the Americanists were common to all of them, such as Catholic acceptance of the separation of church and state in the United States, the very different worldviews of the men involved meant that each had their own unique understanding of what was important in terms of the future direction of the Catholic church. While Hecker may have wanted Catholics to be more open to the inner promptings of the Holy Spirit, Keane was intent on the reunion of Christian churches and the spread of the rights theory of John Locke against the divisive features which he felt characterized European life. Ireland was interested in a Catholic church engaged in the social and political life of the modern age, and Denis O'Connell wanted a new code of canon law. These multiple interests, incremented with each new associate of the Americanist cause (and the numbers became surprisingly large and international), created a situation in which anything "new" was labeled "Americanism." An intelligent approval or condemnation, or a coherent historical reconstruction, of this "mythic" heresy, was and is therefore problematic.

NOTES

1. New York: Harper and Roe, 1937.

2. Henry Steele Commager, *America in Perspective: the United States through Foreign Eyes* (New York: New American Library, 1947).

3. See the author's "Boston Catholic Religious Life in the Era of Cardinal O'Connell," soon to be published in a column of essays on Boston Catholics edited by Robert Sullivan.

4. John Zahm to Denis O'Connell, October 6, 1899, as cited in Ralph Weber, *Notre Dame's John Zahm* (Notre Dame, IN: U. of Notre Dame, 1961) 123.

5. See the article referred to in note 3 above.

6. *Ibid.*

7. On American liberal Protestantism see William R. Hutchison's *The Modernist Impulse in American Protestantism* (Cambridge: Harvard U., 1976).

8. *The Broken Covenant: Civil Religion in Time of Trial* (New York: Seabury, 1976).

9. "Pastoral Letter," *The memorial Volume: A History of the Third Plenary Council of Baltimore* (Baltimore: Baltimore Publishing Co., 1885) 8.

10. See the author's "The Birth of Americanism: 'Westward the Apocalyptic Candlestick'," *Harvard Theological Review* 65 (1972) 415-36.

11. See the author's "American Catholic Expansionism: 1886-1894," *Harvard Theological Review* 75 (1982) 369-93.

12. "Brownson's Road to the Church," *Catholic World,* 46 (October 1887) 6.

13. See chapter 3 of Virgil Michael's *The Critical Principles of Orestes A. Brownson* (Washington, D.C.: The Catholic University of America, 1918).

14. Both were published in New York by the Catholic Publishing House.

15. New York: Office of the Catholic World.

16. On the various 19th. century foreshadowings of transcendental Thomism see Gerald A. McCool, *Catholic Theology in the Nineteenth Century: The Quest for a Unitary Method* (New York: Seabury, 1977).

17. "Inaugural Sermon," *Catholic Mirror* (Baltimore, August 31, 1878).

18. "Bishop Keane's Sermon," *Catholic Mirror* (Baltimore, June 7, 1879).

19. "The Conflict of Christianity and Heathenism," *American Catholic Quarterly Review* 5 (July, 1880) 12.

20. *Christian Education in America* (Washington, D.C.: The Church News Publishing Co., 1892) 7.

21. *Ibid.* 12.

22. "America and Americans as Seen from Abroad," *Catholic World 66 (March, 1898) 721-30.*

23. *"The Parliament of Religions," Pilot* (Boston: January 7, 1893).

24. *Emmanuel* (Philadelphia: J.J.McVey, 1915) 173.

25. "The Pope and America," *Pilot* (Boston: January 7, 1893).

26. "The Philosophy of History," *Church News* (Washington, D.C.: March 7, 1896).

27. Denis O'Connell to John Ireland, December 2, 1897, in the Archives of the Catholic Historical Society of St. Paul.

28. "America and Americans."

29. Patrick Ahern, *The Life of John J. Keane: Educator and Archbishop, 1838-1918* (Milwaukee: Bruce, 1955) 170.

30. "Record of the Administration of John J. Keane, Archbishop of Dubuque, Sept. 27, 1900 to June 29, 1911." This is a 152-page record in Keane's hand preserved in the Archives of the Archdiocese of Dubuque.

31. See the author's "John Ireland and the Origins of Liberal Catholicism in the United States," *Catholic Historical Review* 61 (1971) 621.

32. "The Mission of Catholics in America," in *The Church and Modern Society* (Chicago: D.H. McBride and Co., 1896) 77-81.

33. *Ibid.* 73-76.

34. The best expression of this central position is in the "Introduction" of *The Church and Modern Society,* especially the enlarged version in the 1903 edition.

35. See the author's "The Americanism of J. St. Clair Etheridge," *Records of the American Catholic Historical Society of Philadelphia* 85 (March-June, 1974) 88-105.

36. *A New Idea in the Life of Father Hecker* (Fribourg: Herder, 1897).

THE AMERICANIST ATTACK ON EUROPE IN 1897 AND 1898

Robert C. Ayers

At Fribourg, Switzerland, in the summer of 1897, at the International Congress of Catholic Scholars, Monsignor Denis O'Connell, Roman vicar for Cardinal Gibbons and sometime rector of the American College, gave an address on the subject of "Americanism," which he set forward as "A New Idea in The Life of Father Hecker." This address served to emphasize the effect of the recent French translation of Hecker's *Life,* published that year by Felix Klein. One immediate result of the speech seems to have been to offend the conservatives among the French present. O'Connell blithely had the talk printed and circulated it widely.[1]

In the fall of 1897 the *Führer* of the German ultramontanes in the United States, Monsignore Professor Doctor Joseph Schroeder, was dismissed from the faculty of the Catholic University of America in a move which was interpreted in Europe as an act of anti-foreignism on the part of the Irish-American liberal Catholic faction. Both the curia and the German foreign office recognized that O'Connell, Archbishop John Ireland of St. Paul, and the former rector of the Catholic University of America, John Keane, now titular archbishop of Damascus, had achieved Schroeder's eviction.

In 1897 there existed in Europe a mirror set of conceptions about America and the American style, conceptions which nourished each other. People who were unhappy with the strictures of European patterns tended to admire the openness and opportunity which they thought the American way produced.[2] People who were threatened by the social and economic changes in European life[3] tended to a negative view of the brash, successful young nation of the New World.[4] Particularly in France a democratic pro-Americanism focused on Europe's failings and a possible 'American' solution for them.[5] Conversely, an anti-Americanism criticized America's aggressive capitalism, its adolescent militarism, and its tolerance of Masons and Jews.[6] This attitude was heavy in France, and extended to Catholic Germany and Austria.

For years Archbishop John Ireland had been taking advantage of the pro-Americanism of the 'rallied' Catholics of France, appearing before them as the priest who had left the quiet of the sacristy to live intensely in the modern world.[7] But in the promotion of an ecclesiastical Americanism, O'Connell, Ireland, and their associate John Keane, failed to reckon with the extent of the anti-Americanism harbored within the Church and nations of Europe.

The European stage was well furnished with an anti-Americanism caused by America's growing challenge to Europe's economy and the aspersion which its 'melting-pot' seemed to cast on Europe's festering nationalisms. Now as Europe was presented with a glamorized package of pro-Americanism in the ardently liberal *La Vie du Père Hecker,* flamboyant speeches by Ireland and Keane, and the advocacy by Denis O'Connell of a democratic mandate for the authority of the Church, the scene was ready for a clash of mythologies, a struggle fought over misconceptions and reactions to perceived threats, which gave the 'phantom' quality to the error of Americanism and its condemnation.

By the fall of 1897 the extreme right of the Church of France was able to concentrate its resentments on Hecker, O'Connell and Keane, and attacked, all phobias firing at will. Hecker and Americanism were found to be part of an "anti-Christian conjuration,"[8] dreamed up by the French Catholic right out of its cherished pornography of anti-semitism and hatred for Free Masons.

This French conservative attack culminated in May 1898 in a book by Charles Maignen under the title *Le Père Hecker - Est-il un Saint?* The attack has been well documented by McAvoy, Klein and Fogarty,[9] with a full description of the Americanists' wounded reactions. The book was a direct personal assault on Ireland, Keane and O'Connell.

One contention of Maignen's book may be seen in the following statement: "It was not merely commercial and financial motives which decided the United States to pursue its policy of unjust aggression; it was also the wish to injure Catholicism by taking Cuba away from Spain, (since) the Cuban revolution was promoted by secret societies."[10] The book particularly accused the Americanists of a campaign to install a supra-national pope who would conciliate the state of Italy and re-order an international church along American lines.[11]

A correlation between the development of the Spanish-American war and the condemnation of the "Phantom heresy" had been previoulsy noted[12] but has been de-emphasized. Yet in political and in ecclesiastical affairs the 'manifest destiny' of America was unquestionably asserting itself. Unchecked in war, it could be countered in the church.

It is clear that Denis O'Connell thought that the Cuban war and 'religious Americanism' were aspects of the same inevitable movement, and that he held that 'Anglo-Saxon' superiority was destined to prevail in state and church.[13] In Rome, Archibishop Keane was so much a "single-minded Jingo"[14] that his indiscreet conversation, according to Baroness Eichthal, provided plenty of ammunition for the Merry del Vals, ambassador father and monsignore son, to "sink everything American."[15]

In June of 1898 the German Liberal Catholic writer, F.X. Kraus, under the protection of his pseudonym "Spectator," published his conviction that the progress of the Cuban war demonstrated the decadent condition of the deplorable Ultramontanism of the Latin states and proved that the future of humanity and the church lay with the Germanic or Anglo-Saxon world. Under "Jesuitical Catholicism," he concluded, "peoples lost the ability to cultivate civil interests."[16]

At the Vatican, upon Spain's collapse, the diplomats in the curia, while try-ing to avoid offense to the fallen 'non-Anglo-Saxon' nation, understandably wanted to make peace with the powerful United States. Yet the French mon-archist conservatives continued to howl for the theological condemnation of the Americanists, Father Hecker and all his works, and with them, by association, French progressive Catholics and the republican element in the church of France. To this outrage expressed by the unfortunately non-Germanic children of the eldest daughter of the church was added the voiced unease of the intransigent party at the Court of Rome.

Indeed the first inclination of the curia seems to have been to throw the Americans and liberals to the theological wolves. In 1898 the Index stood ready to condemn the *Life of Hecker,* and with it, John Zahm's book on *Evolution and Dogma.* The German theologian Hermann Schell, who had among other errors supported the Americanists and the ideas of Isaac Hecker, was con-demned in 1898, and his works placed on the Index in 1899. Kraus was narrowly saved from the same fate by the personal intervention of Leo XIII.[17]

Throughout their considerations all of the factions at the Vatican, whether of German or French orientation, transigent or intransigent on the Roman Question, diplomat or theologian, had one thing in common--they were but differing constellations in a general galaxy of hope for the survival of the curia in the best possible condition. While the war continued, the diplomatic apparatus of the Vatican advocated that no unnecessary offense be given to the rising giant of the Americas, the power which would shortly possess Cuba, Puerto Rico and the Philippines, and seven million dollars worth of "Friars' Lands."

At Rome, high parties sought diligently therefore to distinguish between a 'bad' Americanism which could be condemned to the satisfaction of the conser-vatives, and a 'good' Americanism which could be allowed. Denis O'Connell had already put forward a vocabulary of 'political' Americanism and 'religious' Americanism in the Fribourg speech in 1897. Now in letters of defense submitted to Alberto Lepidi, O.P., the court theologian, O'Connell used the terms again.[18] The Master of the Sacred Palace was delighted to be able to refine the terminology of the thorny problem into a 'religious Americanism' which could be castigated to the satisfaction of the old order and a 'political Americanism' which could be allowed to the victor nation.[19]

Fighting for time, the Vatican sent out word that the pope wished all the contestants to *tranquilizzare* the controversy.[20] Shortly, Leo XIII availed him-self of a more articulated vocabulary for a distinction among 'Americanisms.' From her observation post at Rome the baroness Auguste von Eichthal repor-ted to F.X. Kraus that "at the moment, the very word Americanism stirs up a drum roll. But who, besides a few initiates, knows what it really means. That is grist for Leo's mill, who himself set forth. . .for the *Freeman's Journal* that there are many kinds of Americanism: (1) the political kind of the U.S., which only merits acceptance! (2) the French variety, personified by (the broad-minded ex-) Abbe Charbonnel! (3) a German 'Americanism' intent on reform of church and scripture; and (4) an Italian 'Americanism' which was nothing more than Italian liberalism "decked out in the Stars and Stripes" and opposed to the temporal power, the religious orders and the union of church and state.[22]

We may conclude today that in the period leading up to its condemnation, 'Americanism' was being used at the Vatican as a catchword for tendencies which, if effectuated, threatened the absolute authority of the central powers of the Church and the prerogatives of the curia. What might be tolerted in far-off America, chided in France, reproved in Germany, was regarded as truly subversive in Italy where it contradicted the interests of the Vatican and the cherished hope of Leo and many members of the Roman Court that in some future international conflict the temporal power would be restored.

From the standpoint of those who preferred the existing system of what Baroness Eichthal dubbed "episcopal servility and Vatican terrorism"[23] the liberal and Americanist challenge had to be met, else the monarchical authority would fall to the "New Idea" Denis O'Connell had called up out of the *Life of Father Hecker,* the worm of democracy. Yet America, holder of the Islands and steady source of Peter's Pence,[24] must not be openly offended. To Kraus, on Dec. 6th, the sarcastic baroness described the pope's fix:

Meanwhile, the outraged protests from (archbishop) Ireland (over Maignen's book), and *most unusually,* from Gibbons, about the possible results of an alienation of the American Catholics, have produced such a salutary horror in Leo XIII, that the decree, which was prepared months ago, to nail up Hecker's *Life* and doctrine to the Index, has remained lying on Leo's desk, unexecuted. . .

That is related to the political mammoth successes of the United States, their occupancy of the Philippines upon which the future of the monastic orders hangs in such ticklish suspense, so that now far less than before would anyone urge that the Pope proceed harshly against religious Americanism, because its assistance becomes increasingly important.

So Leo has prepared an encyclical which, cautiously handling the theme of Americanism, desired to sail neutrally between Scylla and Charybdis, and which was supposed to appear day after tomorrow. Suddenly he decided to postpone its publication.[25]

Knowing of this postponement, Denis O'Connell concluded that the pope would be slow to act, if indeed he ever acted at all. In this opinion he was strengthened by the warning that Ferdinand Brunetiere, editor of the *Revue des deux mondes* and the most celebrated convert in France,[26] had just transmitted to Cardinal Rampolla to the effect that a condemnation of the liberal Americanist movement would sever relations in France between the church and progressive intellectuals.[27] O'Connell could not imagine that the pope would repudiate the learned convert whom he recently and ostentatiously clasped to his bosom. And Brunetiere had maintained to the pope that the issue for American Catholics was "whether in America one could be a good Catholic and a good citizen at the same time." It was on just such perfectly sound *ralliement* sentiment, thought O'Connell, that the pope still based policy.[28]

Thus O'Connell, departing from Rome for Paris on December 6th, calculated that there would be no encyclical against Hecker and Americanism, and showed the confidence in this matter which has been faulted by a previous writer.[29] But there was great reason for O'Connell's confidence, reason which can only be seen by an understanding of his heightened association with F.X. Kraus.

Since September he had been plotting with the German church-political *savant* in an active arrangement to organize the support of the German government and the other powers of the Triple Alliance on behalf of the moderate candidate for the tiara, Cardinal Serafino Vannutelli.

In 1898 Serafino Vannutelli was a logical candidate for Germany, Italy and Austria[30] because he was known to be 'transigent' on the Roman Question and opposed to Cardinal Rampolla's policy of favoritism toward France. It was the goal of the Triple Alliance to humble and constrain France, and among other things, prevent France from any attempt to restore the temporal power.

Leo XIII's age and failing health seemed to imply an early conclave. Franz Xavier Kraus was the German government's envoy-designate to the impending gathering. For diplomatic reasons the Freiburg professor avoided direct contact with the cardinal, with whose opposition to the Jesuits, the French and Rampolla he became increasingly impressed.[31]

Denis O'Connell was in intimate contact with the cardinal brothers, Vincenzo and Serafino Vannutelli. He was a frequent visitor to their residence in Genazzano in the Castelli Romani, a home which bore witness to their descent from the chief stewards of the Colonna. His friendship provided a secure channel for the German Foreign Office to communicate with Serafino. To *Reichskanzler* Hohenlohe, Kraus' chief patron, the Grand Duke of Baden, wrote: "Only Kraus has the connections to O'Connell's assistance and with the concurrence of chancellor Hohenlohe, Kraus wrote up a *Gravamina nationis teutonicae* which O'Connell was to deliver to Serafino Vannutelli. The document was a specific program for discussions between the German government and the next pope, discussions which could take place between Kraus and Vannutelli before the conclave, or, if Vannutelli indicated agreement and were elected, after the conclave.[33]

At the end of September, with the full knowledge of Hohenlohe and the Grand Duke, O'Connell left Kraus at Freiburg and headed for Genazzano with the *Gravamina*. There the American Denis O'Connell invited Cardinal Serafino Vannutelli to endorse the document as the basis of a programme as pope, a policy which the cardinal could offer in the conclave.[34]

After conferring with the Vannutelli at Genazzano, O'Connell sent their answer to Kraus on October 15th.[35] The Kraus-O'Connell *Gravamina* had been transposed into a *Programme,* which Denis had written down at Serafino's request. The cardinal had completely agreed to their suggestions in an accord in substance which, said Denis, was "nearly spontaneous," and he added that his Italian notation of Serafino's reply was to be taken "with all the significance of an official document."[36] Kraus then presented the O'Connell-Vannutelli reply to the Grand Duke and the Chancellor as a "complete and most important Programme of the future pontificate, one which would not be political, but religious."[37]

We have the Vannutelli 'reply' as translated by Kraus from O'Connell's Italian letter. It was reprinted in Hohenlohe's memoirs.[38] It stands as a meaningful document of the liberal Catholic assault of 1898 because it is a testament to the liberal hopes of Kraus and the American agent, originated and subsequently edited by both. The note is nominally indicative of the measures which Serafino Vannutelli was willing to promise at that stage of his aspirations. Of course it was anathema to all who sought to retain their grip on the church, the powerful orders, the legitimists, the *intransigenti,* and the French, who had already announced that they would accept no papal candidate who would alter French privileges or who would compromise on the Roman question.[39] The Vanutelli Programme may be summarized thus:

(1) The next pope will have a religious orientation rather than political one. The cardinals are convinced that the Holy See should refrain from politics, and abandon dreams of reawakening the days of Gregory VII.

(2) A religious pope will ally himself with no nation, and indeed with no party. The German Empire and the State of Italy will be accepted as accomplished facts. Instead of treating with party leaders and unstable popular elements, the Holy See will deal with governments. Socialism is recognized as an equal danger to the church as to the state, and will be treated as such. The recent interference and partisanship in France will occur no more.

(3) The two extremes of Catholic science, one which will have no progress, the other which will have a progress which is too rapid, will be

treated according to the principle that to the Holy See is reserved the decision about doctrine (*Lehre*) and learning (*Wissenschaft*) in the exercise of the divine magisterium. However, exercise of this magisterium must be taken out of the hands of a gang (*canaglia*) more concerned for their supremacy than for the church. Roundabout attacks on Catholic writers in secret and dishonorable manner will no longer be tolerated.

(4) The implementation of the agreed political program will not be difficult. In the treatment of scientific learning, great battle will have to be given to the local and selfish interests of the orders, who will fight to maintain their supremacy. But the Sacred College is convinced that conflict is inevitable and must be made.

This is comprehended in the formula: A religious pope, and open and honorable methods in the conduct of church affairs.[40]

This 'religious programme' of course represents the liberal Catholic policies for which Franz Xaver Kraus had struggled all his life, and now by O'Connell's involvement, the cause of Americanism was associated with Kraus, the German foreign office and the politics of the Triple Alliance. It was the high water mark in the potential for a union between the Americanist movement and the strength of the "German Orientation" in the Catholic church. Both the accentuation of this combination, made clear by the Vannutelli Programme, provided a more visible target for the counter-attack on Americanism by the French and their allies in the international church.

Denis O'Connell and his American colleagues were soon to discover that to violate Jefferson's advice to Monroe, "never to entangle ourselves in the broils of Europe,"[41] meant to be ground between the upper and nether stones of the great powers. As the world came to know that he and his friends were "in the same boat with Kraus"[42] there descended the wrath of those who had much to lose from a combination which Benedetto Lorenzelli, the *nuncio* to France, would come to describe as that "band of pseudo-intellectuals" who advocated separation of church and state and the "transfer of the Papacy to the Anglo-Saxons;. . .that Italian-German-French-American ecclesiastical group which is. . .in favor of the Triple Alliance in politics."[43]

NOTES

1. "*A New Idea in The Life of Father Hecker*, by the Rt. Rev. D.J. O'Connell, D.D., Domestic Prelate of His Holiness. Read at the International Catholic Scientific Congress at Fribourg, Aug. 20th, 1897. For Private Circulation. Printed by B. Herder, Freiburg im Breisgau, 1897." Example in Kraus Archiv mailed from Munich.

2. Richard Meyer, *Die Ursachen der amerikanischen Konkurrenz: Ergebnisse einer Osterreichisch-ungarisch Studienreise* (Berlin, 1883) 9.

3. William Trimble, *Historical Aspects of the Surplus Food Production of the United States, 1862-1902* (Washington, D.C.: American Historical Assoc. Annual Report [for the year 1918], 1921) 223-39.

4. Address by the Austro-Hungarian Foreign minister in 1897, reported in *The Literary Digest* 15 (Dec. 11, 1897) 964.
5. Felix Klein, *In the Land of the Strenuous Life* (Chicago: A.C. McClurg, 1905).

6. Werner Sombart, *Die Juden and das Wirtschaftsleben* (Munich: Dunecker und Humblot, 1928); Shulamit Volkov, *The Rise of Popular Anti-Modernism in Germany 1873-1896* (Princeton, N.J.: Princeton U., 1977); Uriel Tal, *Christians and Jews in Germany: Religions, Politics and Ideology in the second Reich 1870-1914* (Ithaca: Cornell U., 1975).

7. Archives of the Catholic Historical Society of St. Paul (ACHSSP), Ireland papers, O'Connell to Ireland, Aug. 28, 1897.
8. See Henri Delassus, L'Américanisme et la Conjuration antichretienne (Lille: Desclée de Brouwer, 1899).

9. Thomas T. McAvoy, *The Great Crisis in American Catholic History* (Chicago: H. Regnery, 1957); Felix Klein, *Americanism: A Phantom Heresy (Cranford, N.J.: Aquin Book Shop, 1951); Gerald P. Fogarty, The Vatican and the Americanist Crisis: Denis J. O'Connell, American Agent in Rome* (Rome: Gregorian U., 1974).

10. From the original French version: Charles Maignen, *Le Père Hecker-Est-il un Saint ?* (Rome, 1898), cited in McAvoy, *Crisis* 212, and Klein, *Phantom* 131.

11. From the English version: Charles Maignen, *Father Hecker-Is He A Saint?* (Rome: International Catholic Library, 1898) 222ff.

12. McAvoy, *Crisis,* 204. See also, Colman Barry, *The Catholic Church and German Americans* (Milwaukee: Bruce, 1953), and Fogarty, *O'Connell.*

13. *Archives of the Paulist Fathers, O'Connell to Klein, May 18, 1898. also ACHSSP, O'Connell to Ireland, May 24, 1898.*

14. Kraus Archiv, Auguste von Eichthal File (AVE), Dec. 6, 1898.

15. *AVE, Jan. 15, 1899.*

16. *Allgemeine Zeitung, Kirchenpolitische Briefe von Spectator* (KPBr), KPBr 36, (the articles appeared monthly in the *Beilage,* from July 1, 1895).

17. Franz Xaver Kraus, *Tagebücher* (ed. H. Schiel; Cologne: J.P. Bachem, 1957) 717.

18. Full documentation in Fogarty, Klein, McAvoy, and Patrick H. Ahern, *The Life of John J. Keane* (Milwaukee: Bruce, 1955). Repeated in letters to Kraus; Kraus Archiv, O'Connell File.

19. ACHSSP, O'Connell to Ireland, July 12, July 20, Aug. 28, 1898.

20. McAvoy, *Crisis* 252; Klein, *Phantom* 199.

21. AVE, Jan. 15, 1898.

22. New York: *Freeman's Journal,* Dec. 3, 1898.

23. AVE, May 29, 1898.

24. ACHSSP, Keane to Ireland, March 8, 1898: "...the Holy Father indicated that those Silver Jubilee influences had...impressed him."

25. AVE, Dec. 6, 1898.

26. McAvoy, *Crisis* 254; Kraus, *Tagebücher* 713.

27. *Tagebücher* 713; Archives of the Paulist Fathers, O'Connell to Elliot, Dec. 10, 1898 (cited McAvoy, *Crisis* 273ff.)

28. *Idem.*

29. Fogarty.

30. Christoph Weber, *Quellen und Studien zur Kurie und zur vatikanischen Politik unter Leo XIII* (Tübingen: M. Niemeyer, 1973) 425.

31. *Tagebücher* 720.

32. Political Archives of the German Foreign Office *(Auswärtiges Amt), Kath. Kirche i. d. Ver. St.* 13 A, bd. 3, March 4, 1899. Grand Duke of Baden to Hohenlohe; and also in Chlodwig zu Hohenlohe-Schillingsfuerst, *Denkwürdigkeiten der Reichskanzlerzeit,* ed. K.A. von Müller (Stuttgart: Deutsche Verlags-anstalt, 1931) 487. (Hereafter, HRK III 486).

33. Weber, *Quellen* 42ff., treats this subject but without reference to O'Connell's role.

34. AVE, Oct. 12, 1898.

35. Ornella Confessore, *Conservatismo politico e riformismo religioso. La "Rassegna Nazionale" dal 1898 al 1908* (Bologna: Il mulino, 1971) 84-85, cites Archivio da Passano, La Spezia, Countess Sabina di Parravicino di Revel to Alfredo da Passano, Oct. 22, 1898, to the effect that Denis O'Connell had been at Genazzano, from whence "attendeva di tornarsene per sbrigare tutte la faccende inerenti all'Americanismo..."

36. Kraus Archiv, O'Connell to Kraus, Oct. 15, 1898.

92

37. *Tagebücher* 712.

38. HRK III, 467; Weber, *Quellen* 42ff.

39. KPBr XIV; KPBr XLII.

40. HRK III, 467.

41. Jefferson to Monroe, cited in John Latane, *America as a World Power* (New York: Harper and Bros., 1907) 261.

42. Archives of the Diocese of Richmond, William Gibson to O'Connell, July 29, 1899.

43. Klein, *Phantom* 217; Gerald P. Fogarty, *The Vatican and the American Hierarchy* (Stuttgart: Hiersemann, 1982) 186-87, Lorenzelli to Rampolla, May 24, 1900 and July 21, 1900.

AMERICANISM AND THE SIGNS OF THE TIMES:
RESPONSE TO PORTIER, WANGLER AND AYERS

Margaret M. Reher

It is indeed appropriate, as Portier noted, for this discussion to take place on the centenary of the Third Plenary Council of Baltimore, since all the American protagonists were present there. It is also gratifying to see the scholarly attention that both Hecker and Americanism have continued to attract in the years since I first attempted my own interpretation, particularly since the "Hecker papers" were still under lock and key when I began my work.[1]

(1) *Portier.* Isaac Hecker's vision, as early as 1875, of the European expansion of the Paulists as anticipating the Americanist "movement" of the following decade, has been delineated by Portier. He sees Bishop John Keane as the link which establishes at least a certain "limited continuity" between these two movements. And he has certainly demonstrated very effectively the continuity between the vision of Hecker and that of Keane. Simply put, Keane not only said that Hecker influenced him, his writings reflect that influence.

But I would like to have seen Portier push the dates of Hecker's incipient Americanizing, although clearly not envisioned as any kind of a movement at that time, back to 1857 and his *Civilta* article.[2] There he anticipated a number of the items that formed the Americanist agenda; namely, that America, once Catholic, could of all other nations, lead the Church to new and glorious heights, and that the Catholic Church in America must lose its foreign image. Hecker described the special character of American political institutions, the American system, natural rights, and so forth, as just what Catholicism teaches. In this same article he also displays his naivete to put it kindly, about the materialism of America.[3] As Portier has suggested elsewhere, this blindness was probably due to his close relationship with his beloved brother George who made a fortune developing self-rising flour.[4] Perhaps when Hecker wrote in *Civilta* that American materialism favors conversion because a laborer need not be intimidated by his boss since "lucrative employment is easily found," he had George in mind as a potential employer.[5]

Among other points, it was this aspect of laissez faire capitalism, accepted and even praised by the Americanists, which caused foreign suspicion from the Pope down. Pius IX questioned Hecker about American materialism four months after his *Civilta* article. Hecker agreed that Americans are engaged in material pursuits but, he added, "the holy faith is there."[6]

Archbishop John Ireland, in 1892, admitted that Americans are materialistic but, he added, "they give in princely fashion."[7] As Wangler has stated in another place, Ireland himself had become a millionaire through real estate.[8] The quote I just cited by Ireland seems to be given the lie by Ireland himself, a year later when, as Wangler so marvelously put it, "O'Connell was actively trying to squeeze out of millionaire Ireland some five thousand " to save the *Moniteur de Rome*.[9]

I mention these attitudes toward American materialism because I see them as symptomatic of certain blind spots of the Americanists. Certainly Hecker, Keane, and Ireland had some social interest: all were involved in the temperance crusade; Keane was concerned with the plight of the Negro; Ireland wanted improved social conditions for immigrants. Yet they all failed to be disabused of the myth of "the land of equal opportunity for all," even though Henry George by the late 1860's was already signaling the inequitable distribution of wealth that the expansion of the railroads was effecting, and his celebrated *Progress and Poverty* was published by 1880.[10] It is true that Ireland and Keane defended F. Edward McGlynn who had gotten into ecclesiastical trouble because of his espousal of George's 'Single Tax Theory.' It doesn't matter that they weren't defending McGlynn precisely because they shared his views; the point is that they actually could have, even should have, seen the flaws in America's social fabric.

(2)*Wangler.* Portier ends by citing Wangler's caution that to designate the Hecker-Keane relationship as "Americanist prototype and disciple" with their thought mutually convertible seemed premature" at the time I made it. While I would still hold, with Portier, for a strong connection between them, Wangler has led me to temper my assessment of Keane somewhat. But this is not due to this paper, but rather to his earlier article to which he only alludes in the opening of this paper, "American Catholic Expanisionism: 1886-1894," where he has demonstrated very ably Keane's involvement, more, his leading role in forming and manipulating public opinion in Rome and throughout the world.[11] This plants Keane much more squarely in the packaging and exporting of Americanism than I had earlier suspected. I had pictured Keane, like Hecker, trusting that providence and the Holy Spirit would work things out. The image that Wangler presents is of Keane willingly lending Providence a helping hand, even giving a push and a shove.

I am sympathetic with Wangler's attempts in his current paper to sketch out a metaphysics for each of the Americanists. I have repeatedly said to my students that we all operate out of some kind of metaphysical framework, conscious or unconscious. I would like to add that our metaphysical framework shifts over time and would even like to suggest, although very tentatively, that we may *simultaneously* hold several sets of "metaphysics."

I was very pleased to see Wangler include Hecker in his analysis and I am very congenial to the dialectical framework in which he views both Hecker and Keane. He notes, and rightly, the importance of the role of the Spirit as a key to Hecker's metaphysics, and to an accurate interpretation of it.

While I agree with the dialectical framework, and also find his subject-object position helpful in understanding Hecker's view of Papal Infallibility, some other aspects of Hecker's interpretations of conflict seem more "Hegelian" than Wangler suggests. For instance, both the Nativist conflict in America and the Civil War, Hecker was convinced, would bring Americans to see the truth of the Catholic church.[12] Perhaps Hecker has "several" metaphysics.

Speaking of the role of the Holy Spirit in Hecker's theology brings up the role of Henry Cardinal Manning in Americanism. Wangler, in "The Birth of Americanism: Westward the Apocalyptic Candlestick," argued that it was Manning, not Hecker, who was the idol of the Americanists.[13] I would simply like to point out that Hecker, too, greatly admired Manning's work. His books, *The Temporal Mission of the Holy Ghost* and *The Internal Mission of the Holy Ghost,* Hecker calls "remarkable."[14] Hecker saw his role as effecting a synthesis of these two works and showing their reciprocity.[15] Portier has shown the role which Manning would "hopefully" have played in Hecker's dream of a European Paulist mission. At least in my mind it's easy to see why the Americanists would have patronized Manning. First, and perhaps most important, he was a cardinal; second, he held views similar to theirs and supported their efforts; third, by the time the "movement" got into full swing, Hecker was already dead! Still, I want to emphasize my appreciation of Wangler's thorough study of Keane.

Wangler has stated that Keane made only one public reference to the Holy Ghost after 1888. Still, it was on December 13, 1897 that Keane warned Walter Elliott that Hecker's doctrine of the Holy Ghost was misunderstood as making action of the Holy Ghost too distinct from the Trinity. Keane explained it as the traditional theology of "attribution" which suggests to me that he at least felt quite confident of Hecker's theological position on the question.[16] While I am willing to accept Wangler's Hegelian presentation of Keane, I think he needs to emphasize Keane's continued commitment to "Providence" throughout his life, even though I have admitted his point that Keane was quite willing to help Providence along.

Wangler points out the problematic nature of Keane's faith with this complete identification of the Christian side of his dialectical view with the political and social life of the United States, the philosophy of John Locke, and the separation of church and state.

I think the same problem arises with varying degrees among all of the Americanists, although Edward J. Langlois, C.S.P., in his "Isaac Hecker's Political Thought" has argued that Hecker thought that Catholic natural law in the Thomistic tradition and American natural right in the Lockean tradition were linked.[17] Still all the Americanists, including Hecker, had faith in the "myth" as Wangler calls, it, of Americanism. They, rather uncritically, bought the package, lock, stock, and barrel.

Before we leave Keane, one final and minor question to Wangler: was it really a display of vanity on the part of Keane to write in his diocesan record book, re his appointment to the See of Dubuque, Iowa, that "unlike most appointments, his came with a personal note from the Pope?" Being sent to Dubuque sounds as flattering as Edward McGlynn's having been sent to St. Mary's in Newburgh after he was reinstated in the Chruch.

Wangler is clearly the present expert on John Ireland, and I admit that I may have been excessive years ago in claiming that he should have seen the connection between Ireland and Hecker as I did. I am now willing to accept his description of Ireland's "ecclesiastical imperialism" and his "social ecumenism." He has shown that Ireland did not have the same sense of history nor did he have an historical theology, as Hecker and Keane did. However, I would like him to have shown more clearly how Ireland's distinction between principle, and application of principle "even in the Divine," as he put it, worked out since he saw the Holy Ghost as the preserver of the divine.[18]

Ireland admitted his reservations about understanding Hecker's doctrine of the Spirit, a fact which I interpreted as a weakness in his ecclesiology. But don't forget that Ireland attributed to Hecker "most salutory impressions."[19] Ireland knew enough about him to praise him, in the context of the founding of the Paulists, as one who would advocate a "new" religion suited to the age.[20] Ireland also quoted Hecker almost verbatim in 1897 in his statement that "laymen need not wait for priest, nor priest for bishop, nor bishop for pope."[21] But the question remains: was it Ireland's distinction between the human and divine, as Wangler described it, that caused him in 1903 to express reservations about his involvement in the temporal order?[22]

Nothing has yet appeared which would alter my view of Monsignor Denis J. O'Connell as a pragmatist. At least as far as he is concerned, I am even willing to agree with Emmett Curran's characterization of the Machiavellian use of Hecker by the Americanist.[23] On this point, I think we agree.

(3) *Ayers*. Ayers has centered his investigation upon the close connection between O'Connell and Franz Xavier Kraus and has pointed out O'Connell's convenient distinction between "political" and "religious" Americanism. He has capably shown that the European acceptance of "Americanism" extended beyond England and France into Germany. Ayers and Wangler should get together sometime to discuss their divergent use of "mythology" as a characterization of Americanism. If I read Ayers rightly he uses "myth" as synonymous with "make believe" and "phantom" as "shadow in the dark." If

this reading is correct, Portier and I will, I suppose, also have to join in the conversation.

Ayers argues that O'Connell's confidence that Rome would not condemn Americanism was based on his knowledge of the *Gravamina*, later translated by O'Connell to a "programme" at the direction of Cardinal Serafino Vannutelli. But he does not make at all clear how the content of the Kraus-O'Connell-Vannutelli "programme" became known to the world. This is a critical point if we are to assess the mood of optimism among the Americanists that Rome, in 1898, would not condemn Americanism.

I also do not see why Ayers thinks that O'Connell's association with Kraus and his implication in the *Gravamina* would bolster O'Connell's opinion. After all, the *Gravamina* would take effect only on Leo XIII's death; although ailing, he didn't die until 1903.

This leaves us with a serious point which, I think, none of us has satisfactorily resolved. Why were Ireland, Keane, and O'Connell so confident that Americanism would not be condemned? Heaven knows, there were enough signs.

In 1888, Keane was called up for his "Leo XIII" lecture as Hecker had been earlier for his *Civilta* article. *Longinqua Oceani* in 1895 had less than positive reference both to the separation of Church and State and to the Catholic University of America. Keane had already been removed from the rectorship of Catholic University and O'Connell, from the rectorship of the American College in Rome, before they left Rome so confident, prior to *Testem Benevolentiae.* I have argued that the Americanists really believed that Leo XIII was on their side. If Ayers is correct, O'Connell was looking beyond Leo's pontificate. But if I am correct, then Americanists were absolutely blind to the true political reality. They simply did not read the signs of the times correctly.

CONCLUSION

In attempting to read the "signs of the times," the Americanists had, rather uncritically, attempted to "Catholicize" the American dream. The Americanists, for their efforts, were rejected by some European prelates, as we all well know. Our current American Bishops' *The Challenge of Peace,* is their attempt to come to grips with the "new moment" of history.[24] Their Peace Pastoral is critical of American militarism and capitalism,[25] two of the very points which had bothered the Americanists' critics. Ironically, some contemporary European Bishops are less than enthusiastic about the United States Bishops' evaluation of the policy of deterrance as an American measure.[26] The Europeans, too, are reading the "signs of the times," but from their perspective, caught, as they are, between the two superpowers. So, even reading contemporary "signs of the times" is subject to interpretation. It is certainly not surprising, then, that the papers studied here, dealing with a century-old episode, have not fully agreed in their interpretation of some aspects of Americanism.

NOTES

1. For the background of this response, see Margaret M. Reher, "The Church and the Kingdom of God in America: The Ecclesiology of the Americanists" (New York: unpublished Diss.; Fordham University, 1972).

2. "Riflessioni sopra il presente e l'avvenire de Cattolicisme negli Stati Uniti d'America," *Civilta Cattolica* 8 (3rd. ser.; Nos. 184 and 185, 1857, 385-402, 513-29.

3. *Ibid.* 385ff.

4. William Portier, "Isaac Hecker and Americanism," *The Ecumenist* 19 (1980) 9-12.

5. Hecker, *art. cit.*, 517ff.

6. See Vincent Holden, *The Yankee Paul* (Milwaukee: Bruce, 1958) 409.

7. "America in France," *The Church and Modern Society* (2nd. ed.; New York: G.H.J. McBride & Co., 1897) 356ff.

8. "American Catholic Expansion: 1886-1894," *Harvard Theological Review,* (75 No. 3 1982), 369-393, 387.

9. *Ibid.*, 391.

10. (New York: D. Appleton and Company).

11. *art. cit.*

12. Hecker, *art. cit.*, 517ff. and Hecker to Richard Simpson, "Some Letters of Father Hecker," ed. Abbot Gasquet, *Catholic World*, 83 (Nos. 495, 496, 1906) 362,457.

13. *The Harvard Theological Review* 65 (No. 3, 1972) 415-436, 430.

14. See Xavier DuFresne, "Personal Recollections of Father Hecker," *Catholic World* 67 (1898) 339.

15. *Ibid.*

16. Archives of the Paulist Fathers, Americanism Papers, Keane to Elliott, Rome.

17. *Hecker Studies* (ed., John Farina; New York: Paulist, 1983) 50ff.

18. Ireland, "The Pontiff of the Age," *The Church and Modern Society* (New York: D.H. McBride and Co., 1897) 390ff.

19. Ireland's Introduction to Walter Elliott's *The Life of Father Hecker* (New York: Columbus, 1891) viii.

20. *Ibid.* xvi.

21. "Catholics in America," *The Church and Modern Society* 72.

22. 1903 edition of *The Church and Modern Society* xxiv.

23. *Michael Augustine Corrigan and the Shaping of Conservative Catholicism in America, 1879-1902* (New York: Arno, 1978) 316, 505.

24. (Washington, D.C.: United States Catholic Conference, 1983) p. 40.

25. *Ibid.*, vii.

26. *Ibid.*, p. 58.

III.
WHAT HAS BEEN AND WILL BE

THE DISCOVERY OF THE GENETIC DEVELOPMENT OF THOMAS AQUINAS' THEOLOGY OF HOPE AND ITS RELEVANCE FOR A THEOLOGY OF THE FUTURE

Joseph T. Merkt

With the dialectic taking place today among various theologians of hope and of liberation, and between these theologians and ecclesial and political leaders, it is not inappropriate to once again examine the methodological approaches Thomas Aquinas employed in his theologies of hope. And, in a world whose future is bleak and uncertain, it is not unhelpful to examine the grounds for Thomas' theology of hope.

In the light of the above questions, this article has two goals. The first is to share with the reader the results of recent research which indicates that Thomas' theology of hope developed genetically in three distinct (yet sublating) stages.[1] This discovery is quite a radical departure from previous analyses of Thomas' treatment of hope. These previous analyses presumed that Thomas had only one general and basically unchanging theology of hope that perdured from his earlier *Commentary on Peter Lombard's Sentences* till his later *Summa theologiae* and *Compendium theologiae*.[2] They also presumed there were few, if any, important reflections on hope in Thomas' scripture commentaries.[3]

A second goal of this paper is to note that Thomas' theology of hope does not only *not* merit the criticism it has received from Jurgen Moltmann, but that it can add vital energy to the contemporary theological reflections on the future, on hope and on liberation.

Some Contemporary Criticism of Aquinas' Theology of Hope

Contemporary theologians of hope are not only critical of each others' methods, but they are also critical of the past. Thomas Aquinas is one of the futures from the past whose theology of hope is criticized in the current attempts to bring about a renewal of eschatology or theology of hope.

The most important criticism of Thomas' theology of hope comes from Jurgen Moltmann who states that he does not believe that Thomas really has a true theology of hope. Moltmann believes that instead of a true eschatology Thomas has a theology of hope which is actually an ontology of desire, because his theology of hope relies on the concept of God as final end *(finis ultimus.)*.[4]

Louis Weeks disagrees with Moltmann and even claims that Moltmann could learn much from the theology of hope found in Thomas' *Summa theologiae*.

In sum, the *Summa* does speak incisively to the *Theology of Hope*, although one cannot minimize the differences between a medieval and modern outlook. Because of its sensitivity to the movement of hope, the source of hope, the stance of man in hope, and the place of certainty in hope, the *Summa* can both warn and enrich Moltmann's already refreshing and revolutionary appropriation of that theological category. It declares without equivocation what is the language, origin and limit of hope. The *Summa* cautions concerning the possibility of deception, the sin of presumption, the heeding of science, and the positive use of fear, inherent in a comprehensive Theology of Hope.[5]

Carl Peter is in agreement with Weeks. His address to the American Catholic Theological Society explains that Thomas' theology of hope could be an important factor in a Roman Catholic contribution to the contemporary quest for a credible eschatology. He also develops this contention in an article published about the same time.[6]

Thomas Aquinas' thought is viewed by Moltmann as one of the sources of the problems being faced by contemporary theologians of hope, while his thought is judged by Weeks and Peter as one of the fonts of renewal for today's theology of hope.

Thomas' Theology of Hope--Some Introductory Remarks

There are not many studies of Thomas' theology of hope. Many studies that have been made tend to concentrate on specific aspects of Thomas' theology of hope rather than to examine the totality of his theology of hope.

The more important recent studies of Thomas' theology of hope need to be mentioned. Bernard[7] and Fries[8] approach Thomas' writings about hope from the perspective of the gifts of the Holy Spirit, prayer and the spiritual life. Charles[9] and Pinckaers[10] seek to explain that Thomas does not treat hope as individualistic and self-centered, but as having a communal dimension in charity as well. Ramirez[11] and Conlon[12] investigate the ways that Thomas describes hope's certitude as different than the certitude that is proper to faith. Hill,[13] and Le Tilly,[14] and Urdanoz[15] present translations and commentaries on the *Summa theologiae's* tract of hope, a tract which is considerably more developed than those tracts found in his earlier *Commentary on the Sentences* and his *Disputed Questions on Hope*. Delaney,[16] Harent,[17] Nicolas,[18] Engelhardt,[19] Ramirez[20] and Kerstiens[21] have published encyclopedia articles which summarize Thomas' theology of hope for today's reader. Garrigou-Lagrange[22] and Ramirez[23] have written from within the scholastic tradition to defend the "essence" of Thomas' theology of hope against contemporary challenges. For example, Ramirez is refuting Lain-Entralgo's conclusion that there seems to be a natural virtue of hope.[24]

The above writings are quite detailed, but their concern is more with content than methodology.

Helpful clues to the *Summa's* methodology for treating hope are offered by the more recently published commentaries on the *Summa's* tract "De spe" (II-II, 17-22). Especially valuable are the commentaries by Le Tilly, Urdanoz and Hill. No serious conflicts exist among these three commentaries, though they exhibit slightly different concerns. Le Tilly, for example, seems especially interested in the way the *Summa* relates hope to faith and charity and in the way it discusses whether the virtue of hope existed in Christ.[25] Urdanoz is especially concerned about showing his disagreement with Lain-Entralago who tries to imply that the *Summa* grounds its treatment of hope as a theological virture upon a "natural virtue" of hope that is inherent in each human being.[26] Hill seems especially desirous of putting the *Summa's* thought on hope into historical perspective while emphasizing its ever-present importance.[27]

There is one discussion, not mentioned thus far, that actually focuses explicitly on the methodical dimensions of some questions in all four of Thomas' major treatises on hope. This discussion involves a dialogue between two articles published by the same author--Servais Pinckaers. In 1958, he published an article "la nature vertueuse de l'esperance"[28] which claims that there are significant shifts in vocabulary and methodology from Thomas' earliest treatments of some specific questions on hope to his later treatments of these same questions. This 1958 article claimed that Thomas' earliest tract on hope is to be found in the *Commentary on the Sentences,* his later tracts in the *Summa theologiae* and *Compendium* and his latest and most developed tract in the *De spe.* In 1964, Pinckaers republished the article with major revisions.[29] He reaffirmed the shifts in vocabulary and methodology in these specific questions, but concluded that a closer look at these shifts indicates that the *De spe* is not Thomas' most mature work on hope. Rather, the *Summa theologiae* and the *Compendium theologiae* must be judged to contain his most mature approaches to hope.

These two articles by Pinckaers are very significant. No other studies make detailed comparisons of the methodical differences found in particular sections of Thomas' tracts on hope. Yet there are real limitations to Pinckaers' studies, for Pinckaers' conclusions are based on a concentrated analysis of only a few of the questions found in each of these Thomistic tracts on hope: What are hope's objects? Is hope a virtue? Is it a theological virtue? Pinckaers does not analyze the other questions in these works, especially those pertaining to "spes passio" and to "subiectum spei." Thus these questions can be asked: Is Pinckaers' thesis applicable to the entirety of each of the tracts on hope? Is there general validity to his thesis that there are different methodical approaches in Thomas' various tracts on hope? If so, which of these different methodologies shows the most development of thought?

This article will venture to outline the relationship that exists between method and content in Thomas' treatments of hope and will draw upon the insight of Pinckaers' thought. However, it is to be noted that this article's conclusions go beyond Pinckaers'.

Thomas' Theology of Hope--Schemata I, II and III

Thomas' thoughts about hope develop in such a way that he actually adopts three different schemata for his theology of hope.[30] Schema I occurs in his *Commentary on the Sentences*.[31] Schema II is found in his *De spe*.[32] And, Schema III surfaces briefly in the *Summa contra Gentiles* and is fully developed in the *Summa theologiae* and the *Compendium theologiae*.[33] These three schemata are so distinct that they employ: different analogies;[34] different definitions of virtue;[35] different vocabularies to speak of hope's objects;[36] different approaches to showing that hope is a theological virtue;[37] and different depths of vision when speaking of hope and prayer,[38] hope and divine grace,[39] the subject of the virtue of hope,[40] and hope and fear, presumption and despair.[41]

Reflection on the data indicates that each of the schemata are distinct, but interrelatd. As Thomas moves from Schema I to Schema II to Schema III, his horizon keeps expanding so as to include the previous schema/schemata and to add new questions and insights as well. The distinctness and the interrelatedness of each schema can be illustrated by noting the relationship between these schemata and salvation history.

Schema I, which is found in the *Commentary on the Sentences*[42] employs a definition of the emotion-of-being-hopeful (spes passio) which concentrates on the arduousness involved in this emotion's pursuit of a future good (*bonum*).[43] Its definition of hope as a virtue (*spes ut virtus*) uses this understanding of the emotion-of-hopefulness as an analogy and stresses an understanding of hope's certainty in spite of the arduousness that lies before it in the future.[44] Its analysis of hope's objects notes that the arduousness is due in part to the fact that the hoped-for-object is so distant and future and so beyond human capability, for hope's object is that arduous good which exceeds the faculty of nature and to which one is able to come only through grace, namely God, insofar as he is our beatitude. . .our future happiness.[45]

From this perspective, those scriptural texts which are most easily related to the virtue of hope (as presented in Schema I) are those texts which speak of the arduous future beatitude (which is the object of our hope) and of the assistance that God will offer us in attaining that transcendent future hoped-for-object.

Typical of scriptural passages included in the horizon of Schema I are the following: Matthew 25's parables of the ten virgins and of the talents, and its description of the last judgement's separation of the sheep and the goats. In brief, the focus of the theology of hope in Schema I is directed towards the last things as presented in the typical tract "On the Last Things" (so common to theology up through the Second World War), with special emphasis being put on the nature of hope's certainty.

Schema II, which is found in the *De spe*, employs a defintion for the emotion-of-being-hopeful which stresses the possibility (*possibile habere*)of attaining the future hoped-for-object because one-hopes-for-the-future-assistance-of-another.[46] Schema II speaks of hope's objects from the cognitional (rather than affective) perspective of material and formal objects (*obiectum materiale* and *obiectum formale*).[47] This scema still includes the future supernatural hoped-for-object of eternal life (Schema I), but it transcends the horizon of Schema I to speak more explicitly of the future "material" objects for which we hope[48] and to place much more emphasis on the supernatural and natural future assistance-for-which-we-hope (hope's formal objects).[49] Thus, it is because of our belief in God and our hoping for this natural and supernatural future assistance promised us by God, that we are moved to hope for the natural and supernatural future promised us by God. Schema II, therefore, makes a direct connection between the virtue of hope and God's promises of future assistance through life's journey and ultimately to the beatific vision. This assistance includes not only the supernatural aid of grace, the infused virtues and the gifts of the Holy Spirit, but also the material helps we need as well: "In ordine enim ad hanc fruitionem speramus adiuvari a Deo non solum spiritualibus, sed etiam corporalibus beneficiis."[50]

From this perspective, the scriptural texts which are related to Schema II's presentation of the virtue of hope are not only those that relate to the supernatural-hoped-for-object of Schema I, but also those texts which speak of "material" objects for which we hope and even more importantly those texts which speak of God's promises to us. These promises, and all the promises made over and over throughout the Hebrew Scriptures, basically reiterate in one form or another "I will be your God and you will be my people." These promises reach their fulfillment in the Risen Christ's promise: "I will be with you until the end of time. I ask you to place your hope and trust in the future because of the promises I make to you, and I assure you that one day you will be united with me forever in heaven." It is in looking to these promises of future assistance that Schema II of Thomas' theology of hope goes beyond Schema I.

Schema III, which first appears in a brief and undeveloped fashion in *SCG* III, 153 and which appears in developed form in *ST* II-II, 20-23 and *CT* II, 1-10, is broad enough to include the elements of Schema I and II but goes beyond them.[51] Schema III begins in the past and grows out of the present to the mystery of the future.

Schema III employs a definition of the emotion of being hopeful which stresses that the reception of assistance strengthens hope. In its definition of "spes virtus" hope is a virtue because it attains its rule, being united with God who is present with his loving help and who draws us to hope ultimately for complete union with Him in the beatific vision.[52] Schema III speaks of hope's future objects in terms of the already present divine love and assistance (*divinum auxilium*) as the efficient cause (*causa efficiens*) creating in us a hope for attaining future good (*causa finalis*).[53] The Primary-Efficient-Cause of hope (God) assists us through means of secondary and created agents (of efficient causes) and invites us to hope for the proximate or secondary ends needed to attain our Primary-End (God), as well as to hope for the ultimate attainment of that Primary-End Himself.[54]

It is this focus on the past, the present, and on the affective which makes Schema III so different from Schema I and II, especially since this focus on the present fosters a great reverence for the *mystery* of the future as well. *SCG* III, 153 notes that God's love is expressed in the gift of sanctifying grace, a pre-conscious gift, from which (through the theological virtues) flows our awareness that we are first loved by God in the present, and from which flows an invitation to hope for a continuous growth in that loving relationship with God. This theme is continued in *ST* II-II, 17, 1, ad 2 where Thomas writes that the habit of hope, however, through which a person awaits beatitude, is not caused by merit but solely by grace (which is the giftedness of God's love). Thus hope is seen first of all as a uniting or bonding of ourselves (in the present) with God who first loves us; then as an opening up of ourselves through hope towards the attainment (in the future) of perfect union with God in heaven.[55] This future union is, in a real sense, a mystery.[56]

Such hope, which is grounded in love, reaches out to take on the future hopes and aspirations of all people as our own:

> On this basis, namely because of the union love, it is possible to hope for eternal happiness for another. And just as there is but one virtue of charity whereby we love God, self, neighbor, so there is but one virtue of hope expressing our aspirations for ourselves and for others.[57]

Schema III reaches out to embrace all of God's governance or providence over the world and His action within salvation history beginning with creation itself.

> Man is made by God somewhat as an article is made by an artificer. Something of this sort is said in Isaias 64:8: "And now, O Lord, Thou art our Father and we are clay, and Thou art our Maker." Accordingly, just as an earthen vessel, if it were endowed with sense, might hope to be put to good use by the potter, so man ought to cherish the hope of being rightly provided for by God. This we are told in Jeremias 18:6: "As clay is in the hand of the potter, so are you in My hand, O house of Israel." The confidence which man has in God ought to be most certain.[58]

We should also bear in mind that, while Providence watches sollicitously over all creatures, God exercises special care over rational beings. For the latter are exalted to the dignity of God's image.[59]

As the world grows in its awareness of God's loving providence, it can grow in hope and in understanding of the hope planted within the human heart. Thus Schema III draws hope from all of God's saving actions:

> We should observe, further, that when any perfection is conferred, an ability to do or acquire something is also added. For example, when the air is illuminated by the sun, it has the capacity to serve as a medium for sight, and when water is heated by fire it can be used to cook, and it could hope for this if it had a mind. To man is given, over and above the nature of his soul, the perfection of grace, by which he is made a partaker in the divine nature, as we are taught in 2 Peter 1:4. As a result of this, we are said to be regenerated and to become sons of God. Thus raised to be sons, men may reasonably hope for an inheritance, as we learn from Romans 8:17: "If sons, heirs also." In keeping with this spiritual regeneration, man should have a yet higher hope in God, namely, the hope of receiving an eternal inheritance, according to 1 Peter 1:30-31: "God. . .hath regenerated us unto a lively hope, by the resurrection of Jesus Christ from the dead, unto an inheritance incorruptible and undefiled and that cannot fade, reserved in heaven for you."[60]

Note, by the way, that even human life on a feeling level is affected by the virtue of hope, for the emotions become an integral part of the life of hope. Note also that all of the elements contained in Schema I and II are included in the broader perspective of Schema III. The future hoped-for-object (eternal life) of Schema I and the future hoped-for-help (*divinum auxilium*) of Schema II are still hoped for, but these hoped-for-objects are now grounded in the present and past exerience of God's loving and saving and creating presence. The diagram that follows might be helpful in illustrating how each of the schemata is interrelated.

THE INTERRELATIONSHIP AMONG THOMAS' THREE SCHEMATA
FOR THE THEOLOGY OF HOPE

		SCHEMA III Focuses *also* on God as already present and
SCHEMA I Focuses on future-hoped-for supernatur-al-union-with God	**SCHEMA II** focuses *also* on future-natural-and-supernatur-al-hoped-for-divine-help	causing hope in the future to be born through his already present loving help (integrates feelings and other persons)

Thus each schema builds upon the previous one and includes it, with the final schema embracing the entire Scripture and all of salvation history.[61]

With the understanding that comes from these schemata, some real insight can be gained into some areas of Thomistic study that would be less intelligible without these schemata.

Schema I, II, and III and Some Debates About Thomas' Theology of Hope

Awareness of these three schemata that seem to express variations in Thomas' theology of hope may provide insight into the debate mentioned earlier in this article. The debate to be looked at will be the one between Moltmann, Weeks and Peter regarding the use of finality in Thomas' theology of hope. There will also be an examination of the relationship between Thomas' thought as found in Schema III and liberation theology and contemporary discourse about the last things.

Metaphysical Finalism

In 1967, Jürgen Motmann published the English edition of his *Theology of Hope*.[62] In 1968, as was mentioned earlier in this article he delivered a paper at the Duke consultation on the task of theology today. His paper was entitled "Theology as Eschatology."[63]

Moltmann was concerned, among other things, that God is often perceived as responsible for the world's evils. Moltmann argues in these works that the only way that the real misery of the Cross and the pains of this world can be accepted is if there is belief in the future, if there is belief that at the end of the world, God will finally be God immediately and universally for all. He is convinced that only such an eschatologically oriented belief can adequately address this problem.

> God's being does not lie in the process of the world's becoming so that he would be the unifying good of all tendencies and intentions of transient things: *finis ultimus,* Point Omega. (Rather) God's being is coming.[64]

He further notes:

> Here we find a principal difference between the Aristotelian-Thomist God-idea of the *finis ultimus* and the *Deus adventurus* of the New Testament. As *finis ultimus,* the unmoved mover, in the *appetitus naturalis,* draws all things to himself in virtue of the eros awakened by his perfection. As *Deus adventurus,* however, he comes towards all things with the *novum ultimum* and transforms them. This is the difference between the "theology of hope" of Thomas which is actually an ontology of desire (including anthropology), and an eschatological theology which wants to appropriate and develop an apocalyptic thought form of the New Testament (Cf. Ch. A. Bernard, *Théologie de l'Espérance selon Saint Thomas d'Aquin,* 1961).[65]

This criticism of Thomas Aquinas' use of final causality in his theology of hope opened up a debate.[66] In 1969, Louis Weeks initiated a defense of Thomas with his article entitled "Can Saint Thomas' *Summa Theologiae* Speak to Moltmann's Theology of Hope?[67] In 1974, this defense of Thomas' theology of hope was carried forward by Carl J. Peter's article, "Metaphysical Finalism or Christian Eschatology,"[68] and by his address at the Catholic Theological Society of America Meeting in 1974, "A Roman Catholic Contribution to the Quest of a Credible Eschatology."[6]

Weeks acknowledges that there are severe methodological differences between the theologies of hope of Moltmann and Thomas. In fact, he grants the basic difference noted by Moltmann:

> That Thomas in his *Summa* conceived of the meaning of human existence primarily in terms of cosmological teleology cannot be seriously doubted. The goal of the world in all respects remained in rejoining God who had given it existence. More particularly, in the words of P. Kunzle, what is 'especially characteristic for Thomas' moral theology is that the life of a Christian is conceived of as a return to God from whom he has gone out.' According to Kunzle, Aristotle's teleological *Ethic* gave rise to this concern on the part of Thomas. Whatever its source, the dichotomy still remains; and the resultant chasm in theological methodology between

Thomas and Moltmann cannot be bridged by any simple synthesis.

Nevertheless, even after the Copernican revolution, the technological obsession of modern man, and the ascendency of relativism have been granted the inappropriate places of importance . . . I would assert that the *Summa* can speak in several respects to the *Theology of Hope*.[70]

Though he grants Thomas has a "cosmological teleology," Weeks denies Moltmann's conclusion. Weeks' article is a clear rebuttal of the position that Thomas' theology of hope is bankrupt. It is interesting that the theology of hope Weeks argues from is the theology of hope contained in the *Summa theologiae* (a theology of hope that comes from Thomas' Schema III). The points that Weeks considers meaningful and relevant to Moltmann's thought are truly important: (1) that hope involves movement in time towards the eschaton and movement outwards through charity to the world family (Weeks 220); (2) that hope is a gift issued from God, not from self (Weeks 220-21); (3) that the person of hope is a *viator,* on the way through life's pilgrimage towards a not yet attained end (Weeks 222-23); (4) that hope has a certainty about it (Weeks 223); (5) that precision of language is needed regarding the different kinds of hope, e.g. hope as an emotion and hope as a theological virtue (Weeks 224); (6) that hope comes as a pure gift from God who causes it (Weeks 225); (7) that hope looks for some good from this world, but is only satisfied with the possession of God beyond this mortal life (Weeks 225-26); (8) that discernment of hope is needed to avoid deception, e.g. inebriation or youthful naiveté (Weeks 225-26); (9) that there can be sins against hope (Weeks 226); (10) that hope not only overcomes unhealthy worldly or mundane fear, but incorporates healthy servile and filial fear (Weeks 226-27).

Weeks' main point is that even though Thomas employs final causality in his theology of hope, he does so in a way that is much more sophisticated and nuanced than that indicated by Moltmann's surface perceptions.[71] Weeks is satisfied once he has driven his point home; he does not then go on to explain how it is that Thomas employs final causality. perhaps Weeks might have presented more on Thomas' use of final causality if the distinctions had been clear between Thomas' three schemata for the theology of hope. This is especially so, since the term *causa finalis* is essential to Schema III and can be more easily explained in terms of that schema.

Carl Peter is in general agreement with Weeks' conclusions[72] In fact, even though neither he nor Weeks were familiar at that time with Thomas' three schemata as such, Peter picks up where Weeks leaves off. Peter pursues an understanding of the concepts that are behind the use of final causality in Thomas' theology of hope.

Peter notes, above all, that Thomas' understanding of "participated eternity" gives Thomas a high enough viewpoint that he can overcome the tension that seems to exist between final causality (which sees God as the goal toward which the present world is moving and which it somehow already anticipates) and eschatology (which emphasizes the newness of His coming and contrasts that newness with the "now").[73]

> Careful textual analysis indicates that Thomas Aquinas was not impaled on either horn of the dilemma under consideration. He strove repeatedly to show that the infra-terrestrial finalism of Aristotle and a Christian eschatology minimizing grace in the present are not the only options. There is another, which includes the truths each of these world-views brings into focus. His conviction and the efforts it inspired led him to develop a theory of participated eternity in the beatific vision.[74]

Peter then goes on to explain how it is that the concept of "participated eternity" enabled Thomas to stress the "grace in the present" and the "charity in the present" which bring a hope which dares to seek God as its ultimate end.[75] The concept of participated eternity enables Thomas to stress God's grace in the present without compromising the radical difference between the present and the future. With this concept Thomas can note that God (who is the end of hope) will actualize the potency in the human spirit in such a way in the beatific vision, that the human person will be brought to a state of participation in God's eternity which brings a transcendence of the successive durations of cosmological time and human history.

> The more unactuated potency is eliminated, the more a creature approaches God in his duration or eternity. . .(Angels and human persons) both know and love successively and not all at once. Neither can overcome the law of its being, which is succession, on its own efforts. Nor can they even have an adequate positive idea of what knowledge and love without succession would be like. What is more, nothing they can do on their own resources will let them achieve such perfection. If it comes, it is through GOD'S GRACE. Such a duration, in which knowledge and love are not successive, is what Thomas means by the beatific vision of God, its totally simultaneous character and endlessness are what he makes *participated eternity* stand for. . .Such duration is worlds different from the *now* of man even after Jesus Christ. All the *now*'s in history added together and purified of imperfection to the nth degree do not give one the share in eternity God offers to all who love him.[76]

As can be seen, Peter stresses that hope is not a projection of the human spirit, but is a gift caused by God (*Causa efficiens*) in grace and charity. The goal of hope (*causa finalis*) so transcends the power of the created spirit that it too is a gift caused by God Himself (*causa efficiens*)--Who alone can grant creatures a share of His own eternity. Thus Peter implies that it is not Thomas, but Moltmann, who seems to be caught on one horn of the dilemma.

> Moltmann has so emphasized the future character of history's meaning, so insisted that the latter is now not clear that he has considerably diminished any grounds in the present for making statements about God and providence (Moltmann, "Theology as Eschatology," 13). Promises, he tells his reader, have been made but not yet fulfilled. God will do what he has not done and is not doing. The Lord will negate the powers of evil but is not now doing so in any clear way at all presently. His spirit will renew the face of the earth but the latter still remains literally God-forsaken.[77]

Perhaps, if Moltmann had been aware of the three schemata that Thomas uses for a theology of hope, he might have learned how to include God's present activity in his consideration of the future of God. Certainly he would not have accused Thomas of using final causality in a way that collapses the future into the present. He would have known that Thomas does not even employ the term "causa finalis" in Schemata I and II, and he employs it in Schema III only in conjunction with "causa efficiens," which stresses the ever-new present and future activity of God and his *divinum auxilium*. In fact, the weakness of Schema I is a stress on the arduousness and transcendence of hope's future which tends to ignore the extent to which that future is already operative in the present. Furthermore, Schema II's stress on material and formal causality makes the category of promise (and promise's future) essential to this schema. Only Schema III explicitly refers to the concept of final causality, but it does so only with an emphasis on the ever-new and ever-creative activity of God (*causa efficiens*), which not only gives birth in the present to the virtue of hope but which also will give birth in the future to a radically new life, a life of participation in the ETERNAL life of God Himself.

It might be noted that it is this balance between the present and the future, for which Moltmann strove, that enables Thomas to speak to some other areas of controversy in Thomistic studies: liberation theology and discourse about the last things.

Looking at Schema III, Liberation Theology and the Last Things

Clodovis Boff recently indicated that there have not really been any serious attempts to establish correlations between Thomas' theology and that of contemporary liberation theology.[78] He indicates that a number of critics of liberation theology have cited this or that text of Aquinas, but no critic (or defender) of liberation theology has done sufficient research to fully clarify Thomas' position in this regard (Boff 1).

Boff then goes on to point out four basic points of positive relationship between Thomas' theology and that of liberation theology: (1) the presuppositions of Thomas' method which put the "sacra pagina" in dialogue with the contemporary "questio" (Boff 1-4); (2) the political dimensions of Aquinas' theology (e.g. law, *ST* I-II, 90-97; Justice, *ST* II-II, 57-58; politics and prudence, *ST* II-II, 47-56; property, *ST* II-II, 32, 5 &66; social sin, *ST* I, 91, 4 & I-II, 94, 5; preaching for peace, *ST* III, 42, 2; and dealing with tyranny and oppression, *De Regimine Principorum*, c. 11) (Boff 1, 405); (3) Thomas' use of a popular, nonchristian philosophy which has political overtones--Aristotelian philosophy (Boff 1, 5-6); and (4) Thomas' willingness to speak out on issues that were publicly controversial (e.g. his defense of the mendicants' identification with the poor and his struggle with Siger of Brabant; Boff 1, 7-8). A parallel can be seen between these four areas of Thomas' theology and liberation theology's employment of contemporary questions, its addressing political issues, its use of and modification of Marxist philosophy and its addressing controversial issues.

Clodovis Boff's observations are certainly helpful, for they show certain methodological parallels between Thomas' theology and that of contemporary liberation theology. However, Boff's article only opens the door to further research.[79] If Aquinas and liberation theologians are discussing similar areas, then one can next ask in what way is liberation theology consistent with the principles and conclusions of Thomas' thought? For example, could Thomas' Schema III understanding of the nurturing prayerful support necessary for hope to flourish not shed some insight on the movement to small Christian communities? Would it now raise some critical questions about the dialiectic between poor victims and the wealthy oppressors?

No answer to these questions is ventured here. However it is important to note that Schema III of Thomas' theology of hope, which relates the birth of hope to God's divine assistance in the present as efficient cause, is open not only to God as direct and primary cause of hope but also to creatures and created goods as secondary or instrumental causes of the virtue of hope. Thomas' Schemata II and III also speak of the secondary or created goods for which one should hope with the theological virtue of hope. Thus Thomas establishes a relationship between the material/political world and hope. He understands that in some ways the material/political world is "cause" of hope and an object of hope. It would be very valuable to examine some of the contemporary writings in the field of liberation theology in the light of the principles that Thomas establishes for the interrelationship of the virtue of hope and the material/political world. What correlations would be found?

In addition to analyzing liberation theology in the light of the relationship that Thomas establishes between the virtue of hope and the material/political world, it could be very valuable to analyze liberation theology in the light of the relationship that Thomas also establishes between the theology of hope, the material/political world and the last things.

The last things (the ultimate future) present a problem today not only for the liberation theologian, but for most theologians. Rahner's essays "Towards a Theology of Hope"[80] and "The Hermeneutics of Eschatological Assertions,"[81] show concern about the relationship between hope, human history, and the last things.

The point to be made here is only that Thomas Aquinas' Schema III includes a study not only of the virtue of hope's relationship to the material/political world but also it includes a determination of hope's relationship to the ultimate future, to the last things. Thomas does this in his study of the first and second petition of the Lord's Prayer (*CT* II, 7-10.)[82]

What is perhaps most important here is that by examining these last things, with questions arising out of the four characteristics of hope and employing the general category of participation, Thomas is enabled to see various stages of participation by all peoples in these last things prior to salvation history, throughout salvation history, and into the future--into eternity. He is able to relate them, at the same time, intimately to each individual's desire for perfect beatitude and joy. He asserts nonetheless, the total otherness of the ultimate future of God. He also notes the world's analogous but nonetheless real anticipatory participation in these last things; for in some ways, they are already present and operative in history.

Thus Thomas' Schema III for a theology of hope includes both the material/political world and the last things in dynamic interrelationship and can speak to a liberation theology often devoid of the last things and to treatments of the last things often devoid of practical social consequences and unrelated to the present as they are in Schema III of Thomas' theology of hope.

Certainly there is much more life to be found in Thomas' treatment of the last things from the perspective of hope than is indicated in Albert Michel's *Les Mystères de L'Au-delà*[83] and Reginald Garrigou-Lagrange's *Life Everlasting*.[84]

Thus far, concentration has been on the light that an understanding of Thomas' three schemata for a theology of hope might shed on two different areas of Thomistic studies: (1) the question about finalism and future in Christian eschatology; and (2) the interrelationships between the virtue of hope, the material/political world and the last things. This article will conclude with a few brief references to other areas of study that might be enriched by reflection in the light of Thomas' theologies of hope.

Thomas Aquinas' Schemata for Hope--Some Concluding Remarks

It cannot be stressed enough that Thomas' use of three different schemata (all of which can be dynamically interrelated) enables Thomas' theology of hope to be related to many more areas of thought than would be possible if these three schemata were "harmonized" or "blended" into one amorphous whole.

Because Schema III is so open to the emotion of hope and to the development and actualization of both the emotion of hope and the virtue of hope, it seems that Thomas' understanding of hope could be fruitfully interrelated for example to the developmental psychology of Erik Erikson. He considers the achievement of trust (or hopefulness) to be the first necessary task of early childhood's movement towards psychological maturity.[85] He, like Thomas, sees hope as a gift of love that calls forth a desire for more love.

In fact, one can conclude by asking: Given a world whose future seems so bleak, are there not many areas of modern pastoral life that would be enriched by a better understanding of Thomas' schemata for the theology of hope?

In conclusion, it can be said, as so well stated by Hill in the introduction to his commentary on the theology of hope in Thomas' *Summa*. . .

These are by no means intended to be the last words on Christian hope; on the contrary, it is their function to be suggestive of new dimensions, both horizontal and vertical, of intelligibility. No human theological effort can claim to do more than this. It would be a disservice to St. Thomas to search in his work for what is not there; to fail to discern what is there is an even greater disservice to theology itself.[86]

NOTES

1. Joseph Merkt, "Sacra Doctrina and Christian Eschatology: A Test Case for a Study of Method and Content in the Writings of Thomas Aquinas," (Diss., 1983; The Catholic University of America; Ann Arbor, Michigan: University Microfilms, order no. DA8302486).

2. Most commentaries, it has been found, focus on the *De spe* and/or the tract on hope in the *Summa theologiae* (II-II, 20-23). This article and the dissertation it reflects drew upon the newly published *Index Thomisticus*, which is a computerized index of every word that Thomas Aquinas wrote, including about 3,500 times that he used the word hope (76644:1-721 and 76646:1-2746).

The principal texts that were studied, according to date, are: *AD 1252-1256--In 3 Sent.*, d.23, q.1, a.5; d.23, q.2, a.5; d.26, q.1, a.1-5; d.26, q.2, a.1-5; *AD 1259-1264--SCG* III, 153; *AD 1266-1268--ST* I, 95, 3c; *AD 1268-1270--ST* I-II, 40, 1-8; 62, 1-4; 64, 4; 65, 4 & 5; 66, 6; 67, 4 & 5; 69, 1; 114, 4; *AD 1269-1272--De spe* 1-4; *AD 1271-1272--ST* II-II, 4, 1; 4, 7; 17, 1-7; 18, 1-4; 20, 1-4; 21, 1-4; 22, 1-2; 23, 6-8.

3. *Index Thomisticus*, however, indicated many hundreds of places in Thomas' scripture commentaries where he discusses hope under a great variety of aspects such as: hope's necessity; hope and prayer; supernatural hope; hope's many objects; hope's qualities as a theological virtue; the interrelationship of faith, hope and charity; the relationship of hope and will; hope and the blessed; hope and the damned; hope, purgatory and limbo; attributing hope to Christ; hope and certainty; hope and fear; hope; despair and presumption, etc.

4. Jurgen Moltmann, "Theology as Eschatology" in *The Future of Hope* (ed. Frederick Herzog; New York: Herder and Herder, 1970) 1-5, esp. 13 n. 19.

5. Louis Weeks, "Can Saint Thomas' *Summa Theologiae* Speak to Moltman's *Theology of Hope?*" *The Thomist* 23 (1969) 215-28.

6. Carl J. Peter, "A Roman Catholic Contribution to the Quest of a Credible Eschatology," *The Catholic Theological Society of America: Proceedings of the Twenty-Ninth Annual Convention, June 10-13, 1974*, vol. 29 (Bronx, N.Y.: Manhattan College, 1974) 255-71. Also cf. Carl J. Peter, "Metaphysical Finalism or Christian Eschatology," *The Thomist* 38 (1974) 125-45.

7. Carolo A. Bernard, S.J., *Theologie de l'Esperance selon Saint Thomas d'Acquin*, (Dissertatio ad Lauream in Facultate Theologica Pontificiae Universitatis Gregorianae; Paris: 1961).

8. Albert Fries, C.S.S.R., "Hoffnung und Heilsgewissheit bei Thomas von Aquino," *Studia Moralia* 7 (1969) 133-237.

9. Pierre Charles, S.J., "*Spes Christi* II: Esquisse de l'histoire d'une doctrine," *Nouvelle Revue Theologique* 10 (December, 1937) 1057-75.

10. Servais Pinckaers, O.P., "Peut-on Esperer pour les autres?" *Le Renouveau de la morale: Etudes pour une morale fidele a ses sources et a sa mission present* (Preface de M.D. Chenu; Cahiers de l'actualite religieuse 19; La Sart-Huy: Casterman, 1964).

11. Santiago Ramirez, O.P., "De certitudine spei christianae," *Ciencia tomista* 27 (1938) 184-203, 353-78.

12. Walter M. Conlon, O.P., *De Certitudine Spei Secundum Sanctum Thoman: Fontes et Doctrina* (Dissertatio ad Lauream, 1947; Washington, D.C.).

13. St. Thomas Aquinas, *Summa Theologiae, vol. 33: Hope, 2a-2ae, 17-22* (ed., William J. Hill, O.P.; New York: Blackfriars and McGraw-Hill, 1966).

14. Saint Thomas D'Aquin, *Somme théologique: L'Espérance (2a-2ae Questions 17-22* (trans., L. Le Tilly, O.P., 2nd. ed.; Paris: Desclée, 1950).

15. Santo Tomas de Aquino, *Suma Teologica: Tomo VII, Tratados de la Fe y de la Esperanza* (trans. and introd. by Teofilo Urdanoz, O.P.; Madrid: Biblioteca de Autores Christianos, 1959) 496-507.

16. Joseph F. Delaney, "Hope," *CE* 3. 465-67.

17. S. Harent, "Espérance," *DTC* 5. 606-75.

18. Jean Hervé Nicolas, "Espérance," *DSAM* 4. 1208-33.

19. P. Engelhardt, "Hoffnung," *LTK* 5. 416-24.

20. Santiago Ramirez, O.P., "Hope," *NCE* 7. 133-41.

21. Ferdinand Kerstiens, "Hope," *SM 3. 61-65*.

22. Reginald Garrigou-Lagrange, O.P., *De virtutibus theologicis: Commentarius in Summam theologicam S. Thomae Ia IIae q. 62, 65, 68, et IIa IIae q. 1-46* (Turin: R. Berruti, 1949).

23. Santiago Ramirez, O.P., *La esencia de la esperanza cristiana* (Madrid: Punta Europa, 1960). Note that this book's principal strains of thought are well summarized in Ramirez's later article "Hope," *NCE* 7. 133-41.

24. Pedro Lain-Entralgo, *L'Attente et l'espérance, Histoire et théorie de l'espérance humaine* (trans. R. Disse; Collection Testes et études philosophique (Paris: Desclée De Brouwer, 1966). This very important debate between Lain-Entralgo and Ramirez is discussed in Chapter IV, the conclusion of my dissertation (see above, n.1.).

25. S. Thomas D'Aquin, *S. Theol.: L'Espérance* 216-41.

26. S. Tomas de Aquino, *S. Teol.: Esperanza* 477-96.

27. S. Thomas Aquinas, *S. Theol.: Hope* 123-79.

28. Servais Pinckaers, O.P., "La nature vertueuse de l'espérance," *Revue Thomiste* 54 (1958) 405-42 and 623-44.

29. Servais Pinckaers, O.P., "La nature vertueuse de l'esperance," *Le Renouveau de la morale: Etudes pour une morale fidèle a ses sources et a sa mission présent* (Preface de M.D. Chenu; Cahiers de l'actualite religieuse 19; La Sart-Huy: Casterman, 1964) 178-240.

30. Cf. Merkt, *Sacra doctrina* esp. 153-83 and 322-36.

31. *In 3 Sent.,* d. 26, q.1 & 2 (1252-1256).

32. *De spe.* 1-4 (1269-1270).

33. *SCG* III 153 (1259-1264); *ST* II-II 20-23 (1271-1272); *CT* II 1-10 (1272-1273).

34. Cf. Merkt, *Sacra doctrina* Chap. III Sect. 4, *Spes passio* and *Spes virtus theologica* 114-24.

35. *Ibid.* Chap. III, 5, Hope as a Virtue: The First Principles--The Truths of Faith (MP I-II) 133-148.

36. *Ibid.* Chap. III Sect. 6, the objects of Hope as Presented in Thomas' Various Treatises on Hope 159-184.

37. Cf. *Ibid.* Chap. III Sect. 7, Hope as a Theological Virtue: A Discursive Reasoning Process (MP III-IV) 201-5.

38. CF. *Ibid.* Chap. III Sect 2, Prayer and Hope, 86-106.

39. Cf. *Ibid.* Chap. III Sect. 8, That Divine Grace Causes Hope in us, 209-19.

40. Cf. *Ibid.* Chap. III Sect. 10, The Subject(s) of the Virtue of Hope, 244-69.

41. Cf. *Ibid.* Chap. III Sect. 11, Hope and the *Homo Viator,* 269-97.

42. Preliminary analysis indicates that Thomas employs Schema I thinking in his commentaries on *Matthew* (1256-1259), *Job* (1261-1264) and *Galatians, Ephesians,* 1 *Thessalonians,* 2 *Thessalonians and Titus.* In fact he employs this schema even when the text itself would be more apropriately interpreted by Schema II or Schema III thought. Note that there seems to be general agreement that Thomas' commentaries on *Matthew* and *Job* are among his earliest works. (The dates of the other works cited here are not known.)

43. Cf. Merkt *Sacra doctrina* Chap. III Sect. 4, *Spes passio* and *Spes virtus theologica, 114-24.*

44. Cf. *Ibid.* Chap. III Sect. 5, Hope as a Virtue: The First Principles (MP I-II) 133-48 and a Discursive Process (III-IV) 148-50.

45. *In 3 Sent.* d.26, q.2, art.1.

46. The thought patterns for Schema II also seem to be present in Thomas' commentaries on *Isaiah, Jeremiah,* 2 *Corinthians, Philippians* and 1 *Timothy* and 2 *Timothy.* (Note: there is no agreement as to the dates of these commentaries.)

47. Cf. Merkt, *Sacra doctrina* Chap. III Sect. 6, The Objects of the Virtue of Hope, 153-84. Also cf. *De spe* art.1.

48. Cf. *Ibid.* Chap. III Sect. 5, Hope as a Virtue: The First Principles (MP I-II) 133-48 and A Discursive Reasoning Process (MP III-IV) 148-50. Cf. *De spe* art.1, c: "omnia quae materialiter sperantur, ordinantur in unum finale aperatum, quod est fruitio Dei."

49. Cf. *De spe* art. I c: "formale obiectum spei est auxilum divinae postestatis et pietatis, propter quod tendi motus spei in bona sperata, quae sunt materiale obiectum spei. . .In ordine enim ad hanc fruitionem speramus adiuvari ¦a Deo non solum spiritualibus, sed etiam corporalibus beneficiis."

50. *De spe* art.1 c.

51. The thought pattern of Schema III also seems to be present in Thomas' scripture commentaries on *John* (1269-1272) and his commentary on the *Psalms* (1272-1273), especially on *Psalms* 21, 22, 23, 24, 30, 31, 33, 37, 39, and 43-51 as well as *Romans*, 1 *Corinthians* and *Hebrews*. Note that Thomas' commentary on *John* and the *Psalms* are among Thomas' later and more mature commentaries. There is no agreement as to the dates of the other commentaries.

52. Cf. Merkt, *Sacra doctina* Chap. III Sect. 5, Hope as a Virtue: The First Principles (MP I-II) 133-48.

53. Cf. Sect. 6, The Objects of the Virtue of Hope: *SCG* III 153, 161-2; *ST* II-II 17, 1 & 4 and 2 & 3, 168-78; and *CT* II 7-10, 178-84.

54. *Ibid.*

55. Cf. *ST* II-II 17, 2 c.

56. *Ibid.* ad 1.

57. *ST* II-II 17, 3 c.

58. *CT* II 4.

59. *Ibid.*

60. *Ibid.*

61. Perhaps a very good illustration of how Thomas' thought developed and how each new schema developed can be seen in Thomas' commentaries on God as "Father": Schema I in Thomas' discussion of God as Father in his *Collationes Super Pater Noster*; Schema II in Thomas' discussion of God as Father in his *Commentary on Galatians*, Chap. 5, Lect.2; and Schema III, of course, in the *Compendium's* discussion of God as Father.

62. Jürgen Moltmann, *Theology of Hope* (trans. J.W. Leitch; New York: Harper, 1967).

63. Jürgen Moltmann, "Theology as Eschatology" in *The Future of Hope* (ed. Frederick Herzog; New York: Herder and Herder, 1970) 1-51.

64. *Ibid.* 13.

65. *Ibid* 13 n. 19.

66. Note his criticism is quite similar to that of Per Eric Persson (cf. n. 35 above).

67. Louis Weeks, III, "Can Saint Thomas' *Summa Theologiae* Speak to Moltmann's *Theology of Hope?*" *The Thomist* 23 (1969) 215-28.

68. Carl J. Peter, "Metaphysical Finalism or Christian Eschatology," *The Thomist* 38 (January, 1974) 125-45.

69. Carl J. Peter, "A Roman Catholic Contribution to the Quest of a Credible Eschatology," *The Catholic Theological Society of America Proceedings of the Twenty-Ninth Annual Convention, June 10-13, 1974,* vol. 29 (Bronx, N.Y.: Manhattan College, 1974) 255-71.

70. Weeks, "Can Saint Thomas' *Summa Theologieae* Speak to Moltmann's *Theology of Hope?*" 216-17.

71. Moltmann, in a brief conversation in Spring, 1973, stated that he had relied heavily on Bernard's book for his assessment of Thomas' eschatology because so few other materials were available. He added that he would be happy to revise his assessment of Thomas' eschatology as more was published on it and as he had more time to become more familiar with it. A copy of this article and the dissertation is being sent to him. His thought has developed much since these works in 1967-1968.

72. Carl Peter, "Metaphysical Finalism" 125 and 144-45 and "The Quest" 257-58 and 262.

73. Peter, "Metaphysical Finalism" 129-30.

74. *Ibid.* 125.

75. Cf. Peter, "Metaphysical Finalism" 143-44 and "The quest" 262-63.

76. Peter, "Metaphysical Finalism" 143. Very helpful background is provided in Peter, *Participated Eternity in the Vision of God* 44-49. Here Peter explains why hope ceases in the blessed as they begin to participate in God's eternal NOW and are brought to such fulfillment that the celebration of the present eliminates the future with its hopes and desires.

77. Peter, "The Quest" 259.

78. Clodovis Boff, "St. Tomás de Aquino y la teologia de la liberación," *Paginas*, Separata no. 42 (Dec., 1981). Note that Clodovis Boff was recently censored (Spring, 1984), and lost his authorization to teach as a Roman Catholic Theologian because of some of his views about liberation theology. [He was reinstated in 1986 -- editor.]

79. For example, could not Thomas' Schema III's understanding of the prayerful support necessary for hope to flourish shed some supportive insight on the movement to develop base Christian communities? Would not his Schema III raise some critical questions about the dialectic between poor and wealthy oppressors?

80. Karl Rahner, "Towards a Theology of Hope," *Theological Investigations* 9. 242-53.

81. Karl Rahner, "The Hermeneutics of Eschatological Assertions," *Theological Investigations* 4. 323-46.

82. Thomas' analysis of these petitions in the light of the last things was examined several times in the course of Merkt, *Sacra doctrina,* Chap. III, 153-94. The most explicit treatment was Chapter III, the Objects of the Virtue of Hope: The Virtue of Hope and the Last Things, 184-186. Note that the last things were discussed by Thomas in all three schemata, but the most comprehensive relationship between them and the virtue of hope was established in Schema III.

83. Albert Michel, *Les Mystères de L'Au-delà (4th. ed., Paris: P. Tequi, 1963).*

84. Reginald Garrigou-Lagrange, O.P., Life Everlasting (trans. Patrick Cummins, O.S.B.; St Louis, MO.: B. Herder, 1952). Yves Congar highly criticizes this approach in the *Revue des Sciences Philosophiques et Théologiques* 33 (1949) 463-4. He considers it to be a "type of physics of the last things."

85. Erik Erikson, *Identity: Youth and Crisis* (New York: W.W. Norton 1968) 82, 96-97, 103-4 and 106.

86. *Summa theologiae: Hope* (ed. Hill) p. xxii.

RE-CONCEIVING THE TRINITY AS MYSTERY OF SALVATION

Catherine Mowry LaCugna

If we move beyond ancient liturgical or dogmatic formulations about the trinity, it is not at all obvious what it means to speak of the threefoldness of God. Certainly, trinitarian theology is not obviously relevant for the life of most believers in this century. But while a trinitarian framework is necessary for Christian theology, merely repeating dogmatic formulae will not well serve us today. Christians today are inclined to ask what the doctrine of the trinity means in one's life as a Christian. If the doctrine of the trinity is really the central mystery of the Christian faith, ought we not more readily be able to answer such a query? The polite neglect of the doctrine of the trinity in most contemporary theological works signals that something is wrong--either with the concept and confession of a triune god, or with its desuetude. In the latter case, the future of Christian theism would seem to depend on its restoration to life and theology.

Among the several possible ways of re-conceiving trinitarian theology, one is to revise the classical "models" or analogies of the immanent trinity. Instead of working with the "three persons, one nature" formula, theologians construct new models of trinitarian relations: interpersonal (H. Mühlen); community of persons (J. Bracken); processive relations of divine becoming (L. Ford); temporal unsurpassability (R. Jenson); semiotic relations (G. Tavard); eschatological consummation (J. Moltmann).[1] This approach has many merits for it helpfully recasts archaic terms (e.g., hypostasis, subsistent relation) along with their accompanying metaphysics. But at the same time, this approach disguises a more fundamental problem: how is the reformulated inner trinitarian analogy related to the 'economic' trinity, that is, to God's activity in salvation history? How does the new analogy convey God as being God *for us?*

We may raise in addition to his theological question, a preliminary methodological and hermeneutical one: what is the reality to which any theoretical model of God refers, and how may we link up our speculations about God's 'inner' life with the divine reality? What are the theological warrants for seeing a connection between what we say about God and who or what God *is?* What is the connection between our experience of God in Jesus through their Spirit, and God's transcendent reality? What does it mean to speak of God as being threefold internally and constitutively, that is, as eternally prior to the divine excursion into history and time?

In Karl Rahner's monograph on *The Trinity*[2] he proposes an axiom which is accepted by most trinitarian theologians: "The 'economic' trinity is the 'immanent' trinity and *vice versa.*"[3] The axiom provides a grammatical and theological perimeter within which one may re-conceive the relationship between

God and all that is other than God ("the world"). According to the axiom, who God is and how God acts in the economy of salvation *is* (the same as) who and how God is and acts eternally and transcendentally. That is, what one says about God's economic-historical activity is true as well of God's 'inner' history or immanent life.

Evidently an adequate trinitarian theology, Nicene, Cappadocian, or contemporary, will adhere to the equivalence indicated by the copula. One easily could make a twofold historical observation: first, that the two classic distortions of Christian teaching on God, Sabellian modalism and Arian subordinationism, resulted from not taking seriously enough the equivalence indicated by the "is." Second, contemporary theologies likewise run aground in either of the same directions.[4] Rahner's axiom stands in contrast to much of "orthodox" western trinitarian theology from Augustine onwards, for the precise reason that analogies were developed for the 'immanent' trinity while the 'economic' trinity largely passed out of theological and religious consciousness. This had the consequence of emptying the Christian doctrine of God of its salvific focus.

I plan to look very briefly at Rahner's understanding of the axiom both as a formal theological principle and as a constructive proposal incorporating the data of salvation history. What is the meaning of the axiom? What is the justification for it? And what are the consequences of postulating it? Later I will suggest what a contemporary trinitarian theology might look like if it adhered to Rahner's axiom.

I. The Axiom in Rahner's Trinitarian Theology

A. *The Need for the Axiom*

Trinitarian doctrine is virtually irrelevant in both life and theology. Rahner says, "Christians are, in their practical life, almost mere 'monothesists'."[5] He means to imply not that trinitarian Christianity entails tritheism, only that orthodox Christians ordinarily do not connect events in salvation history (creation, the incarnation; the sending of the Spirit) with God's own inner reality. Moreover, many theologians since Augustine thought that any of the divine persons could have become human. This reasoning contributed to the view that the economy of salvation can tell us little or nothing about 'inner' divine life. Rahner's fundamental purpose in *The Trinity* is to restore to Christian consciousness and theology the deep meaning of the threefold God in order to work out a "permanent perichoresis" (mutual indwelliing) between salvation and theological theory.

It was not always so in Christian tradition. The tendency in antiquity had been to begin (as does the New Testament) with the Father as the origin of divinity and source of unity, and to discuss Son and Spirit as recipients of divinity. Both the creeds and Greek theology concerned themselves with the divine activity in the economy, hence the emphasis on the threefoldness *(Dreigaltigkeit)* of God rather than the unity *(Dreieinigkeit)*. Augustine, however, reversed the order, beginning with the oneness of the divine nature and by requiring that whatever be predicated of one person be predicated of all. Differences among persons, therefore, no longer were seen to be bound up with the unique activity of each in the economy, but became a matter of *appropriation*. Since each person is identical with the divine substance, whatever belongs to the divine nature is singular (e.g., one divine 'will'). the doctrine of appropriations (in Augustine) leads to abstract formulas such as, the Father is Father as one who begets; the Son is Son by being begotten; the Spirit is Spirit by being bestowed.

The Latin starting point led to the separation in medieval theology between the two treatises, *De Deo Uno* and *De Deo Trino;* the first topic studied is not God the Father as the unoriginate origin of divinity but the essence of the godhead *(deitas)* common to all three. Rahner comments, "Thus the treatise of the Trinity locks itself in even more splendid isolation, with the ensuing danger that the religious mind finds it devoid of interest."[6] The One God may remain quite unconnected with salvation history; assertions about God's threefoldness can only seem to be super-added to the treatment of the divine nature.

Rahner's axiom is meant to correct the isolation of trinitarian theology by joining the mystery of salvation with theological theory. He shows that the very nature of christian theology, in its effort to comprehend the mystery of God's self-communication, requires a formal connection between the historic self-communication and the Communicator.

B. Rahner's Proof of the Axiom

There are two parts to Rahner's 'proof' of the axiom, the doctrines of incarnation and of grace. He correlates these two doctrines with the two internal processions in God and argues that the incarnation of the Logos must not be viewed as arbitrary (as if any person could have become incarnate) but must disclose to us something about God's internal life as God. Likewise with grace, Rahner's thesis is that each one of the three divine persons communciates itself to us in gratuitous grace in its "own personal particularity and diversity."[7] God's indwelling in the justified is a personal act, thus it is a communication of 'persons'. Therefore the "three self-communications are the self-communication of the one God in the three relative ways in which God subsists."[8] God's self-communciation, Rahner says, is not a copy or analogy of the inner trinity but *is* the trinity itself; this means that the communication can occur only in the intra-divine manner of the self-giving of Father to Son and Spirit. Both *ad intra* and *ad extra* then, the divine persons "do not differ from their own way of communicating themselves."[9]

God's self-communication is threefold because God *in se* is threefold. God communicates Godself *as* one God but according to the uniqueness of the divine persons. The double self-communication of God in Word and Spirit occurs according to the order (*taxis*) which exists already in the structure of God's being. That is to say, Word precedes Spirit in God's eternal being. God the Unoriginate ('Father') remains ever incomprehensible and yet communicates "himself" through Son and Spirit. The two moments of the divine self-communication entail and require each other; in this connection Rahner notes that Catholic theology in general "is convinced that the Spirit might well exist without the incarnation."[10] But Word and Spirit should be understood as "the inner, mutually related moments of the *one* self-communication, through which God (the Father) communicates himself to the world unto absolute proximity."[11] By way of Rahner's axiom, then, we see that insofar as divine *self*-communication is free, and its two moments are also free, still, the two missions--incarnation and sending of the Spirit--are necessarily connected with each other, otherwise salvation history tells us nothing about the inner life of the threefold God.

II. Consequences for Theology and Methodology

Rahner's theology of the trinity provides us with a soteriological focus which will help us reinvigorate the venerable dogmatic and liturgical formulations as we revise them in new theological models and analogies. I turn now to some of the concrete theological and methodological ramifications which I see entailed by adhering to Rahner's axiom.

A. *Theological Implications*

Recovering the tradition. The doctrine of the trinity pertains, above all, to the *mystery of salvation.* This emphasis might better be served by retrieving other options in the trinitarian tradition, specifically, the Greek rather than the Latin trinitarian tradition, the Cappadocian rather than the Augustinian, the emanationist rather than the rationalistic. A soteriologically-oriented contemporary reformulation will mean, therefore, incorporating Christology in its soteriological dimensions. While dialectical and evangelical theology would emphasize the mystery of the cross (Barth, Jüngel, Moltmann) and Catholic theology the mystery of the incarnation (Rahner, von Balthasar), there is only one mystery: "God was in Christ reconciling the world to himself" (2 Cor 5:19). When trinitarian speculation moves away from this, its center, it becomes a one-sided 'immanent' speculation on God. Such a mirror image is distorted; it reflects the ability of the human intellect to construct analogies and theories of God, but not necessarily with reference to God's saving activity.[12]

Missions and processions. Second, a severe disjunction between missions and processions no longer can be retained. It was Augustine's genius to employ neo-Platonic categories to construct a Christian trinitarian theology. But the attendant doctrine of divine timelessness, which entailed the metaphysical and temporal disengagement of *ad intra*, eternal processions ('begetting' and 'breathing') from *ad extra,* temporal missions (incarnation, sending of the Spirit) is problematic for us. Even though for 1500 years the Augustinian approach did not cause for Christian theologians difficulties of the sort we have today, it does explain why someone like Schleiermacher thought that Christian theology was better off without the doctrine of the trinity.[13]

But according to Rahner's trinitarian axiom, any discussion of Son or Spirit must be conducted in the context of their salvific missions, since the missions in history are constitutive of their divine 'personhood' and *vice versa.* Likewise, reference to what "God has accomplished in Christ in their Spirit" must not be conceived apart from the inner-trinitarian reality of which it is expressive. A remark of Rahner's bears repeating here: Catholic theology in general "is convinced that the Spirit might well exist without the incarnation."[14] In this same connection we would have grounds for reversing the traditional aporia concerning the indifferent appropriation of the creative and salvific events to the divine persons.[15]

Contemporary challenges to Christian theism. Third, a trinitarian theology which is focussed on *mysterium salutis* might respond quite differently to the contemporary challenges to theism. Feminist and Latin American liberation theologies, linguistic theory, atheistic theology and new metaphysical systems, notably that of process theology, each has already questioned classical Christian theism on various counts.[16] These include its patriarchalism and imperialism, its frequent appeal to special or exempt linguistic and logical canons, its self-restriction to a static metaphysics, and its inability to articulate a 'real' relationship between God and world. I am suggesting that a re-conceived trinitarian theology would challenge the generally unitarian or Christomonistic character of most Christian theology as well as provide a fresh approach for answering the critiques generated by these contemporary theological challenges. Contemporary trinitarian theologies should point up the inadequacy of Christian dogmatics which in the west, from the fifth century on, had concentrated on the 'immanent' trinity and developed its doctrine of God in a non-soterioloigcal, a-historical fashion. Our efforts in the area of the doctrine of God will need to be rooted in the mystery and death of Jesus rather than abstractly theistic. The closeness of God will become more important than God's incomprehensibility, for the second of these too easily is a metaphysical rather than a religious affirmation.[17] Similarly, God will continue to be worshipped as mystery yet not anonymity in the style of an earlier apophatic theology[18], Christian theology will concern itself with identifying *which* God--

the God of the outcast or the God of the elite, the God who led Israel out of bondage or the God of Freud's illusion--it professes to know and love. In this respect, trinitarian theology helps us articulate the who and how, rather than the whether of God.[19]

Theological language and spirituality. Fourth, the emphasis on the history of salvation has implications for our view of theological language. Presently we are witnessing a rather widespread interest in narrative theology, imaginative theology, symbolic theolgy, metaphorical and parabolic theology,[20] all of which have acknowledged that theology can become vapid when it is developed apart from the variety and richness of religious imagery. Certainly no one has suggested that theological language and religious language amount to the same thing, nor even that theological precision and conceptual reification are undesirable. As long as a soteriological concern is at the center of our doctrine of God, we ought to use the images and words which have emerged in the community's experience of salvation. This implies a new kind of trinitarian theology, one that is not only more self-consciously soteriological but one which is comprised of the various images, symbols, metaphors, parabolic experiences and narrative truths which give rise to the doctrine in the first place.

Fifth, with respect to spirituality, there is a burgeoning movement back towards the center point of the intersection between theology and spirituality. Regardless of the difficulty of defining the latter term, at least we can say that the increasing separation of theology from spirituality since the 13th c. has made each to some degree arid. A contemporary trinitarian reformulation, were it to be the fruit of a contemplative theology (and all great trinitarian theologians have been contemplatives--Augustine, Gregory of Nyssa, Bonaventure, Aquinas, Richard of St. Victor), it just might give us the combination of religious imagery, theological creativity, and soteriological rootedness we are seeking. After all, trinitarian theology should be the prime exemplar of the encounter between specualtive and mystical theology.

B. Methodological Implications

The place of the trinity in a dogmatic scheme. First, if the doctrine of the trinity concerns above all the mystery of salvation, then we might ask about its place in a theological or dogmatic schema. Were we to survey the tradition on this point, we would find two major methodological decisions; in the first, "the triune God" is treated as a separate theme (e.g., Aquinas); in the other, the theologian creates an infra- or super-structure of threefoldness (including perhaps a theo-logic such as Calvin's or Barth's, or a theo-dramatik such as von Balthasar's). One would expect advantages and disadvantages in either case, and there is no intrinsic reason to prefer one to the other. Each approach is suitable for explicating the basic trinitarian model, God-in-relation. But let us take note of some of the pitfalls of each.

If we elect the first course, which makes sense for the practical reason of the "division of theological labor," still the temptation will be to formulate a doctrine of God, not a doctrine of the triune God, that is, a doctrine which ostensibly does not have a soteriological focus. The questions we often hear now, such as, "Can we believe in God after Auschwitz?" indicates the yearning we have for a God who will save us and for a theology which will carry the assurances of a God who actively, assiduously, is "for us." In terms of Christian theology we are, I think, frequently deceived into thinking that if we could only get our house in order on "the one God," we might be able to rehabilitate our rather dysfunctional theism and put to rest the liberation-theological, linguistic-theological, atheistic-theological and metaphysical-theological critics. At that point, we need never get around to "the triune God" since it would once more have been shown to be superfluous. *But salvation history forbids such a foreclosure.* Christian theists have to face up to the fact: either the Christian doctrine of God is first and foremost a truth about salvation in Christ and therefore it is trinitarian, or, it is only another metaphysical theory. Christian trinitarian theology is in fact both.

The second methodological option--a structural trinitarianism--has the advantage of any undergird: it provides continual support. But the disadvantage lies in the easy fascination with the number three, so that one is always trying to find three characteristics, three effects, three features, forms, or types.[21] Whatever the doctrine of the trinity might have meant in the first place, it comes to mean more of a numerical or dialectical arrangement. In this connection Rahner's overall theology is to be admired, for while it exemplifies the kind of structural trinitarianism we are referring to, it resists the magic of threefoldness; in fact, one is surprised to find in his explicit thematic treatment of the trinity, *four* aspects of *two* self-communications. There is a lot to be said also for any approach which resists easy correlation of Father, Son and Spirit with creation, redemption, and reconciliation, since the biblical and patristic records on this score are mixed.[22]

The trinity in relation to other doctrines. Second, if missions and processions are theologically in "permanent perichoresis," then methodologically speaking, three conclusions follow. First, both Christology and pneumatology ought to be developed in a manner which makes explicit the connection between the salvific missions of Word and Spirit, and their origin in the eternal divine processions. This is in order to uphold the axiomatic unity of 'economic' and 'immanent' trinities, of missions and processions. Second, since the two *ad intra* processions of Word and Spirit entail and imply each other, then doctrines concerning the two *ad extra* salvific missions ought to be developed in tandem with, not independently of each other. This would mean a more pneumatological Christology, and a more incarnational pneumatology. The two "modalities" of God in Word and Spirit need not work at cross-purposes with each other at the level of doctrine. And third, Christology and ecclesiology/ pneumatology ought to be consdiered as *portions* of the more comprehensive Christian theological task. We might say that Christology and ecclesiology are "tracks" within the wider enterprise of theology as such which seeks to articulate its experience of salvation in trinitarian terms.

The trinity and apophasis. Third, the experience of salvation always entails some recognition of one's inadequacy before God, and therefore one sees the appropriateness of silence before God's ever greater reality. And when one breaks the silence, one recognizes the haltingness of one's speech and the smallness of one's imagination. We are in that respect like Moses who protests to Yahweh, "I am a slow speaker and not able to speak well." (Ex 5:10b) Now it is perfectly clear that a theology which would speak univocally or literally about God's being would run contrary to the whole of the biblical view of God as well as violate the most basic precepts of all theology and mystical experience. Is the alternative utter silence?

The apophatic tradition in theology (whether that of mystical or negative theology) has tried to embody this distinctive dimension of the experience of salvation. However, negative theology in the Greek patristic tradition was entangled with a doctrine of God's immutability, impassibility, and nontemporality.[23] Today we need a positive incorporation of the spirit of apophasis[24] without adopting its tendency towards agnosticism and certain accompanying metaphysical assertions (at least, they cannot be all that is "said" about God). We therefore need a theological doctrine of God which is able to conjoin the insight of negative theology (in Augustine's words, "a thing is not ineffable which can be called ineffable") (*De Doct. Chr. I.6*) with the urge of the theological *ratio* and *explicatio* which feel licensed actively to think and speak of God, and which produce content-statements about God ("There is one God in three subsistent relations."). Both an agnostic theology and a one-dimensional theology flatly are impossible. Images remind us that our abstractions tend to collapse the distinction between God's reality and our thoughts and words about God, and concepts serve to reattach our images to the referent, God-in-relation. Notice that the trinitarian framework preserves God's hiddenness and inscrutability (which is associated with "Father") and God's manifestedness and concreteness (associated with the Son). The methodological result, then is this: a theology of God in its totality must be both silent and forthcoming, just as God is both silent and yet utters a word. It must balance the two sides of the experience of salvation, just as it must conform to the God who saves. I have suggested elsewhere that the model of God as trinity is the vehicle for doing just that.[25]

The trinity and religious imagery. Fourth, I suggested that a trinitarian theology which takes seriously Rahner's axiom will be shaped by the religious imagery and symbols of our experience. Liturgies and creeds are already trinitarian and often narrative in part; speculative theology must claim them for its own. Yet systematic theologians often are chary of the 'merely' symbolic and revert to a view of metaphor as mere ornamentation. This implies that non-discursive terminology is less well-suited to the experience of God than the technical.[26] However, even a superficial survey of doctrinal definitions shows a church not afraid to use metaphors: the 'Father' 'begets' the 'Son',[27] or in an even more inventive vein (at the Eleventh Council of Toledo in 675), the 'Son' 'proceeds' from the 'womb of the father' (*de utero patris*).[28] The point is that since God is not directly graspable by human intellection nor exhaustible by human locution, imagistic and ostensive language in all its forms (analogy; symbol; metaphor; parable; narrative) will have as decisive a role to play in theological formulations as will concepts and definition. While it is true that "trinity" is a narrative truth insofar as it is the story of Christian salvation, it also can be given conceptual precision and systematic elegance when elaborated as a speculative and comprehensive theological *model*. Models insure that all kinds of language are given hearing, which is to say nothing more than that our understanding of God gains by being articulated in several different modes of discourse.

The trinity and comtemplation. A final methodological corollary has to do with what we described as a "contemplative" style of theology. Ordinarily contemplative theology has been associated with the mystical Greek and the medieval monastic traditions, in contrast with the Latin speculative and medieval scholastic traditions, respectively. History shows that the monastic and scholastic in fact complemented each other as theological styles. Today we should not want to drive such a hard distinction between the monastic-contemplative and scholastic-speculative approaches, perhaps by caricaturing the former as biblical, subjective, personal, liturgical, imagistic, moral-psychological, synthetic, and the latter as philosophical, objective, universal, scholastic, conceptual, intellectual, analytic.[29] If theology is above all a disciplined and faithful search to understand the mystery of salvation, then a theological style is called for which incorporates both emphases. In the modern theological context we are not suggesting that theology once again be the province of monks, but that theology be regarded as a participatory rather than spectator activity. Therefore it will not imitate the modern *scientia* which equates 'objectivity' with personal distanciation, nor will it surrender its passion for rigorous logic and precision.[30] In a contemplative-speculative theology, the theologian will be engaged with God affectively as well as cognitively, imaginatively as well as discursively, silently as well as expressively, doxologically as well as academically. The style is perhaps illustrated by the difference in English between "conceiving" (the divine) and "conceptualizing" it.[31] If I am correct, the contemporary task is to re-conceive the doctrine of the trinity as the mystery of salvation, and to do so in both contemplative and speculative fashion.

III. Summary

We began by wondering what it might mean today to speak of the immanent and economic threefoldness of God. Rahner's axiom provided a starting point for reflecting on the connection between the doctrine of the trinity and the mystery of salvation. Given the connection between the God who *saves* and the *God* who saves, it was then possible to explore theological and methodological changes which would be brought about by adhering to the axiom. We saw that by conceiving of God as "God for us" in such a way that "God for us" *is* "God as God," trinitarian faith might once again be restored to the center of Christian doctrine and spirituality.

NOTES

1. See Heribert Mühlen, *Der Heilige Geist als Person* (Münster: Aschendorf, 1963) and *Una Mystica Persona* (Munich: Schöningh, 1964); also Robert Sears, "Trinitarian Love as Ground of the Church," *Theological Studies* 37 (1976) 652-79; Joseph Bracken, "The Holy Trinity as a Community of Divine persons," *Heythrop Journal* 15 (1974) 166-82, 257-70, and "The Triune Symbol" (unpublished ms.); L. Ford, "Process Trinitarianism," *Journal of the American Academy of Religion* 43 (1975) 199-213; Robert Jenson, *God After God* (Indianapolis: Bobbs-Merrill, 1969) and *The Triune Identity* (Philadelphia: Fortress, 1982); George Tavard, *Vision of the Trinity* (Washington, D.C.: Univ. Press of America, 1981); Jürgen Moltmann, *The Crucified Trinity* (New York: Harper and Row, 1974) and *The Trinity and the Kingdom* (New York: Harper and Row, 1981).

2. *The Trinity* (New York: 1970) is a translation by J. Donceel of "Der dreifaltige Gott als transzendenter Urgrund der Heilsgeschichte," in *Mysterium Salutis: Grundriss Heilsgeschicht liche Dogmatik.* Bd. II (eds. J. Feiner & M. Löhrer; Einsiedeln: Benziger, 1967). See also Rahner, "Remarks on the Dogmatic Treatise 'de Trinitate'," *Theological Investigations* 4. 77-102, and "The Mystery of the Trinity," *Theo. Invest.* 16. 255-259.

3. Rahner, *The Trinity* 22.

4. For example, Maurice Wiles, in *Working Papers in Doctrine* (London: SCM, 1976), and in *The Remaking of Christian Doctrine* (London, SCM, 1974), Geoffrey Lampe, *God As Spirit* (Oxford: Clarendon, 1977), and Claude Welch, in *In This Name: The Trinity in Contemporary Theology* (New York: Scribner, 1952) uphold the Schleiermachian view that only the "economic trinity" can be the subject of theology. On the other side, P. Schoonenberg holds that God is not eternally self-differentiated; rather, God 'becomes, triune in the event of Jesus Christ. Cf. "Trinität--der vollendete Bund. Theses zur Lehre vom dreipersönlichen Gott," *Orientierung* 37 (1973) 115-117, translated as "Trinity -- The Consummated Covenant: Theses on the Doctrine of the Trinitarian God." *Studies in Religion* 5/2 (1975-76) 111-116.

5. Rahner, *op. cit.* 10. 'Unitarianism' might have been more precise than 'monotheism' since Christians do believe in only one God.

6. Rahner 17.

7. *Ibid.* 35.

8. *Ibid.*

9. *Ibid.* 36.

10. *Ibid.* 83.

11. *Ibid.*, emphasis mine.

12. Hegelianism exemplifies that a trinitarian theory need not be attached to the threefold God. G. Lampe's work (*op. cit.*) is, interestingly enough, explicitly soteriological yet not trinitarian; he considers 'Spirit' to refer not to God's essence but to God's activity; salvation and creation are conflated as one divine activity "toward us." Lampe's theory shows the liability of not observing both the "is" and the "*vice versa*" of the axiom.

13. Friedrich Schleiermacher, *The Christian Faith* (eds. H.R. Mackintosh and J.S. Stewert; Edinburgh: T. and T. Clark, 1928).

14. Rahner 85.

15. Cf. The challenge of M. Wiles on the traditional way of appropriating activity to the divine persons, in "Some Reflections on the Origins of the Doctrine of the Trinity," *Journal of Theological Studies,* n.s., 8/1 (1957) 92-106.

16. Notice that Eberhard Jüngel, *God as the Mystery of the World* (Grand Rapids: Eerdmans, 1983), Walter Kasper, *Der Gott Jesu Christi* (Mainz, 1982), and J.P. Mackey, *The Christian Experience of God as Trinity* (London: SCM, 1983), each begin their books on the doctrine of the trinity with sections on contemporary atheism.

17. These remarks should not be construed as being antimetaphysical. Any trinitarian theology reconceived along the lines I am suggesting will be metaphysical in its own way. At the same time, the early history of trinitarian theology demonstrates that the shift to the Augustinian preference for beginning with the divine nature and unity makes it impossible to introduce God's relation to the world into God's own being. Thus Aquinas distinguishes between God's 'logical' relation to creatures, and the creatures' 'real' relation to God. In *Summa Theologiae* I. q.13 a.7.

18. Cf. J. McLelland, *God the Anonymous* (Patristic Monograph, Series 4; Philadelphia: Philadelphia Patristic Foundation, 1976).

19. Cf. R. Jenson, *The Triune Identity 115.*

20. The reader is referred to the vast literature in this area, including Robert Funk, *Language, Hermeneutic and Word of God: The Problem of Language in the New Testament and Contemporary Theology* (New York: Harper and Row, 1966); Sallie McFague, *Metaphysical theology* (Philadelphia: Fortress, 1982); Ian Barbour, *Myths, Models and Paradigms* (New York: Harper and Row, 1974); Max Black, *Models and Metaphors* (Ithaca; Cornell U. 1962); Ian Ramsey, *Religious Language* (London; SCM., 1957); F. Ferré, "Mapping the Logic of Models in Science and Theology" in Dallas M. High, ed., *New Essays on Religious Language* (New York: Oxford U., 1969); R. Scharlemann, "Theological Models and Their Construction," *Journal of Religion* (1973).

See also D. Burrell, *Analogy and Philosophical Language* (New Haven: Yale Univ. 1963); D. Tracy, *The Analogical Imagination* (New York: Crossroad, 1981); W. Lynch, *Christ and Apollo* (Notre Dame, 1960); A. Wilder, *Early Christian Rhetoric: The Language of the Gospel* (rev. ed.: Cambridge, MA: Harvard Univ., 1971); John D. Crossan, *In Parables: the Challenge of the Historical Jesus* (New York: Harper and Row, 1973); Norman Perrin, *Jesus and the Language of the Kingdom* (Philadelphia: Fortress, 1976); Leander Keck, *A Future for the Historical Jesus: The Place of Jesus in Preaching and Theology* (Philadelphia: Fortress, 1981).

21. The work of T.F. Torrance exemplifies in an extreme way a Barthian trinitarianism which has become a trichotomy. See for example *Theological Science* (Oxford U., 1969).

22. Again, cf. Wiles' essay, in n. 15 above.

23. McLelland *(op. cit.* 160) notes that we need to recover the intent of the patristic doctrine of God: "Immanence asserts God's trustworthiness, impassibility his moral transcendence, anonymity his eminence beyond our linguistic and conceptual categories."

24. See, for example, Thomas J. Altizer's theology in *The Self-Embodiment of God* (New York, 1977) and *Total Presence: The Language of Jesus and the Language of Today* (New York; Seabury, 1980). See also L. Dewart, *The Future of Belief* (New York Herder and Herder, 1966) and *The Foundations of Belief* (New York: Herder and Herder, 1969).

25. C.M. LaCugna, "Trinity: Metaphor and Model," paper presented to 1983 Catholic Thelogical Society of America meeting, summarized in *Proceedings of the Thirty-Eighth Annual Convention;* (Bronx, N.Y.: Manhattan College, 1983) 101-3.

26. We must remember that all philosophical terms (accident, form, substance, et al.) are themselves metaphors. See Black, *op. cit.* 40-42.

27. I. Ramsey suggests that Arius' inability to see the figurative-imaginative dimensions of the metaphor of begetting accounts for his rejection of it. See Ramsey, *op. cit.,* pp. 158ff.

28. DS 276.

29. Based on the discussion in J. Leclercq, *The Love of Learning and the Desire For God* (New York: Fordham U., 1961) 233-5

30. In contemporary science "objectivity" is often understood to obtain in inverse proportion to one's distanciation from the "object" being studied. But if in theology the "object" (who is really also a "subject") is God-in-relation, such distanciation would involve a logical contradiction. If God can be known only in-relation, one can not prescind from this relation without invalidating one's method.

31. There is support for this distinction in the study by J. Gibbons, "Concept and Verbum: Reproductive Metaphors and the Inner Life in the 12th century." (Unpublished paper, presented to the 1983 Medieval Conference at Kalamazoo, Michigan.) She contrasts the monastic-devotional and scholastic-technical approaches to God. In general, the monastic use of the conception metaphor refers to conception in the heart, which is maternal. The monastic attitude stresses the change in one's life brought about by conceiving God's word in the heart. The schools, on the other hand, saw conception as an intra-mental process, the mind being in this case the image of God.

FEMINIST SPIRITUALITY AS SELF-TRANSCENDENCE

Denise Lardner Carmody

My topic is "Feminist Spirituality as Self-Transcendence."[1] I propose first to deal with self-transcendence, showing some of the ways in which it escapsules Christian spirituality. Then I shall suggest some of the nuances or colorings that self-transcendence receives when one sets it in sympathetic dialectic.

I. On Self-Transcendence

My first thorough exposure to a spirituality, or view of the human person's vocation, in terms of self-transcendence came through my doctoral dissertation on Bernard Lonergan's notion of person.

In Lonergan's dynamic view of human consciousness I found a powerful endorsement for spirituality-as-intelligent-growth. For the student who apprentices herself to Lonergan soon realizes that becoming whole, advancing in wisdom, is a matter of always being willing to move beyond, following the Spirit's allurements. Be it through science, art, theology, prayer, or any of the many varieties of practical service, one finds a steady pressure to understand more widely and deeply, judge more soberly and fairly, decide more generously, further open one's heart to a love that would be unrestricted, enamored of goodness wherever found. Eric Voegelin's writings tend to the same conclusion, but with more attention to the history of human consciousness. For Voegelin the order of history, the intelligibility we can discern, best emerges when we study the history of order; how the various civilizations and epochs have spoken to themselves about the constitution, the organization, of reality.

For Voegelin one of the most important insights into the human vocation came through Greek philosophy. The key finding of Greek philosophy, which reached fullest vigor in Plato and Aristotle, was that human consciousness is a light with a metaxic or "in-between" character. It stretches from the unbounded of primal matter to the One or the Mind that gives the world order. The golden mean is a life lived in consonance with this insight, a life that stretches upward toward the One but never forgets its roots in primal matter. At the richest moments in the history of Greek philosophy reason itself is clarified as a movement, a *zētēsis,* that takes the form of a knowing ignorance, an unease with one's present confusions, that turns out to be the drawing of divinity itself. Thus fully human life takes the form of a pursuit of the ground of existence, the foundation of reality.

Voegelin's own language describing this view of human life is difficult, but one cannot read it carefully and fail to see the self-transcending, dynamic character that it imparts to human spirituality:

Consciousness is the area of reality where the divine intellect (*nous*) moves the intellect of man (*nous*) to engage in the search of the ground. Aristotle has carefully analyzed the process in which the divine and the human intellect (*nous*) participate in one another. In his language, man finds himself first in a state of ignorance (*agnoia, amatheia*) concerning the ground (*aition, archē*) of his existence. Man, however, could not know that he does not know, unless he experienced an existential unrest to escape from his ignorance (*pheugein tēn agnoian*) and to search for knowledge (*epistēmē*). . . The search, thus, is not blind; the questioning is knowing and the knowing is questioning. The desire to know what one knows to desire injects internal order into the search for the questioning is directed toward an object of knowledge (*noēton*) that is recognizable as the object desired (*orekton*) once it is found. . . The search from the human side, it appears, presupposes the movement from the divine side: Without the *kinēsis,* the attraction from the ground, there is no desire to know; without the desire to know, no questioning in confusion; without the questioning in confusion, no knowledge of ignorance. There would be no anxiety in the state of ignorance unless anxiety were alive with man's knowledge of his existence from a ground that he is not himself.[2]

Implications abound but the point I would underscore is the enormous religious potential latent in the unrest of those--my students in women's studies classes among them--who are searching for sense, order, a grounding for their lives. They are restless for an object or a goal, that God is luring them toward: a grasp of the real divinity that is the final cause of both the world and themselves. One need not go apart from people's existential unrest, their pains and confusions, to find a realistic spirituality. When we have exegetes who show us the significance of our confusions, the spirituality is revealed to lie right in the strivings to make order in our lives.

The achievement of the classical Greeks was what Voegelin calls a "differentiation" of consciousness. From what had previously been an undifferentiated whole (cosmological consciousness), Plato and Aristotle, built on the work of their forebears and distinguished a precisely noetic component. They came to appreciate the structure of the human mind, and they were convinced that this structure applied wherever members of the human species thought, worked, pursued (however vaguely) the ground of their existence. Naming this noetic strand and clarifying the general structure of human intelligence was an epochal achievement. For Voegelin history demarcates itself and reveals its structure, precisely through such achievements. They are breakthroughs, "leaps in being," that become points of no return. As long as people continue to think in the train of the epochal achievers, they cannot go back to a pre-epochal state of awareness. And so it has been first in the West and then in the entire world. Despite the fact that the classical Greeks' achievement was blurred in Hellenism, and has suffered other forms of derailment, Western consciousness, science, political theory, philosophy, religion--would have taken a far different path without it.

The same is true of the second great leap in being that Voegelin distinguishes, the break-through of Israelite revelation. This, too, was an epochal differentiation, a point of no return. Even more than the Greek clarification of noesis, Israelite revelation broke with the cosmological myth. By symbolizing beyond any doubt a God who transcends the world, who is not immanent but beyond and independent, Israelite revelation created a revolution in human consciousness. With Abraham or whoever actually received the experience of a God independent of the natural world, history brought forward another new thing.

The difference between the two differentiations, the Greek and Israelite, is the difference between mind and spirit. Voegelin has compared Paul (as heir of the Israelite prophets who clarified the revelations of the transcendent God) and Aristotle on this point, bringing out the different ways that they express an equivalent understanding of human existence:

> The symbols are equivalent, but the dynamics of existential truth has shifted from the human search to the divine gift (*charisma*), from man's ascent toward God through the tension of Agape. The Pauline *pneuma* is, after all, not the philosopher's *nous* but the rendering in Greek of the Israelite *ruach* [spirit] of God. Hence, Paul does not concentrate on the structure of reality that becomes luminous through the noetic theophany [revelation of God], as the philosophers do, but on the divine irruption which constitutes the new existential consciousness, without drawing too clear a line between the visionary center of the irruption and the translation of the experience into structural insight. Paul distinguishes between *pneuma* and *nous* when the order of the community compels him to do so, as in the case of the tongue-speakers, but he does not expand this effort into a philosopher's noetic understanding of reality; the dividing line will remain rather blurred as, for instance, in 1 Corinthians 2:16, with its quotation from Isaiah 40:13, where the *ruach* of Yahweh is rendered as the *nous* of the Lord, preparatory to the assurance that we, for our part, 'have the *nous* of Christ.' The theophanic event, one may say, has for Paul its center of luminosity at the point of pneumatic irruption; and the direction in which he prefers to look from this center is toward transfigured reality rather than toward existence in the cosmos.[3]

This is another mouthful, but several points here can be easily extricated and turned to our account. First, revelation stresses the divine gift it experiences its truths to be. In other places Voegelin has noted that the philosphers, too, spoke of their vision as free happenings, matters of grace, so that we should not make hard and fast distinctions between philosophers and prophets. Nonetheless, it is the initiative of the love of God, rather than the anxious questing of the human seeker, that captivates the prophet's interest. Even though the quest of the human seeker turns out to have been stimulated and supported by God, in the experience of revelation the action of God is much more overt and unavoidable. It is as though God's spirit or breath breaks (irrupts) into a human situation or personality, giving it a new center of awareness, a new point for viewing. Paul is so overwhelmed by this new center of awareness that he does not bother to work out all of its correlations with other faculties or strata of consciousness. The theophany that riveted him (the Christ event) means a new transfigured realty. After all, God has resurrected Jesus--a completely unheard of thing--and thereby revealed a zone of glory, an inward reaching of heavenly power, previously unknown. The first task is to describe and communicate this irruption that people may grasp its world-shaking implications. It is a later task to think through how this irruption correlates with existence in the ordinary natural world (which of course continues).

By focusing on the spirit that the grace of God transforms, Paul has given us a second locus of self-transcendence. His imagery is not so dynamic as the Aristotelian imagery of questing. It is more passive and mystical. But its ultimate import is even more transforming than that of the Greek noetic insights. Through revelation God has taken the world up into the divine order of existence. If the philosophers discover a mind-to-mind connection between God and human beings, the recipients of revelation discover a spirit-to-spirit connection. In the movements of our spirits to love, for example, we can discern the drawing of God's spirit. In the still moments when we abide with a sense of the divine presence, the spirit of God is at work transforming us. This Pauline set of instincts will be crucially important when one deals with the issue of Christian prayer. Because of the biblical tradition of pneumatic differentiation, we now can speak of a God who always remains other, beyond, but whose work in our prayer transforms us into what She herself is eternally.

The third of my guides in self-transcendence, Karl Rahner, has emphasized the pneumatic presence of divinity as an irreducible Mystery, a fullness of light and love that for our limited minds is bound to seem dark and will often appear empty. This means that "God," the reality we try to name with our received three-letter word, is *sui generis*, very different from the other realities with which we contend each day:

> "The individual realities with which we are usually dealing in our lives always become clearly intelligible and comprehensible and manipulable because we can differentiate them from other things. There is no such

way of knowing God. Because God is something quite different from any of the individual realities which appear within the realm of our experience or which are inferred from it, and because the knowledge of God has a quite definite and unique character and is not just an instance of knowledge in general, it is for these reasons very easy to overlook God. The concept 'God' is not a grasp by which a person masters the mystery, but it is letting oneself be grasped by the mystery which is present and yet ever distant. This mystery remains a mystery even though it reveals itself to man and thus continually grounds the possibility of man being a subject. There can then follow from this ground, of course, the so-called concept of God, explicit language about him, words and what we mean by them and try to say to ourselves reflexively, and certainly a person ought not to avoid the effort involved in this process of reflexive concep-tualization. But in order to remain true, all metaphysical ontology about God must return again and again to this source, must return to the transcendental experience of our orientation towards the absolute mystery, and to the existential practice of accepting this orientation freely. This acceptance takes place in unconditional obedience to conscience, and in the open trusting acceptance of the uncontrollable in one's own existence in moments of prayer and quiet silence."[4]

This is a very rich, pregnant quotation, so let me presume to explicate it in more commonsensical terms. The pneumatic reality that irrupts into history through Israelite revelation and the Christ event is not like the things with which we ordinarily find ourselves dealing. We cannot easily differentiate God from the finite things that we regularly experience, because God is neither finite nor a thing (a circumscribed entity). To know God one must participate in the movement that has brought God into the world as the ground of reality that the questing mind seeks or as the breath-like force that takes human spirit where it has unknowingly longed to be. Since a participation depends upon God, as well as our own dispositions, our own alertness to a possible disclosure and hunger for it, we can overlook God and live as though there were nothing but definite entities, missing the subtle solicitations of the spirit.

Moreover, there is no way that we can pin God down or mount up to God as a secure end to a chain of reasoning. We never master the Mystery, the totality of being, that revelation shows is the constant presence of the Creator to creation. The only way to know the real God is to give oneself over to the Mystery, to abide, watch, and pray. We can do this in formally religious ways, with considerable agony, knees sore from long hours on hard chapel floors, imaginations filled with gripping icons. Or we can do it almost casually, by letting ourselves enjoy the incalculable splendor of a spring day or keeping ourselves present to sources of deep grief because we can lick our wounds in no other way. At such times we can experience that the "more" into which our joy takes us, or the void of our grief, is an "existential," a constant objective feature of our spiritual horizon. The Mystery we somehow intuit as the most significant thing about us is always there, whenever we avert to it, yet it is ever far from us, always exceeds our comprehension.

Rahner says this mystery may reveal itself to us, but that even in such revelation (for example, the experiences recorded in the Hebrew Bible and the Christ event) it remains a mystery, a fullness we cannot fathom. We are who we are, recieve our subjectivity, from the "call" of this Mystery, its allurement of us, but we never become its masters, and always find ourselves its dependents (Muslims would say: its slaves). To be sure, we fashion words, images, and propositions about this mysterious God, so as not to be entirely helpless, and to be able to share our experience of it with others, but these words risk doing more harm than good if we detach them from the basic, originating experience of the mystery itself. In the concrete order of human life as we actually struggle to live it, the best posture is to accept the Mystery, open up to it, let it more and more become the religious (ultimate) horizon of our lives.

When we strip away external pressure and conventions, simplifying ourselves so that we listen in utter stillness to the voice of conscience, we sense the holiness of the Mystery, what it means for Rahner to say that the Mystery grounds the possibility of our being subjects, people called to respond. It is the ultimate norm or criterion of our lives. It is the same when we accept what is beyond our control, and acknowledge the transhuman dimension to life, what earlier cultures called fate. This, too, can magnify the Mystery for us, and break our lives free of the constrictions to which Madison Avenue would confine them. Like Lonergan, Rahner ends at an unrestricted view of human destiny. The climax of self-transcendence is the Mystery as which the eternal God has a constant presence in daily human history.

For Karl Raher, the human person is a listener for a Word of revelation from the divine Mystery. Take human drives to know and love to their limit and you will place the human personality before the Mystery, open and expectant. In analyzing what the human being is "owed" by its Creator, Rahner--like most Catholic theologians--finds that revelation is not included. For the Creative Mystery to disclose itself as personal, loving, and forgiving is an utter gratuity. Yet Christianity stems precisely from this utter gratuity. Christianity is the religion that derives from Jesus of Nazareth, the Christ, whom his followers have long believed to be the incarnate Word of God. The actual order of Rahner's theology has the Incarnation as the starting point, for Rahner never denies that his faith in Jesus Christ orients his analyses of the dynamics of human consciousness. He thinks that these analyses have an integrity and persuasiveness of their own, such that one need not believe in Jesus Christ to find them attractive, but he quite frankly admits that his faith has shaped his understanding of human nature through and through.

The center of Christian faith is Jesus, in whom God has spoken a once-for-all, irreversible, "eschatological" Word of grace and forgiveness. Where philosophic probings of the Mystery leave the prober uncertain of the status human beings have before God, theological probings in the aftermath of the Christ event can build on the New Testament's assertions that nothing can separate us from the love of God in Christ Jesus (Romans 8:39). Jesus therefore is the mercy of God, the divine compassion. In his flesh the Christian finds the basic sacrament of the divine will to free human beings from their sinful bondage, love them out of their irrational closures and communicate to them the divine life.

In terms of God's loving initiative, Jesus is an unthinkable condescension: in him the divine has emptied itself of its privileges and taken on our lowly human status, even suffered our human malice. In terms of his human achievement, Jesus is the revelation of what we images of God can become, when we do wait upon the mystery and take its revelations to heart. For Rahner Jesus is the perfect exemplar of a potentiality that all human beings share, insofar as their spiritual dynamics open them to the Mystery. We are the peculiar creatures who, without in any way having the divine life owed to us, can be elevated by God so that we become sharers in the divine nature, subjects of what Eastern Christianity has called *theōsis*: divinization. Rahner somewhat breaks with the typical Western stress on soteriology, which has made the Incarnation mainly God's way of saving fallen humanity from sin. He doesn't deny this at all, but the Eastern theme of divinization seems to him of equal importance. The two themes converge in the iconic Christ whose "emptying" reveals the paradoxical form that the divine life tends to take within history. So when Rosemary Haughton in her book of that name speaks of "the passionate God,"[5] she means much more than God's ardor to unite with human beings like a romatic lover. The divine love is a suffering, self-spending love (*agapē*).

More than Rahner, but in line with his thought, Haughton skates poetic pirouettes around the notion that Jesus' followers now compose with him one Body. The extension or ongoingness of the Incarnation is the flesh of those who bear the passionate divine love like a stream within the flood of evolutionary history. When Christian believers let their imaginations feed on biblical imagery, they can sense that after Christ all human culture takes on overtones of passion and resurrection and somewhat reenacts the emptying of the Incarnate Word. Certainly for Paul the resurrection made possible Jesus' gathering of his followers to himself in a new way, incorporating them as members of his freed body. Loosed of the limits of mortal life, Jesus could associate with his followers in degrees of intimacy previously impossible.

None of this sort of probing, in the nature of the case, can be very exact. All of it remains but a glimpse of what God has intended through the resurrection. Yet all of it suggests that the Incarnation is now our human affair as much as God's historical affair. The Body of Christ in which the saving Mystery now reveals itself is the lovely flesh of the servant saints, the torn flesh of the poor and persecuted. Wherever the Spirit uses human openness, even human brokenness, to infiltrate love, make new beginnings, and combat infections of the heart, the Incarnation of the Word gains another turn of nuance, another quantum leap of helical progress. The flesh of Jesus therfore is the exact hinge of Rahner's profound understanding of grace. God gives this ultimate self irrevocably in the body of Jesus, who lives now as the resurrected Christ who is the head of many members.

For a spirituality of self-transcendence, Jesus represents an iconic ideal. The self-giving love through which he revealed the most intimate nature of God made him a new paradigm of human perfection. As Lonergan has emphasized, love takes over the initiative in the order of grace. Under the guidance of the Spirit of love, Jesus was willing and able to love to the extremity of his death on the cross. When Christians make the cross the focal point of their faith, they should make sure that Christ's love, rather than his sufferings, is their cause of wonder. Otherwise they can seem to be promoting a strange glorification of pain, a sadistic notion that God's ways are blood and gore. God's ways deal with blood and gore and have something overwhelming to say about all the sunderings that creation suffers. But God's ways in themselves are always ways of love, overtures to exchange, gracious efforts to heal human flesh and raise it into the divine community of Father, Son, and Spirit. The Incarnation, then, should serve us as a startling model and concretion of the self-transcendence that God's Word made possible when it emptied itself and identified with our historical neediness.

II. Feminist Colorings

Having given you some notion of how I would cast Christian spirituality in terms of self-transcendence, let me now suggest some of the shadings, nuances, or colorings that contemporary feminist reflection invite. I begin with what Carol Gilligan has called women's "different voice."[6]

In Gilligan's view, the female moral voice is distinguishable from the male as early as the eighth year, and by the eleventh year it is unmistakably different. For example, a typical eleven year old boy, answering Kohlberg's famous dilemma about Heinz, construes the dilemma as an opposition of rights. The dilemma is this: Heinz needs a drug if he is to save the life of his dying wife. He has no money and the druggist who possesses the drug will not give or loan it to him. Should Heinz steal the drug? An intelligent eleven year old boy usually will answer yes, Heinz should steal the drug, because the right of his wife to life is stronger than the right of the druggist to make a profit on his wares. A typical eleven year old girl, however, will not construe the dilemma in terms of opposing rights. (This immediately places her outside the Kohlbergian expectations.) Rather, she will approach it as a problem in human relationships, and she will seem uncomfortable with the limited choices that the test has laid down before her.

Consider, for example, the response of Amy, a bright eleven year old, when she is asked whether Heinz should steal the drug:

> Well, I don't think so. I think there might be other ways besides stealing it, like if he could borrow the money or make a loan or something, but he really shouldn't steal the drug--but his wife shouldn't die either. . . If he stole the drug, he might save his wife then, but if he did, he might have to go to jail, and then his wife might get sicker again, and he couldn't get more of the drug, and it might not be good. So they should really just talk it out and find some other way to get the money."[7]

Other girls' responses tend to take a similar tack, avoiding a stark confrontation between legal rights and probing the possibilities of solving the problem by changing the relationships. So, for instance, many girls castigate the druggist for his inhumanity, pointing out that if he weren't insistent on his right to a profit, and saw more clearly the much higher value of a human life, the dilemma wouldn't arise.

That this more contextual and relational approach to a moral dilemma such as Heinz' places girls lower on Kohlberg's scale of moral development than boys, in effect penalizing them for their instinctive inability to think only in legal terms, is a small shame within the province of psychology. I would not minimize the implications of this shame, since ours is a narcissistic age, with millions overly interested in measuring how they are doing according to some chart of maturation. But the penalties that girls suffer by being scored lower in such research is by itself rather small beer. It is the unconscious bias of the test, and the relation of this bias to the biases of all the other tests, formal and informal, acknowledged and unconscious, on which our society relies that is the real problem. For if women do construe moral (and, no doubt, other) conflicts differently than men, at least in our American society of the late twentieth century; and if this feminine construction is ignored by the paradigms that shape business, law, religion, education, and our other social institutions; then the injustice of the Kohlbergian gradings is repeated all across the land. In place after place, women are almost automatically being scored as less reasonable, decisive, less able to solve hard problems, and the like, because the regnant models have ignored them.

This reflection would be but a little exercize in logic, laying out the hypothetical inferences, were it not so apparent that the discriminating pattern is in fact a grim feature of real life. Certainly in all the institutional areas that I mentioned--business, law, religion, education--men still control the flow of money and power, men still legislate and enforce most of the rules. It is true that women have become more prominent in business and law. It is true that women have, in some important statistical ways, long been preponderant in education and religion. It is not true that business or law shows any sign of turning to androgynous paradigms in the near future. It is not true that education or religion runs by female models. Why? Mainly because men occupy most of the positions of power in all of these institutional areas; but it is partly also because women have taken in the regnant paradigms, and so judge their own sex less astute at decision-making (at least the formal, institutional kind) than the male.

So, women meet in other areas the same sort of injustice we suffer in the Kohlbergian tests. And, perhaps more ominous, other areas suffer the imbalance that affects recent developmental psychology. Business, for example, suffers from a lack of "feminine" contextual sensitivity, a feminine creativity about relationships. Law is much less able to deal with subtle, contextual and atmospheric matters than adequate justice would demand. Education has canonized scientifico-male models of knowing that have shortchanged the humanities (and are now crumbling before the newest physics). Religion has made sacred lore men's business (for example, in Judaism) or has denied women's competence to represent Christ (for example, in the Roman Catholic controversy about women's ordination to the priesthood).

In each case, the resources and needs of half the species have not factored into the decision-making processes. In other areas, such as medicine and the military, the situation is quite parallel: small hearing given the voices calling for a holistic medicine; little appreciation shown for non-violent ways of making peace and avoiding war. The grossness of this sexism is astounding, when one steps back and ponders it whole. It is a remarkable measure of our sin and distance from Lady Wisdom. In fact, as racism was the great symbol of nineteenth century American evil (and, of course, continues today), so sexism is the great symbol of our twentieth century evil (although it may more easily be overcome, since this could serve the advantage of white women, who are potentially a quite powerful force).

Let us return to Gilligan. Often the different psychological orientation of the women she studied expressed itself as a much stronger investment in relationships. On the whole, women seem considerably more concerned about keeping connections, ties to other individuals and groups, than men do. Much more than men, women typically define themselves not as isolated individuals but as group members, participants in such and such a family or work circle, swimmers in such and such a general stream. Their whole bulks larger than their individual parts. The maintenance of connection or relationship is so high a value that women will often subordinate to it many personal goals. For women being is being-with, work is collaboration, a sense that we best decide by talking things through. So constructive building, rather than men's negative objecting or destroying, characterizes most women's group interactions. Therefore, dialogue and consultation tend to be more important than solitary brooding.

This is not to say, of course, that no women are destructive and no men can build. I am painting in broad strokes, combining Gilligan's descriptions of women's developmental orientations with my own observations of how women and men tend to behave. But I have no serious qualms about the broad characterization that has been emerging. From the popular stereotypes that one encounters in the mass media, to the refinements being brought forward by contemporary social science, the more relational pattern of women's ways of coming to understand and decide stands out again and again. For most women reality is markedly more ecological, symbiotic , relational, and processive than it is for men.

Now, my point is not to begin building a new philosophy of relationship or a new theology of connection, but to reveal some of the implications that women's relationality would seem to hold for an adequate model of self transcendence, a spirituality likely to be viable for both sexes in the future. Recall the instinct of the eleven year old girl Amy to solve Heinz's dilemma by finding alternative ways to get the money, and so the drug. Amy does not conceive Heinz, his wife, or the druggist as isolated individuals. She sees them as ingredients in a holistic gestalt. Moreover, Amy quickly imagines further ramifications at which the test-problem itself merely hints: the possibility of borrowing the money. Further, Amy is more concerned about the druggist than any simply legal rendering of the dilemma is able to be. She does not want Heinz to steal the drug, and one likely reason (in addition to her acceptance of our general proscription on stealing, and to the possibility that Heinz would be jailed) is the hurt that stealing would inflict on the druggist. As we shall soon see, *care* is a central ingredient in a distinctively feminine moral reasoning, and following closely to care is a strong desire not to inflict pain. Clearly, however, care also is based upon relationship, the fact that for women we are all in it together.

This sense that we are all in it together has, to date, kept feminism more an ally than a competitor of other liberation movements. Rarely, for instance, does a feminist pit women's rights or needs against those of peoples of color or other groups that are marginal to the centers of American prosperity and power. Part of this inclusiveness may stem from women's having been moved by the pathos in other underlings' sufferings. Another part, however, likely stems from women's aboriginal orientation toward the whole, the all of us, that makes cooperation more natural than competition. It is not that women have a special virtue that helps them see unattractive people like the druggist in gilded terms. Some women may have such a special virtue, as may some men, but most women would not judge the druggist an attractive person. Rather, most women simply are less able than are most men to exclude the druggist from the moral calculus or make him simply the enemy. The situation is something whole, so the solution has to be something whole, a formula to which all of the participants have contributed. The same with the situations of real life, the social conflicts tearing apart real neighborhoods. The feminine instinct is to try to get all the parties talking, to try to bring all the sufferers some relief.

From the relationship comes care, a sense of responsibility for all the members of the gestalt. If the etiology of care is somewhat murky, its potency is very clear: the prophet said that God could no more abandon Israel than a nursing mother abandon her child. For the prophet, a nursing mother was the *ne plus ultra* of loving concern, the example beyond which one could not go. Indeed, through history much of women's praise has developed from their special caring. The beery songs that spell out M-O-T-H-E-R play on self-sacrificing care, as do many more estimable forms of laud. Women themselves tend to focus on caring, praising it in their female role-models and expecting it of themselves. This is probably more helpful than harmful, especially in view of the needs of the species as a whole, but lately it has become obvious that care can be a great problem for women, a source of considerable frustration, retardation, and guilt.

For the care that society has praised has been the care that has redounded to society's direct profit. With "society" here being largely its male spokespersons, women have been praised for spending themselves at home for their spouse and children, taking on the volunteer work that makes our nobler institutions run, doing the cleaning and typing at the economically bottom rung of many work situations. Society therefore has been rather hypocritical in the praise it has lavished upon feminine caring. The 59¢ female dollar is inconceivable apart from such hypocrisy, as is the exclusion of feminine care from the boardrooms of power. As mentioned, none of the major institutions that one sees when surveying the cultural landscape has adopted androgynous, let alone feminist paradigms. The praise of feminine care that wafts through religion, education, medicine, or government is quite tainted, and more than vulnerable to the charge of being proffered in bad faith.

Still, women seem unwilling to give up caring, and their only caveat nowadays is that caring be extended to the feminine self. The daughters who look back in awe at their mothers' careful self-spending are starting to realize that often such spending was beyond measure, to the point that it gave away capital mother herself could ill afford to lose. Mothers overextended and underrewarded tend to become mothers with axes to grind, grievances to parade, injustices to redress by fair means or foul. Easily do they weep, lament, manipulate, and drive others to teeth-grinding with their dizziness or incompetence. Had such women cared more for themselves, been less pressured by hypocritical models of care that lost sight of the self, they might have served everyone thay encountered less ambiguously.

Relationships do not flourish when care is excessive, smothering, spending more of the carer's substance than it should. Care for the self should be like the love on which Jesus predicated his love of neighbor. We are to love our neighbor, he said, as we love ourselves. The fairest assumption, then, is that we are to love ourselves fully, with an eye to our own good, a strong striving for health and the development of our talents. If we are to be helpful we must be strong. If we are to be effective we must take the time to become competent, good and glad in our work.

Granted this, however, women still want to be caring. They still reject models of social existence in which individualism and competition threaten relationship. Although they have been going into law in greater numbers, few women are completely happy with the law's adversarial structure, and many women only put up with the law's unattractive forms because working through them may prove helpful to their needy clients. The same with medicine and education. The women I see entering these professions are willing to try to take what is good in them, what these professions have grown to be under male auspices, but they are not willing to canonize what is impersonal or ruthless. Indeed, a large number of women in my field of education have a long agenda of reforms they are trying to push forward. Against the streams of power, they are trying to promote interdisciplinarity, consensual models of governance, humane support and evaluation of teaching, bias-free treatment of students (no more sexual harassment, for example), and other off-shoots of an at least implicit rootage in care.

I have introduced the notion and contemporary setting of a feminist spirituality conceived as self-transcendence, worked through some of the major findings of recent transcendentalist thinkers, and reflected on some of the shadings that feminist reflection might take on such major findings. By way of summary and conclusion, let me now put to myself a single pointed question: Would you please make as sharp as possible how you see the self-transcendence that could serve women well as their spiritual focus, in what they are trying to achieve in their struggles after personal relgious growth?

The two general words that I would use to characterize such self-transcendence are freedom and love. Freedom carries much of the load which the onward-pushing, over-going motifs of the male transcendentalists assemble. In Lonergan's model, for instance, the person is free to experience, understand, judge, decide (love), and following out this freedom (this call of human nature to grow) will increase it. Indeed, it will bring the person to the point of an unrestricted love, an opening of mind, heart, soul and strength that tries to match itself to the unboundedness of the divine Mystery. The free person therefore is on the move, underway, convinced that her inbuilt drives to know what is real and embrace it in love are a beautiful birthright, an imperative from the muses of authenticity. No heteronomous, outside agency can rightly contradict this drive, because to contradict it is to oppose the way that God has construed the human personality. We are made ever to question, ponder, and try to achieve what is good. Realism and goodness are the inalienable goals or achievements for which the spark in our clod burns. Any institution or foreign body that does not share these goals, or that tries to prevent us from pursuing these goals, is inauthentic. As inauthentic, it cannot be a work or servant of God. The old Platonic criterion remains completely valid today: Something is not good because people say that it is "godly" (revealed, inspired, traditional). Something is godly because it is good (consonant with light, productive of welfare).

Freedom alone, however, is not the holistic spirituality I find women to covet. The feminist spirituality I see aborning would synthesize freedom with love. And "love," of course, is just as grand a term as freedom, capable of just as many interpretations and abuses. I could mean several things by it, but in the first place "a positive care." Love is the animating spirit behind healthy relating, tactful nurturing, self-spending that is not masochistic but admirably generous. It can be strong as death, as the *Song of Songs* knows. It can be bereft as crucifixion. The Pauline hymn to love in Corinthians 13 is a good bit of Christian phenomenology. The reflections in John bring out love's kinship with God's life and the soul of a religious community. The passionate, romantic love that Haughton applies to God comes from the singular litera-ture of medieval Provencal. The much older Confucian notion of *jen* and Hindu notion of *bhakti* pitch in with helpful similitudes from the East. We are what we love, even more than what we eat. We are what we want to love, for where our treasure is, there will our heart be. And so it goes, this playing with "love," gilding of "love," that theologians can no more avoid than poets. Without love we are nothing: tinkling brass and clanging cymbal. Without love we do not do justice to women's historic grandeur, women's contem-porary spiritual needs.

So, my model has love, and I find it to soften the crudeness and hurt unbridled freedom can bring. I find it to make the helix more graceful, more like the good witches' spiral dance, less like a metallic screw. When love is syn-thesized with freedom, it does not veto pushing ahead, striving to grow. Erotic love is very much like freedom's striving. Its pursuit of beauty, personal fulfill-ment, the world that might be is, in fact, the self's most energetic, delight-filled pushing ahead. On the other hand, love does have chastenings in store for freedom, purifications that freedom may not initially want. At the heart of the religious matter, converse with God is dialogue, and in a dialogue one listens as well as speaks, is receptive as well as productive. There would be no honest dialogue with the Christian God, Father or Mother, if the human partner came with a rigid list of non-negotiables. The bible, like any sacred book is the judge of its reader, as well as a collection of texts today's reader has critically to sift. Love enables us to bear the judgement of God that comes through scripture, tradition, the example of the saints. The same Spirit who insinuates God's love-life of *agape* is Mother enough occasionally to brood our needs to die, so that we may rise to fuller life. She is like a refining fire, a living flame, that would burn away any sin keeping us in bondage, any fetter on our self-transcendence.

I realize that this is rather traditional language, and that it has often been abused. But I see no way around it. Unless we are to separate ourselves from prior female Christian exemplars, who have blazed with the gospel's passion for what is right, we shall have to contend with sin, purification of the self, the ways of God that are as far above our ways as the heavens are above the earth. If we care about God, we care about God's ways and try to make ourselves disponible to them in the Spirit. If we care about other people we listen to what they tell us they need, how they perceive God's will for them. Even if this demands that we shift away from egocentricity, and abrade our selfishness. The question we should ask about any language or practice is not whether it is traditional but whether it serves well today, (in a time of raised feminist consciousness). Opinions will differ about particular practices, but I myself would doubt a wicca who made no place for converions, asceticism, the love that makes loss the condition of many gains.

Nor is this all. There is also the matter of loving our enemies, doing good to those who persecute us--Jesus' most harrowing command. Qualifications are in order, of course, and justice does not fly out the door. But Christian love is inseparable from forgiveness, reconciliation, and pledges to make new starts. I think that Mary Daly[8] is right to write herself out of the Christian camp, for she seems unwilling to accept this central doctrine. Her spirituality becomes, as Elisabeth Schussler Fiorenza sees, something for a coven of outsiders, a group that wants no truck with either oppressive men or incompletely liberated women.[9] The several chapters she writes on the injuries that women in several cultures have suffered from men makes Daly's position understandable, but they also color her care splenetic. As a result, her humors are dark and gnashing, like old furies nursing grim grievances. Like Schüssler Fiorenza, I want no cheap grace that would erase the evils of past history without repentance and reparation. But I also want no future that stands under a dark cloud of militant hatred, and has no place for shafts of forgiveness and new starts. Where would any of us be without forgiveness? How could any spirituality make progress? We all have sinned and fallen short of God's glory. We all need to be freed by her careful love, which looks more to what we want to be than to

154

what we are or ever have been. In that careful love, finally, lies our freedom. In our freedom lies our true spirituality.

NOTES

1. This paper is excerpted from *Seizing the Apple: Feminist Spirituality as Personal Growth* (New York: Crossroad, 1984).

2. Eric Voegelin, *Order and History* (Baton Rouge: Louisiana State U., 1974) 189-90.

3. Ibid. 246. See Kenneth Keulman, "The Tension of Consciousness: The Pneumatic Differentiation" in *Voegelin and the Theologians* (eds. J. Kirby and W. Thompson; New York: Edwin Mellen, 1983) 61-103.

4. Karl Rahner, *Foundations of Christian Faith* (New York: Seabury/Crossroad, 1978) 54. See *A World of Grace* (ed. Leo J. O'Donovan; New York: Seabury/Crossroad, 1980) for interpretive essays that clarify many rough spots in Foundations of Christian Faith.

5. Rosemary Haughton, *The Passionate God* (Ramsey, N.J.: Paulist, 1981).

6. Carol Gilligan, *In a Different Voice* (Cambridge, MA: Harvard University, 1982).

7. Ibid. 28.

8. Mary Daly, *Gyn/Ecology* (Boston: Beacon, 1978).

9. Elisabeth Schüssler Fiorenza, *In Memory of Her* (New York: Crossroad, 1983) 21-26.

THE CHICAGO DECLARATION
AND THE CALL TO HOLY WORLDLINESS

Rodger Van Allen[1]

As the second lay president of the College Theology Society, and speaking about laypeople, I trust my topic will not be one of mere personal interest but will also have general appeal and timeliness.

I will center my remarks on the Chicago Declaration as follows: (1) a review of recent changes in the profile of the professional religious personnel within Catholicism in the United States; (2) an explanation of the Chicago Declaration; (3) a review and assessment of four major themes entered in critique of the Declaration; (4) a suggestion about what went wrong with the worldly vocation theme of Vatican II, and finally, a comment on the ecumenical and ongoing significance of the basic point that has been made by the Declaration.

I.

There is a Chinese proverb: May you live in interesting times. These last twenty-five years have indeed been interesting times. The Second Vatican Council is likely to be regarded by history as the most important religious event of the twentieth century. It may even be regarded, along with the Reformation, as one of the major turning points in the whole history of Christianity. The changes in the self-understanding of Catholicism and its relationship to the world brought exciting developments in ecumenism and religious and church renewal.

Changes in personal religious meaning, a sense of vocation and a sense of ministry have been at the roots of the shift of life-style that has been notable in Roman Catholicism since the Council. The total number of priests, seminarians, brothers and sisters is now about 90 percent of what it was in 1954. After an increase of about 20 percent, the trend downward came in 1968, and it has been going down ever since.[2] About 10,000 priests, 50,000 sisters and 4,000 brothers have resigned since 1968.[3] Still, however, there are many more priests, seminarians, and sisters in American Catholicism today than is generally recognized. Poland, whose media image is quite clerical, in fact has about one-half the number of priests per Catholic population as does the United States. It has about one-third the number of nuns per Catholic population, and it has only about three-fourths the number of seminarians per Catholic population.[4] Perhaps these numbers help us to recall how pervasive was the presence of those in black garb, if with all the changes there is still such a striking edge in these numbers for American Catholicsm over Polish Catholicism.

Today there is striking growth in the permanent diaconate. In about ten years there has been a tenfold increase to more than 6,000 permanent deacons. But it is especially among laypeople that the most striking changes are evident. About four-fifths of all teachers in Catholic schools today are laypersons. In addition there are hundreds of professional religious education directors working full time in local churches. In addition, there are about 125 lay mission volunteer programs. The Maryknoll lay missioners may serve as an indicator of recent trends among these groups. Between 1975 and 1981 the annual number of inquiries about their lay mission program increased tenfold--from 300 to 3320. This dramatic increase in inquiries during the last ten years suggests that interest in short-term religious service is growing. Lay persons are working in campus ministry, in pastoral plannng offices, in youth ministry, ministry to the aged, bilingual ministry, ministry to the handicapped, clinical pastoral education and marriage encounter, just to mention a few of these specialized ministries. The introduction of eucharistic ministers and lectors has added many numbers of parishioners to the list of personnel giving service. Eugene Hemrick summarizes his thoroughgoing report on the trends we have been sketching here with the following assessment:

> It would seem as we look at the restoration of the permanent diaconate, the advances in religious education, the growth of lay volunteers, the increase in new offices of planning and the various other types of ministries and their support systems, the data would indicate that neither the number serving the church in a special manner nor church services have diminished. The type of personnel, however, has changed. We are going from a big clerical and religious visibility to an integrated visibility of lay persons and ordained permanent deacons with the world of clerics and religious. All things considered, it would seem church vitality is very strong.[5]

Projecting ahead from this contemporary assessment to the year 2000, one would find the number of priests changing from 60,000 serving today's 50 million Catholics, to 30,000 priests serving 65 million Catholics.[6] Deacons, religious and lay men and women serving the church in a special manner will be reasonably numerous if recent trends continue, but adjustments may have to be made in terms of who can celebrate the eucharist, administer the rite of reconciliation, or anoint.

Returning to Hemrick's contemporary assessment, with laity numerous in all kinds of special manners of service within the church, does this indicate the coming of age of the laity in Roman Catholicism? Has that "emerging" laity that Donald Thorman wrote about a quarter of a century ago finally made it?[7] This is one of the questions the forty-seven signers of "A Chicago Declaration of Christian Concern" wanted to address, and their response to his question and their other comments deserve our attention.[8]

II.

Issued in mid-December of 1977, the Chicago Declaration charged that

> a wholesome and significant movement within the Church--the
> involvement of lay people in many Church ministries--has led to a
> devaluation of the unique ministry of lay men and women. The
> tendency has been to see lay ministry as involvement in some church
> related activity, e.g., religious education pastoral care for the sick and
> elderly, or readers in church on Sunday. Thus lay ministry is seen as the
> laity's participation in work traditionally assigned to priests or sisters.

The signers feel that the welcome involvement of lay people in many church
ministries has in fact upstaged, distracted and confused many laity into thinking that this was what religion was all about. Where is that compelling vision of
lay Christians in society, a vision nurtured historically in Chicago and
elsewhere, and eventually accepted and celebrated by the Second Vatican
Council? Has this historical development been aborted? The laity, who spend
most of their time and energy in the professional and occupational world
"appear to have been deserted," while many in the Church exhaust their
energies on internal issues "albeit important ones, such as the ordination of
women and a married clergy."

> 'Without a vision the people shall perish.' Who now sustains lay persons
> as they meet the daily challenges of their job and profession--the arena
> in which questions of justice and peace are really located?

Movements, organizations and clergy should be devoting themselves to
"energizing lay leaders committed to reforming the structures of society."
Quoting Vatican II, the Declaration strongly emphasized the distinctive
ministry of lay people.

> What specifically characterizes the laity is their secular nature. It is true
> that those in holy orders can at times be engaged in secular activities and
> even have a secular profession. But they are, by reason of their particular
> vocation, especially and professionally ordained to the sacred ministry.
> Similary, by their state in life, religious give splendid and striking
> testimony that the world cannot be transformed and offered to God
> without the spirit of the beatitudes. But the laity by their special vocation,
> seek the kingdom of God by engaging in temporal affairs and by ordering
> them according to the plan of God. They live in the world that is, in each
> and all of the secular professions and occupations. They live in the
> ordinary circumstances of family and social life, from which the very

160

web of their existence is woven. Today they are called by God, that by exercising their proper function, and led by the spirit of the Gospel, they may work for the sanctification of the world from within as a leaven. In this way they make Christ known to others, especially by the testimony of a life resplendent in faith, hope and charity. Therefore, since they are tightly bound up in all types of temporal affairs, it is their special task to throw light upon these affairs in such a way that they may be made and grow according to Christ to the praise of the creator and redeemer.[9]

Beyond this central theme of the Declaration, other items given subordinate consideration included tempered criticism of some dimensions of the Detroit "Call to Action" program, diaconate programs, clergy and religious who have sought "to impose their own agendas for the world upon the laity," and the steady depreciation of the ordinary roles through which the laity serve and act upon the world.

The impression is often created that one can work for justice and peace only by stepping outside of these ordinary roles as a businessman, as a mayor, as a factory worker, as a professional in the State Department, or as an active union member and thus that one can change the system only as an "outsider" to the society and the system.

Who were these forty-seven signers of the Chicago Declaration? They included veterans of Catholic social and political efforts such as Ed Marciniak, Russell Barta and Patty Crowley, scholars such as Sister Agnes Cunningham and Fathers John Shea, John Pawlikowski, and Carroll Stuhlmueller, and other persons from an unusually broad range of occupations in business, journalism, labor, medical care and law.

Initially two thousand copies of the Declaration were printed and distributed. Within a few months, however, it had been so widely reprinted that more than one million copies were in circulation and eventually more than two million copies. It was highlighted in *Newsweek*, *The New York Times* and *The Los Angeles Times*, and discussed in the *London Times*. Editors used the following headlines to describe the Declaration: *National Catholic Reporter,* "Church Must Take Laity Seriously"; *Our Sunday Visitor,* "Laity's Role in the World Being Devalued Says Chicago Declaration"; *America,* "Recovering the Lay Apostolate"; *Chicago Sun-Times,* "Prominent Area Catholics Rap 'Inward-Turned' Church." *Commonweal* editorially praised the Declaration and pointed out that reaction to it "had been overwhelmingly favorable." They stated that "sources as different as the radical Center of Concern in Washington and *Our Sunday Visitor* welcomed the concern about the devaluation of the laity's secular tasks." The Declaration was issued with a return address and letters of support and encouragement came from Congressmen Paul Simon (Ill.) and Robert F. Drinan (Mass.), Notre Dame's Theodore Hesburgh, Cynthia Wedel (co-president, World Council of Churches), Harvey Cox, David O'Brien, James Hitchcock, George Gallup and many others.[10]

In March 1979, a major conference on the Declaration was held at Notre Dame with papers presented by John A. Coleman, Ed Marciniak, Michael Novak, Sargent Shriver and Margaret O'Brien Steinfels.[11] These papers have been published and the book *Challenge to the Laity*, is now in its second printing. Those who have entered the discussion substantially in addition to those at Note Dame include Robert Hoyt, Rosemary Ruether and John Garvey in an excellent *Commonweal* symposium,[12] and Joseph Komonchak in a lengthy essay in *The Jurist.*[13]

III.

The major theme to emerge in the critique of the Declaration is that it seems to maintain as Msgr. George Higgins for one put it "too sharp a distinction between the respective roles of the laity and the clergy in the social ministry of the Church."[14] Robert Hoyt, in his response, stated:

> On the whole I think the fuzzing of what is lay and what is clerical is a good thing. I don't want a clear definition that will bar Robert Drinan from sitting in jail, Mary Luke Tobin from rallying the sisters, or Andrew Greeley from counting noses. None of them is usurping my place or imposing an agenda on me.

Joseph Komonchak felt that the Declaration appeared to confine the political significance of the gospel in rather narrow channels in general and particularly with regard to the ministries of the clergy and religious. There are different gifts in the Church, he points out, some of which are more useful and suitable than others for articulating in theory and practice the political character of the gospel. These gifts, however, are not likely, says Komonchak to be distributed neatly within the lines of the distinctions among clergy, religious and laity.[15] John Coleman contributes the proper contemporary nuance to the discussion when he points out that the Declaration is wrong in drawing a line "mainly between clergy and laity instead of one between the new professional class (ordained and lay) and the laity in a worldy calling."[16]

I accept Coleman's helpful specification of this new religious professional class, and I agree with Komonchak that gifts are not likely to be distributed in neatly canonical lines, but I find it curious that a broadside like the Chicago Declaration, attempting to explode some general sense of ordinary lay participation in the world, is somehow turned into another discussion of the one percent or less of Catholics who comprise the religious professional class. That such a theme should emerge as the leading one in discussion of the Declaration may only confirm the original need for such a Declaration.

A second major area of discussion concerns the Declaration's charge of an inward turning church. The last few lines of the Declaration read as follows:

> The Church must constantly be reformed, but we fear that the almost obsessive preoccupation with the Church's structures and processes has diverted attention from the essential question: reform for what purpose? It would be one of the great ironies of history if the era of Vatican II which opened the windows of the Church to the world were to close with a Church turned in upon herself.

It should be made clear at this point that the Chicago Declaration is a document that comes forth from persons that are, in my view, properly regarded as committed to structural reform within Catholicism. This is no reactionary group. They do feel, however, that great opportunities may be being missed or relatively neglected for assisting the development of religious meaning and impact on the world for many lay persons.

Robert Hoyt is among the commentators addressing this dimension of the Declaration. He comments:

> . . . though I yield to no man, women or Declaration in the depth of my distaste for churchiness, I will argue that people should not be called away from considering the nature of the Church and its processes, specifically including papal infallibility and authority, until the full implications of the issuance of *Humanae Vitae* have been faced and dealt with. Agreed: It is to yawn. But I suspect that to many signers of the Declaration, the birth control encyclical demonstrated that the Church is not what it says it is. So what is it? It *will be* what faithful Catholics who attend to its inner life make it to be.[17]

In similar fashion, Rosemary Ruether points out that it is not surprising that movements such as the "Call to Action" focus, in part, on changes within the Church itself, "not because they want to focus on the internal workings of the institution, but because it has become evident that, until the power relations within the institution itself are reordered, the Church indeed will not be the base for activating any new vision and mission to the world."[18]

I agree with Hoyt and Ruether that these essentially internal questions cannot be neglected. They are important in themselves and in the negative impact that they exert pastorally.[19] I believe, however, that Ruether's wording may overstate the case. I don't believe that a new vision and mission to the world need be held hostage "until the power relations within the institution itself are reordered." That could be a long time. I think this is the way the Chicago Declaration feels too.

A third area in discussion of the Declaration involves its expression of concern with "steady depreciation during the past decade [1967 - 77] of the ordinary social roles through which the laity serve and act upon the world." The Declaration doesn't like the impression "often created" that one can work for justice and peace "only" as an 'outsider' to the society and the system. It is this theme, it seems, that prompted Andrew Greeley to see in the Declaration a "healthy return from the romantic revolutionary style of the Berrigan era" to an earlier Catholic social action vision.[20] John Garvey also referred to the Berrigans in his comments, though their names appear nowhere in the Declaration. "What I am afraid the Declaration is saying," said Garvey, "is that if only people like the Berrigans had consulted politicians and State Department sorts, they would have learned the error of their ways, and would have worked within the system to reform, say, operation Phoenix or the CIA."[21] Garvey points to the lay experience of Dorothy Day, Jim Forest, Tom Cornell and others that favors the outsider's role. Garvey's reference to operation Phoenix reminds us of those Vietnam War days and how necessarily and properly influenced many of us were to a needed outsider role. The Declaration, however, is not out to dismiss Tom Cornell or Daniel Berrigan or any other so-called outsider. Indeed, it leaves open the possibility that structural change in some situations may only come from outside. But it clearly does not accept the proposition that all structures in society are somehow damned. One does, in some circles, it seems to me, hear so much of sinful social structures, that the inference is easily given that any and all structures are sin-filled. Let me contrast this with the following careful exposition from Francis Meehan's *A Contemporary Social Sprituality*:

> . . .structures. . .have moral values embedded in them. They can be good or evil. They are rarely neutral. Sometimes a structure is so deeply oppressive as to be unredeemable. . .but not always are things so clear. Sometimes structures contain a mixture of good and evil. That is another way of saying that they often have elements of hurtfulness and helpfulness, elements that foster the dignity of some and may conflict with the needs of others. . . .This awareness of both good and evil delivers us from a modern mindset where one too easily sees all structure as evil, or all bureaucratic impersonalness as evil. One must sometimes

look more carefully . . . Social structures are often like human personalities. Pieces of our personality are evil, but in eradicating the evil we must be careful to treasure the good that is often the flip side.[22]

John Coleman holds that the Declaration is correct in rejecting the proposition that outsiders to the system are the principal actors in changing the social order. To hold that outsiders to the system are the principal actors in changing the social order "lacks historical validity and deviates widely from the traditional Catholic sensibility for concrete political wisdom," says Coleman. He grants that there are societies in the world which merit that judgement, but he does not find America at present to be one of them. He asks if a "too facile importation of social action models from other countries"[23] might explain their current prevalence in the American Church.

I agree with Coleman's estimate of American society, and I agree with the Declaration's appreciation and value of those who do attempt to work as insiders with structures. It is more Coleman than the Declaration that seeks to measure whether it is the insider or the outsider to the structures that makes the most difference. For the Declaration, it is enough to maintain that those who work in ordinary roles with the structures of society can and do make a significant contribution which ought not be dismissed.

A fourth area of critical response to the Declaration maintains that Catholic lay people shouldn't really need any clerical, religious or lay professional class energizing them to the reform of the structures of the society, stirring them to see a Christian vision in society or galvanizing them in their secular-religious role. John Garvey says that "lay people in need of galvanization by priests wouldn't have done us much good anyway, galvanized or not."[24] He adds: "There is no reason why lay people can't organize themselves; and if they fail to do so, it is because of an absence of lay leadership.[25] Rosemary Ruether says: "'Let the dead bury the dead.' If the clergy don't want to 'inspire' and 'activate' us, why not inspire and activate ourselves? Why not really come of age as laity?"[26]

There is, perhaps, a certain visceral and rhetorical attractiveness to these remarks by Ruether and Garvey, but they may be too contextualized to the theological and existential shoes of Ruether and Garvey, i.e., because Ruether and Garvey stand in no need of any religious professional class activating or inspiring them, can it therefore be inferred that no lay people have these needs? I don't think the forty-seven signers of the Declaration were particularly expressing their personal needs for inspiration or vision. I do think they were looking much more broadly at the religious needs and creative potential of the more than fifty million Catholics in the United States. The Declaration states:

In the last analysis, the Church speaks to and acts upon the world through her laity. Without a dynamic laity conscious of its personal ministry to the world, the Church, in effect, does not speak or act. No amount of social action by priests and religious can ever be an adequate substitute for enhancing lay responsibility. The absence of lay initiative can only take us down the road to clericalism.

The Chicago Declaration is not a perfect document. Readers of it would get the notion that the Catholic Church in the United States has many more priests and religious involved in radical social action and ministry than my perceptions reveal. Second, its analysis of clericalism is too tightly drawn in terms of priests and religious, instead of the more generic and lay populated religious professional class, which class it has obviously noted. Third, the Declaration can be read in a way that would minimize the significance of the continuing effort toward internal *aggiornamento* in Roman Catholicism, instead of seeing a necessary inter-relationship between the inner life of the church and its attempt to influence the world. John T. Noonan, in his reflections on the Declaration, points out that the church needs to be made effective and attractive if it is to have an impact on the culture, and thus structural renewal is needed, in parishes, the diocese, the National Catholic Bishops Conference, and the Vatican.[27]

We have focussed at length on some particular criticisms of the Delcaration. Its fundamental strength, however, is more significant, and has been noted approvingly by every commentator I have mentioned and many more. The Declaration's message is one of confidence that a broad based lay impact on the world is both possible and necessary both for the needs of the world and the need for religious fulfillment and meaning for many persons. As John Coleman has pointed out, only religious resources can retrieve a new sense of worldy vocation for a genuine renewal of church in service of society.[28]

IV.

But what went wrong, we might ask? Isn't this sense of worldy vocation for genuine renewal of church in service of society, what was thought to have been achieved in the Second Vatican council? Avery Dulles' commentary introducing the "Constitution on the Church" document maintained that the Constitution provided "an excellent foundation for a new and creative approach to the role of the laity in the Church." He said the dignity and responsibilities of lay Christians were presented "in an inspiring manner."[29] Albert C. Outler, in his response to that crucial Vatican II document, said that its notion of the laity as the presence of the church in the world had restored yet another biblical emphasis upon the general priesthood of all believers (as constituted by their baptism and confirmation) and had laid out the theory for their apostolate in and for the world.[30] Writing in 1962 of his hopes for the Council, Philip Scharper stated that the recovery of the sense of this priesthood of the faithful seemed to him "a particularly hopeful line of development." Scharper pointed out that the priesthood of the faithful, a fundamental tenet of the Protestant Reformation, had been spoken of by Pope Pius XII who had declared that the laity should be informed of the priesthood that is theirs by virtue of baptism, and that the fact of their priesthood "should neither be minimized nor denied." In spite of this strong papal directive, however, Scharper reported that in the years since it had been given he had never heard a single sermon on the topic, nor was it a subject of discussion in general Catholic periodical or newspaper literature.[31] Standing before you twenty-two years after these remarks by Philip Scharper, and after the most official Catholic reaffirmation of the priesthood of the faithful in Vatican II, I must report that I have never heard a single sermon on the topic. Further, none of the more than two hundred students I taught during the past year had ever heard of it. The Catholic Periodical index still has no subject heading "Priesthood, Universal" as does the Religion Index which covers mainly Protestant Journals. Occasionally one encounters a nervous reference to it, but the context typically is one mainly pointing out that this differs "in essence and not only in degree" from the hierarchical priesthood. There are more balanced counter currents. For example, Raymond Brown has contributed an excellent essay on "The Challenge of the Three Biblical Priesthoods."[32] which is quite worthwhile, and to be sure there are other counter currents, but the broad picture is one of serious neglect of what Scharper had called "a particularly hopeful line of development." In 1965, Albert Outler had praised the themes in the Constitution on the Church, but he had also pointed out that there was of course the "tragic possibility" that such themes would not be "widely read or actually implemented in the ongoing life of the Church."[33] The priesthood of all believers shared by laity and clergy alike is too rich a theme to be neglected. It is a priesthood which, as 1 Peter 2:5 says, manifests itself in "offering spiritual sacrifices acceptable to God." As Raymond Brown says, "The heart of the believers' priesthood in which we all share is the giving of our whole lives, not just in the Eucharist, but in everything that we do."[34]

We have been asking what went wrong in the last twenty years in the move to achieve some sense of worldy vocation? One thought that has been shared is that the priesthood of all believers has been neglected. Surely there is more to say on so broad a question, but even this single theme could easily be linked in a positive way to themes of work, family, liturgy, and more, and such linkage need not be a merely individualistic kind of religious vocationalism, but can and must include the knowledgable structural analysis that comes from this kind of experience.

We began this paper by reporting on the emergence of what some would call a "churchy" laity in Roman Catholicism. We reported too on the Chicago Declaration and its call for a "worldly" laity in Catholicism. But the question in these terms transcends Roman Catholicism, and one of the most worthy books I've come across is Richard Mouw's *Called to Holy Worldliness*[35] which addresses these questions in a broad ecumenical perspective. He uses the terms "churchy" and "worldly" laity in descriptive rather than disparaging ways and without depreciating the value of the "churchy" laity, he emphasizes the significance of the "worldly" laity, their exercise of the priesthood of the faithful, and their ministry to the structures of society in and through their work, family and recreation. Such notions of ministry may strike some persons of Catholic background somewhat by surprise. They typically have hazy notions of ministry -- it's something a minis*ter* does, and a minis*ter* is a Protestant. One such Catholic summed up his dawning consciousness of ministry this way: "Yesterday, I didn't know what minister meant; today, I find out I am one!"

Such notions of ministry, linked up with occupation in a way that emphasizes both competence and a critical posture, may present important avenues of religious meaning to be explored by us as professors whose students typically enter our classrooms at least partly because of credit requirements they must fulfill on their way toward degrees in accounting, engineering, nursing, etc. To be really good at your job and a critical and creative member of your profession and world is authentically religious. Sad to say, that thought strikes some students as novel!

I am grateful for the Chicago Declaration and the discussion that it has stimulated. Another conference on the themes of the Declaration was held in Chicago in 1982, and those Proceedings have been published.[36] Russell Barta of Mundelein College has established a Center for the laity at Mundelein and has capably edited continuing periodic newsletters containing further dialogue and discussion growing out of the Declaration.

One feature I especially admire about these newsletters and I find it in Richard Mouw too is the attempt to relate to the ordinary layperson. Mouw questions the neglect of the ordinary layperson which he found in the unbalanced attention given "the decision makers" by a recent and well publicized Congress of the Laity. The impression is given, he says, that the "real" laity are politicians, football coaches, bank presidents, corporate executives, orchestra conductors and others of that ilk. Little attention is somehow given to the callings of the waitress, the water boy, the telephone operator, the third chair violinist, the clerk in the florist shop, or the parent whose primary task is managing a home.[37]

In 1965, Thomas Merton in his introduction to Philip Berrigan's *No More Strangers,* said that the renewal of the Church depended on the difficult task of "changing a clerical church back into a lay church," and by that Merton did not mean simply adding lots of lay people to the professional class in the Church. In words that would cheer some framers of the Chicago Declaration, Merton said the task of creating a fervent and profoundly enlightnened Christian laity was one involving "indispensable" efforts of the clergy. The task, for clergy and others, was to convey the fact that "ordinary life with its work, its insecurity and its inevitable sacrifices is for the Christian just as much a part of the 'sacred' realm as anything else, because, like everything else, it has been consecrated to God by the Incarnation, the Death and the Resurrection of Jesus Christ." The call of all, as Merton put it so well, is to "the world of everyday reality, of common duty, of work, of play, of sorrow and joy."[38] It is this call to holy worldliness that remains the great challenge as we look toward the future in 1984.

NOTES

1. This paper represents the written text of the presidential address of the 1984 annual meeting.

2. The basic statistical source on Catholics is the *Official Catholic Directory,* published by P.J. Kennedy and Sons.

3. Cf. Barbara Backwith, "Manpower/Womenpower in the Church: Who Will Be Tomorrow's Ministers?" *St. Anthony's Messenger* 86, No. 10 (March, 1979) 30-39.

4. Cf. Adam Nowotny, "The Church in Poland: a Faith Forged by History," *New Catholic World* 226, No. 1355 (September/October, 1983) 214-18.

5. Still, there are many problems and questions, as the author capably shows. Eugene Hemrick, "Report on Church Personnel: Developments in Ministry," *Origins* 13, No. 34 (February 2, 1984) 561-66.

6. Alfred McBride, "The Church in the Year 2000" *St. Anthony's Messenger* 91, No. 9 (February 1984) 33.

7. Donald J. Thorman, *The Emerging Layman: the Role of the Catholic Layman in America* (Garden City, N.Y.: Doubleday, 1962).

8. Published in numerous periodicals and in Russell Barta, ed., *Challenge to the Laity* (Huntington, Ind.: Our Sunday Visitor, 1980) 19-29.

9. "Constitution on the Church" (No. 31).

10. Cf. *Initiatives* (May, 1978; National Center for the Laity, 6363 N. Sheridan Road, Chicago, Ill. 60660).

11. Barta, ed., *op. cit.*

12. John Coleman also contributed; cf. *Commonweal* 105 (February 17, 1978) 108-16.

13. Joseph A. Komonchak "Clergy, Laity, and the Church's Mission in the World," *The Jurist* 41 (1981) 422-47. Many others are part of the discussion too in their columns (Andrew Greeley, George Higgins and others), reviews of *A Challenge to the Laity,* and contributions from varied sources of experience reported in the issues of *Initiatives*.

14. *Commonweal, op. cit.* 108.

15. Komonchak, *op. cit.* 447.

16. *Commonweal, op. cit.* 115.

17. *Ibid.*, 112.

18. *Ibid.*, 113.

19. For some evidence of this impact, cf. Andrew M. Greeley, *Catholic Schools in a Declining Church* (Kansas City: Sheed and Ward, 1976) 103-57.

20. *Commonweal, op. cit.* 108.

170

21. *Ibid.*, 114. For the Phoenix program cf. Stanley Karnow *Vietnam: a History* (New York: Viking, 1983) 601-02.

22. Francis X. Meehan, *A Contemporary Social Spirituality* (Maryknoll, N.Y.: Orbis, 1982) 9-10.

23. *Commonweal, op. cit.* 116. Coleman's examples of other countries: Korea, the Philippines, Brazil.

24. *Ibid.* 114.

25. *Ibid.* 115.

26. *Ibid.* 113.

27. John T. Noonan in *The Catholic Laity Today* (Chicago: FADICA, 1982) 52-53. He adds: "Intelligent, experienced, disciplined lay people would have a great deal to contribute [to this structural renewal] which they are not now permitted to do . . . there is still a division keeping us out."

28. *Commonweal, op. cit.* 116.

29. *The Documents of Vatican II* (Ed., Walter M. Abbott; New York: Association, 1966)12.

30. *Ibid.* 104.

31. Philip Scharper, "Renewal of the Church," *Commonweal* (June 8, 1962) 276-8.

32. Raymond E. Brown, "The Challenge of the Three Biblical Priesthoods," *Catholic Mind* 78 (March, 1980) 11-20.

33. Abbott, *op. cit.,* 105-106.

34. Brown, *op. cit.*

35. Richard J. Mouw, *Called to Holy Worldliness* (Philadelphia: Fortress, 1980).

36. *The Catholic Laity Today* (Chicago: FADICA, 1982).

37. Mouw, *op. cit.* 17.

38. Thomas Merton, Introduction to Philip Berrigan, *No More Strangers* (New York: Macmillan, 1965) xi-xx.

BECOMING PEACEMAKERS:
MORAL PERSPECTIVES FOR DWELLING IN PEACE

J. Milburn Thompson

Edward LeRoy Long, Jr. begins his book, *Peace Thinking in a Warring World*, with this declaration, "For too long we have thought about war and peace in terms of handling war as a problem rather than seeking peace as an achievement."[1] I think Long is correct about theology in general; I know he is right about this theologian. For years I have struggled, personally and before local audiences, with the question of the morality of war. I have given far too little attention to accomplishing peace. Professor Long goes on to forge a new approach to peace. This paper represents an attempt to walk with Long on some of the paths he has cleared.

Basically, Long contends that the first step toward peace is to change our way of thinking. We need to move from war thinking to peace thinking.[2] Long's brief analysis of "myth" or "paradigm" in his chapter discussing truth, helps us to understand his first and fundamental point.[3] Our perspective or horizon colors everything we see. We are now thoroughly immersed in a war mentality and mind-set. War resisters even make war on war.[4] We need to change our perspective; we need to think peace.

Theologically, this is hardly new. It is the Gospel call for *Metanoia*, specifically directed at peace. We need shalom vision, a peace perspective. Yet the importance of this shift in horizon can hardly be exaggerated. Peace thinking involves both an inner and an outer transformation, a spiritual and social conversion. I would like first to briefly explore the spiritual dimension of peace thinking, and second to develop some of the moral movements, the changes in attitudes, the virtues, necessary for transforming society toward shalom.

Shifting Our Vision

Henri Nouwen suggests that we live in the house of fear and that we will never create peace until we dwell in the house of Love.[5] Fear is a strange land for Christians, or at least it ought to be. We are the ones who know clearly that we have been loved into life by a God who is our Parent, our Father and Mother. "If this is how God loved us, then we should love one another . . . There is love, and whoever lives in love lives in God and God in him or her . . . There is no fear in love; perfect love drives out all fear." (1Jn 4:11, 16, 18) Our fear, then, is a sign of our lack of conversion, of our need for spiritual transformation.[6]

The fear that Nouwen refers to is not so much our atomic anxiety, fueled by movies like "The Day After" and "Testament." Rather it is our fear of the Russians, the fear that couples us to the false security of "Gods of Metal." Nouwen locates the source of this fear in our "illusion of control."

> In the final analysis, isn't the nuclear arms race built upon the conviction that we have to defend--at all cost-- what we have, what we do, and what we think? Isn't the possibility of destroying the earth, its civilizations, and its peoples a result of the conviction that we have to stay in control--at all cost--of our own destiny?[7]

The antidote to our fear, which germinates from control and competition, is love, which is born of prayer, service, and community. Love transforms us into a new self, a person of compassion.

> In and through Christ we receive a new identity that enables us to say, 'I am not the esteem I can collect through competition, but the love I have freely received from God' . . . This new identity, free from greed and desire for power, allows us to enter so fully and unconditionally into the sufferings of others that it becomes possible for us to heal the sick and call the dead to life."[8]

This spiritual transformation from fear to love, from competition to compassion, is the fertile inner field for Long's concept of peace thinking.[9]

Characteristics of Peace Perspective

This experience of God as Love and compassion is mediated to the world through persons and communities characterized by particular perspectives or postures, by certain moral attitudes and virtues.[10] Conversion to Christ, then, would seem to make one socially subversive. The movement from fear to love requires further change in our moral perspective and attitude. Long suggests six moral movements that might be indicative of peace thinking.[11] I would like to re-prioritize and further develop four of the characteristics of a peace perspective. Each of these movements in moral attitude should characterize transformed persons and contribute to the transformation of society.

(1) From Macho-Militarism to Feminist Humanism

First we need to disengage thoroughly from the macho-militarism that pervades our society and firmly embrace a feminist humanism. Militarism is at the root of war thinking. Machismo spawns militarism. Macho-militarism expresses a

philosophy of human nature along these lines: to be a man is what it means to
be human. To be a man is to be dominant, uncaring, rational, calculating,
selfish, hard and exploitive. This is harldly an expression of Christian
orthodoxy regarding human nature.

Tracing the roots and offshoots of macho-militarism in our society is a
consciousness-raising, but ultimately depressing, even disgusting, experience.
After the initial insight it is interesting to begin to make connections. Macho-
militarism accounts for the dehumanization of military training techniques.[12]
President Reagan, the cowboy, can be fruitfully viewed as a macho-militarist.
This would explain his response to Paul Nitze, the cold warrior he chose to be
our chief "negotiator" at the Intermediate Nuclear Force talks with the
Soviets, when Mr. Nitze suggested that our negotiating position was simply
unreasonable. "Well, Paul," said Reagan, "you just tell the Soviets that you are
working for one tough son of a bitch."[13] Macho-militarism may help us
understand our penchant for competitive, even violent, sports. "We are #1"
applies equally well to the superbowl race and the arms race. But soon these
interesting connections become depressing. We begin to see that militarism,
formed from machismo and fostering materialism, is the taproot of violence
and war. Alan Geyer notes the pervasive and sinister influence of militarism.

Militarism tyrannizes politics, sabotages diplomacy, plunders the
economy, corrupts science, subverts education, scorns the laws and
morals of warfare itself in the name of 'military necessity'--and does all
these things as a functional theology, even to the point of manipulating
established religions.[14]

Depression gives way to disgust when we recognize that uprooting this evil
is about as easy as uprooting the centuries old oak tree in our backyard.

Disgust might yield to despair were it not for the feminist movement.
Feminism gives us the tools to topple macho-militarism and replace it with a
more creative philosophy of human nature and human nurture. As I understand
it, feminism holds that being human is a balancing act; it is the task of integrat-
ing emotion and ideas, compassion and courage, love and power, creativity
and diligence within our characters and our social structures. This sort of
balance, integration, wholesomeness could be characterized by the Hebrew
concept of Shalom or the Chinese construct of Yin-Yang.[15] The connections
from this initial insight are also interesting, and they yield hope. Images of
Yahweh as Mother in Hebrew scripture can correct those of the Warrior
God.[16] Daniel Maguire has ably catalogued the perils of macho-masculinity in
terms of violence, hierarchy, abstractionism, consequentialism, and hatred of
women, and he contends that feminism is necessary to rejuvenate ethics, by,
for example, recovering affectivity, and linking private and public

morality.[17] A feminist perspective subverts our image of God, of ourselves, and of our world. We may dare to hope that it will grace us with peace.

(2) *From Deceit to Truth*

Secondly, we need to develop a critical consciousness oriented toward truth. War thinking is founded on deceit. Peace thinking requires the laying bare of lies, the exposing of false myths. Theology is well-suited for abetting this demythologizing process.

> Demythologizing has become the indispensable theological tool of peacemaking: it is the operation empowering the people of God to understand the stratagems by which inhuman speech violates the word of God. Those stratagems include a relentless outpouring of myths about weapons, strategy, security, enemies, history, and human nature--from government bureaucracies and adjunct think tanks and co-opted media and electronic theologians.[18]

This search for truth must be engaged on many levels, from our image of God, to our image of ourselves and the meaning of life, to our language and behavior. Having at least suggested how we might address some of the deeper levels, here we will concentrate on language, because our words communicate and shape our perspective.

George Orwell's novel, *1984*, with its "Doublethink" and "Newspeak" propoganda and its slogans, "War is Peace," "Freedom is Slavery," and his essays, such as, "Politics and the English Language" (1946), make us conscious of the manipulative power of language. Thomas Merton, writing with the concern of a poet, exposes the malaise of language with special reference to war in his essay, "War and the Crisis of Language" (1969). The context, of course, is the Vietnam War. Merton begins with general remarks on the sickness of language, the history of the problem, the contributions of religion and advertisement. Then he focuses on war. He begins with the now famous statement of a U.S. Major regarding the Vietnamese city, Ben Tre, "It became necessary to destroy the town in order to save it." Merton points out the sinister connotations of words like "pacification," "liberation," and "Free Zone" as they were used in Vietnam. Merton goes on to explain the logic of all war-makers, the logic of power.

> The Asian whose future we are about to decide is either a bad guy or good guy. If he is a bad guy, he obviously has to be killed. If he is a good guy, he is on our side and he ought to be ready to die for freedom. We will provide an opportunity for him to do so: we will kill him to prevent him falling under the tyranny of a demonic enemy.[19]

He concludes:

> The effect of this, of course, is a vicious cirle: it begins with a tacit admission that negotiation is meaningless, and it does in fact render the language of negotiation meaningless. War-makers in the twentieth century have gone far toward creating a political language so obscure, so apt for teachery, so ambiguous, that it can no longer serve as an instrument of peace; it is only good for war.[20]

The war mandarins have manipulated and murdered language allowing them to victimize truth and peace, and us.

Another monastic, Joan Chittister, a Benedictine Prioress, expresses similar sentiments regarding our preparation for nuclear war.

> As an educator, I am first of all confused and concerned by the language that masked the reality of the nuclear age. To distance ourselves from the unacceptable effects of annihilation, we use words with acceptable overtones or connotations. We talk about surgical strike or precisely targeted attacks, presumably on military installations, as if in a nuclear attack there could really be contained contamination. Americans, of course, feel strongly that anything 'surgical' is curative, humanitarian, of lofty purpose . . . Why don't we simply say attack and destroy and annihilate and contaminate; that is what we are really prepared to do.[21]

When our language masks the truth, we lose touch with reality. When our language expresses the logic of tautology, dialogue is impossible. When the Soviets withdrew from the negotiating table in the fall of 1983, they simply witnessed to the truth--negotiation had never begun.

In the midst of lies and false myths, telling the truth is essential for the development of peace thinking. "There is a largely unheralded connection between peace and truth which must be made firm if all the other themes in a theology of peace are to hold together."[22] On the level of language this involves a struggle analogous to the elimination of sexist terminology. For example, I have personally concluded that the military, whose purpose is war, no longer *serves* the best interests of society. Therefore, I try to avoid speaking of "military *service."* Perhaps our "Defense" Department ought to return to its original title, "War" Department.[23] As with sexist language many will contend that language is a trivial matter, but the issue is truth and reality, and, ultimately, peace. The critical passion for telling the truth must, of course, be exercised on many levels. Language is but an illustration of the larger task. Gandhi reminds us of the depth and importance of seeking the truth, and subtly warns us of the danger of self-righteousness.

> If we had attended the full vision of truth, we would no longer be mere
> seekers, but have become one with God, for Truth is God. But being
> only seekers, we prosecute our guest, and are conscious of our
> imperfection.[24]

We should witness to the truth with lives willing to suffer, not kill, for our
vision of reality.

(3) From American Justice to Biblical Justice

Thirdly, to paraphrase Paul VI, if we want peace, we must work for justice.
True peace is not merely the absence of conflict, but the presence of justice
and community.[25] St. John speaks of God as Love, Gandhi of God as Truth,
Nouwen of God's compassion. Stephen Mott claims that "Justice is a chief
attribute of God. God is the one who vindicates the oppressed and defends the
weak."[26] The justice that is to characterize our peace perspective is based in
our understanding of God.

Three recent writers, Mott, Long, and Daniel Maguire, are unanimous in
contrasting the retributive or preserving concept of justice that is characteristic of
American policy with the creative and subversive idea of justice found in
Christian revelation.[27] Long formulates the inadequate thinking about justice
that we take for granted. "Justice, as we most commonly think of it,
adjudicates claims, redresses grievances, protects the majority from socially
destructive behavior, and legitimizes means of defense against danger and
exploitation."[28] Biblical justice, in contrast, is primarly positive action on
behalf of the disadvantaged and marginal in society in order to redress
inequality and create an egalitarian community.[29] Daniel Maguire draws out
the contrast more fully and most consciously. American justice reacts to an
indiviudal offense in a supposedly impartial, but strictly punitive way. Law in
America effectively conserves the status quo through minimal involvement
and strictly limited jurisdiction. For example, U.S. courts have consistently
refused to look beyond the scope of property damage and national boundaries in the trials of nuclear weapons protestors. Judges refused to officially
acknowledge the humanistic purposes of the defendants or to hear their
appeals to international law. Biblical justice, on the other hand, is
unequivocally biased in favor of the poor and oppressed. Yahweh calls for
preemptive and effusive positive action to overturn inequality and create a
universal community. Whereas American justice is abstract, rationalistic,
cold, and calculating, oriented to winning,[30] biblical justice is characterized
by a feminine compassion that passionately seeks to subvert society in favor of

Shalom.[31] Biblical justice realizes that, "The equal provision of basic rights requires unequal response to unequal needs. Justice must be partial in order to be impartial."[32]

Christian revelation, then, provides us with a clear concept of justice, all the more attractive because it cuts through the myriad abstract philosophical distinctions that have clouded this idea. We are required to see the world from the perspective of the oppressed, to make the cause of the poor, which is God's cause, also our cause. This is truly subversive; it turns our world upside down, like the Magnificat suggests. "God brought down mighty kings from their thrones, and lifted up the lowly. God filled the hungery with good things, and sent the rich away with empty hands" (Lk 1:52-3). This means, for example, that, in our dealing with each other and other nations, we ought not be motivated by self interest, but by our interest in the oppressed. Such compassion is born of solidarity.[33] To accomplish justice, this compassion needs not be incarnated in concrete action, motivated not by a concern for effectiveness or productivity, but by a sense of gratitude, a knowledge that everything can be shared because all is gift.[34] This justice, born of compassion and birthing community, is the fertile womb of peace.

(4) From Indifference to Transforming Initiatives

The biblical command to do justice in society[35] gives rise to the fourth characteristic of our peace perspective. Long expresses it in terms of a movement from indifference to advocacy and action.[36] My inclination is to specify this characteristic of conversion in terms of a call to undertake transforming initiatives[37] or to develop catalytic strategies[38] for practicing justice and making peace.

A brief exploration of the sources of our indifference and apathy brings us back to fear and its brother, despair. James Forest suggests that fear's genuine function is to awaken us, like an alarm clock, to stir us to conscientious response to fearsome evil. "But alarm clocks are useful for only a few moments; they are not meant to ring throughout the day. When fear becomes a constant howling, instead of awakening us, it paralyzes and deadens us. Imagination and conscience, rather than being stirred to life, are stunted."[39] As we have seen, God's transforming love can heal our hearts, fill us with hope and vision, empower us to be agents of reconciliation who create community and subvert society. Fear drives us to despair and powerlessness.[40] Our satiety leaves us listless and selfish. Love, however, invokes hope and gratitude, solidarity and altruism, action and joy.

Our conversion to peace thinking, then, prods us to become peacemakers. But what are we to do? How do we make peace? I do not, of course, pretend to have a definitive answer to this question, nor do I want to imply that there is any one way to be a peacemaker.[41] I do want to suggest that one might do two things. First, gather together with other folks. Second, take a transforming initiative.

Besides being an imperative of the Gospel, forming community is simple common sense if one is serious about social change.[42] Among other advantages, community contributes significantly to forming a peace perspective and to transforming society. There are, of course, many kinds of community. Because community is a very familiar notion among Christians, though too significant not to at least mention here, I will leave the subject after one further remark. The movement of transformed persons into community should continue through the community toward the transformation of society. That is, social change is not an option for the church. Justice and peace are constitutive of Gospel mission.

I owe the idea of transforming initiatives to Dr. Glen Stassen. In his small group study guide, *The Journey into Peacemaking*, Stassen ingeniously interprets Paul's letter to the Romans in terms of the question of peace. He perceives Paul's admonitions in Chapter 12 as a call to engage in "transforming initiatives" against evil and on behalf of good. That is, Paul, encourages Christians to do something surprising and imaginative, to take a creative risk in the interests of transforming our personal enemy or an oppressive social situation.[43] Although their words do not quite convey the excitement of Stassen for the idea, the U.S. Bishops seem to call for transforming initiatives when they write, "While we do not advocate a policy of unilateral disarmament, we believe the urgent need for control of the arms race requires a willingness for each side to take some *first steps*. . .Certain risks are required today to help free the world from the bondage to nuclear deterrence and the risk of nuclear war."[44] Because of our love and compassion which leaves us fearless, and because of our vision of justice and reconciliation, we are able to make the first move, take a risk, be imaginative. Such initiatives can transform and subvert a situation.

When I think of transforming social initiatives, Gandhi comes immediately to mind. Remember his dramatic march to the sea where he galvanized the Indian revolution by the simple act of making salt. I think of Dorothy Day and the Catholic Worker community picnicking in Central Park during civil defense drills. I think of Anwar Sadat's journey to Jerusalem, Jesse Jackson's trip to Syria, and Randall Forsberg's idea of a nuclear freeze. On a more personal level, I remember visiting a storefront Mennonite meeting on a Wednesday evening. The previous week a drunken driver had smashed into one of the brothers' cars that was parked out front, causing damage to several other cars belonging to members of the meeting through a chain reaction. Their discussion that evening focused on developing a strategy for ministering to the drunken driver and his family. They decided to send a couple to the family's house on the pretense of discussing insurance claims, but with the not-so-hidden agenda of ascertaining if they could be of service to a possible alcoholic and/or his wife and children. It was a beautiful transforming initiative.

Alan Geyer outlines a more political version of transforming initiatives in terms of "catalytic strategies."[45] He suggests guidelines for making creative political initiatives and points to current examples. Paul Walker in his booklet, *Seizing the Initiative: First Steps to Disarmament*, outlines a similar strategy.[46] What if the U.S. announced a unilateral nuclear freeze and invited the U.S.S.R. to respond in kind? What if we unilaterally adopted a comprehensive test ban? What if we submerged ourselves in the efforts of the Contadora group to achieve at least a cease fire in Central America? What sort of creative and imaginative actions might churches and other communities do to move our government toward transforming initiatives? Such are the questions born of peace perspective.

Conclusion

The U.S. Catholic bishops have urged theologians to develop a theology of peace.[47] They add their voice to a growing chorus.[48] Theologians are beginning to respond. This paper has attempted to record the early rumblings of what I hope will be a landslide of creative literature from theologians on the subject of peace. According to theology, Shalom requires a transformation, a revolution of perspective, that propels one into becoming a creative social subversive. This peace conversion is rooted in the movement from fear and competition to love and compassion, and it is characterized by at least four further movements: From macho-militarism to feminist humanism, from deceit to truth, from American justice to biblical justice, and from indifference to transforming initiatives. This infant peace theology will join, and relate to, the already extensive and still developing corpus on the morality of war. Perhaps the urgency of living in an end-time requires that, for the moment, we leave the study of war and devote ourselves to exploring and enacting peace.

NOTES

1. Edward LeRoy Long, *Peace Thinking in a Warring World: An Urgent Call for a New Approach to Peace* (Philadelphia: Westminster, 1983) 9.

2. Long, Chap. 1.

3. *Ibid.* 63-73.

4. *Ibid.* 23-25.

5. Henri Nouwen, "The Spirituality of Peacemaking," presentation in Oct., 1983, in New Britain, CT as part of a nationwide tour on this topic.

6. Jim Wallis says, "The root cause of war is our lack of conversion, our utter lack of love," in "The work of Prayer: The Heart of Christian Witness," in his *Waging Peace* (San Francisco: Harper & Row, 1982) 197.

7. Henri Nouwen, "Letting Go of All Things: Prayer as Action," in Jim Wallis, ed., *Waging Peace.*

8. Donald McNeill, Douglass Morrison, and Henri Nouwen, *Compassion* (Garden City, N.Y.: Doubleday, 1982) 21.

9. James Douglass ably explores this spiritual transformation in his *Resistance and Contemplation* (Garden City, N.Y.: Doubleday, 1972) and *Lightning East to West* (New York: Crossroad, 1983).

10. See Long 90-93 on compassion.

11. Long's movements are from retribution to creative justice, from repression to ordered fredom, from misunderstanding to truth, from suspicion to trust, from hostility to composure and compassion, and from indifference to advocacy and action. My debt to Long's work is enormous.

12. See Helen Michalowski, "The Army Will Make a Man Out of You," *WIN* 16 (March 1, 1980) 6-12; U.S. Catholic Bishops, *The Challenge of Peace* (NCCB, 1983) Nos. 313-15.

13. Strobe Talbott, "Behind Closed Doors," *Time* (Dec. 5, 1983) 32.

14. Geyer, *The Idea of Disarmament* 207. Geyer connects militarism with anti-humanism, but not with machismo.

15. See James Douglass, *Resistance and Contemplation*, for a very provocative discussion of Yin-Yang and liberation.

16. I am indebted to an unpublished paper by Jean Myers, then a student at Southern Baptist Theological Seminary, titled, "Peacemaking and the Church: The Feminization of God," 1982. Ms. Myers refers to Leonard Swidler, *Biblical Affirmations of Women* (Philadelphia: Westminster, 1979) 30-34, and Phyllis Trible, *God and the Rhetoric of Sexuality* (Philadelphia: Fortress, 1978) 40-51.

17. Daniel Maguire, "The Feminization of God and Ethics," *The Annual of the Society of Christian Ethics*, 1982, and "The Feminist Turn in Ethics," *Horizons* 10 (1983) 344-47. Long is also concerned with the continuity between private and public morality throughout his *Peace Thinking in a Warring World*.

18. Geyer 194-5.

19. Thomas Merton, "War and the Crisis of Language" in *The Nonviolent Alternative* (New York: Farrar, Straus, Giroux, 1971) 239.

20. *Ibid* 244.

21. Joan Chittister, in Jan Wallis, ed., *Peacemakers* (San Francisco: Harper & Row, 1983) 42. See also Otto Friedrich, "Of Words That Ravage, Pillage, Spoil," *Time* (Jan. 9, 1984) 76, and June Jordan, "The Language of the Powerful Inprisons the Powerless," *Hartford Courant* (May 9, 1984) op-ed page.

22. Geyer 194.

23. Long 14.

24. M. Gandhi, *ALL Men Are Brothers* (New York: UNESCO, 1958) 61.

25. Martin Luther King, Jr., *Stride Toward Freedom* (San Francisco: Harper & Row, 1958) 24.

26. Stephen Charles Mott, *Biblical Ethics and Social Change* (New York: Oxford U., 1982) 60.

27. Mott, p. 65, correctly links American justice with the concept of justice in Aristotle.

28. Long 31.

29. Mott 63, 65, 66.

30. Along these lines a Connecticut lawyer, Kathleen Stingle, has reflected on the insights found in Carol Gilligan's, *In a Different Voice*, and suggested that women (and others) might practice law differently, seeking to resolve conflict and reconcile persons, rather than win the case. "Lawyering in a Different Voice," *Hartford Courant*, (May 20, 1984) D1, 4.

31. Daniel Maguire, "The Primacy of Justice in Moral Theology," *Horizons* 10 (Spring, 1983) 74-80.

32. Mott 66. See also Long 34-40.

33. Long 89-92.

34. McNeill, Morrison, and Nouwen 126-9.

35. Mott 77-79.

36. Long, Chap. 6.

37. Glen Stassen, *The Journey into Peacemaking* (Memphis, Tenn.: Brotherhood Commission, SBC, 1983), chaps. 5, 6, 9. Stassen draws on the work of Robert Fisher.

38. Geyer 179. Geyer draws on the work of Charles Osgood.

39. James Forest, "Astonishing Hope: Good News in a Time of Despair," in Jim Wallis, ed., *Waging Peace* 183.

40. For a more political analysis of powerlessness see Geyer 142-5.

41. Long examines several alternatives and pleads for a recognition of the legitimate diversity of responses in Chap. 6 of *Peace Thinking*. Geyer examines "Scenarios of Disarmament," in Chap. 7 of *The Idea of Disarmament*. Ronald Sider and Richard Taylor, *Nuclear Holocaust and Christian Faith* (Ramsey, N.J.: Paulist, 1982) explore a wide variety of peacemaking responses in Parts III, IV, and Appendices.

42. See Mott. Chap. 7. Stassen's emphasis on peacemaking groups is one way of gathering into peacemaking communities either within or outside of local churches.

43. Stassen, Chaps. 5 and 6.

44. U.S. Catholic Bishops, *The Challenge of Peace* No. 205. [Emphasis mine]

45. Geyer 171ff.

46. Paul Walker, *Seizing the Initiative* (Nyack, N.Y.: FOR, 1983).

47. Bishops, Nos. 304, 25, 26.

48. See Thomas Shannon, *What Are They Saying About Peace and War?* (Ramsey, N.J.: Paulist, 1983) Chap. 5.

IV.
NEW VISIONS AND CHALLENGES

A SPIRITUALITY FOR THE FUTURE:
SITUATIONAL AND SYSTEMATIC

James C. Bacik

My approach to the question of a spirituality for the future, while drawing upon my pastoral experience as a spiritual director and counselor, also takes its dominant analytical perspective from the theology of the late Karl Rahner who, as David Tracy has suggested, is one of the four or five most influential theologians in the history of Catholic theology.

The word "sprituality" in the title points to the depth dimension of the full range of human experience; and it suggests a call from a transcendent source to achieve full self-actualization and active involvement in helping to create the community of love. The future, which is essentially unknowable, is nevertheless subject to a descriptive analysis in which we attempt to identify probable trends, as well as subject to a prescriptive analysis in which we dream about how we would like things to be from the perspective of the kingdom or reign of God proclaimed by Jesus. With these points in mind, let me recount the stories of two people, both happily willing to have their experiences shared in order to help others, who represent different directions for spirituality for the future.

I

A woman came to me seeking guidance in deepening her spiritual life. She felt she was at a standstill and had not made much progress lately. The real obstacle to further growth in her estimation was her failure to adhere to a systematic approach. She needed more structure, a tighter schedule, a definite plan, clear directions. There was a certain plausibility to her analysis and so I agreed to help her work out a more organized procedure for making progress in the spiritual life. We then discussed the advantages of a daily schedule which would include meditation, spiritual reading and formal prayer as well as regular exercise, proper diet and sufficient sleep. We also spoke of the importance of the scriptures and liturgy, the value of regular self-examination, and the benefits of periodic days of recollection. As a way of getting started and sorting out what was valuable and possible for her in this traditional wisdom, she decided to set aside 20 minutes each day for reflection. During this period she would try to put herself in the presence of the Lord and plan how to incorporate into her day some of the other components of an ideal spiritual regimen. This struck me as a reasonable beginning point and it seemed a solid plan was in place. We prayed together and agreed to meet monthly to discuss her progress and to refine the general approach.

However, something happened on her way to spiritual perfection. The plan didn't work. It produced more guilt feelings and self doubt than it did progress and growth. Often she was too busy or simply forgot and the 20 minutes of reflection did not happen. On these days, for reasons she did not understand, it became more difficult to control her diet and to get the motivation for her daily exercise. She did do some spiritual reading but it seemed unfocused. She found it harder to concetrate in formal prayer situations including Mass and attributed this to a vague feeling of having let God down or perhaps herself. As I listened to this report, my intuition told me that a solution would not be found in fine tuning the general plan. Rather, the regimen itself had become part of the problem. The effort to systematize the spiritual journey had led to failure and consequent guilt. Further efforts to impose a set routine would likely lead to the same results.

What, then, was to be done? How could her spiritual journey be resumed in a healthy and constructive way? The woman's own experience provided the clue to a general direction. On one occasion, a beautiful sunny day just naturally put her in a reflective mood. She felt the presence of the Spirit and a prayer of gratitude flowed from her heart. She decided to get some exercise outside and the whole day went well. On another occasion, she was celebrating the anniversary of her mother's death and spontaneously fell into a brief period of deep prayer in which she found her grieving surrounded by a mysterious comforting presence. It seemed quite natural at that point to pick up her Bible and read a few familiar passages. These experiences suggested a radically different method for achieving spiritual growth. Instead of placing a new regimen on top of her ordinary routine, she should allow her daily experience to guide the process. Thus, rather than demand 20 minutes a day in formal reflection, she should try to be more attuned to the happenings throughout the day which could lead to a few minutes of heightened awareness of the abiding presence of the Lord. These brief moments might occasionally lead to extended periods of meditation, but for the most part they should be prized as times of genuine prayer with a power to illumine the rest of the daily routine. The trick would be to increase the number of situations already present in life which actually trigger the moments of prayerful reflection. As a matter of fact, the woman realized in the course of the conversation that this already occurred naturally and without much thought in her daily life. For example, she was in the habit of using time spent waiting in lines for a bit of conversation with God about the virtue of patience. Reflection on this particular methodology quickly revealed many other catalysts for brief prayer scattered throughout her busy day. When I articulated and affirmed much of what she was already doing, the woman experienced a great sense of liberation and spoke of a renewed energy for getting other parts of her spiritual life together. Once the burden of an imposed regimine was abandoned, her spiritual journey continued to be lighter and more productive.

This woman's story is typical of an increasing number of serious-minded individuals today who find a systematic regimen to be more burdensome than helpful. The pattern is familiar: busyness causes neglect of the spiritual exercises which produces guilt which prompts giving up. Rather than abandoning the quest or living with constant guilt, it seems better to strive for an integrated spiritual life which is more spontaneous and responsive to the actual rhythm of one's life. We might call this approach a "situational spirituality" since it is an effort to find meaning and depth in the real life situation which already constitute our existence. For example, we could imagine prayer being induced by a wide variety of daily events: becoming aware of increased tension prompts a few minutes of relaxing meditation; driving the car provides a chance for prayerful reflection on the day's activities; unexpectedly running into an old friend issues in a prayer of gratitude; failing to meet a responsibility leads to a longing for forgiveness from the merciful One; glancing into the starry night evokes a word of praise; doing routine household chores forms a backdrop for prayer; feeling anxious or depressed produces a petition for peace and strength; experiencing joy brings a spontaneous thank you addressed to the Source of all gifts. Busy persons might not have 20 minutes for formal prayer, but they do have more than enough experiences thoughout a day which can generate a brief moment of genuine prayer.

If we extend this analysis of a situation prayer life to other areas, similar catalysts for development appear: boredom with TV leads to a ½ hour of spiritual reading; attendance at Mass suggests a more careful reading of Scripture; sensing burn-out prompts a couple of days of retreat; dissatisfaction with one's physical condition leads to more regular exercise and a better diet; stimulating conversation flows into journal writing. The point is to allow real life to suggest the frequency and style of one's program for spiritual growth. In doing this it is vital to avoid feeling guilty or inferior because one is not doing it the traditional way or with the same frequency as others.

There are, of course, limitations and even dangers in following such a methodology. It can degenerate into aimless drifting while we passively await clear-cut triggers to move us to action. It can be used to follow our own whims while neglecting the traditional wisdom. On the other hand, a situational sprituality has the great advantage of actually being workable for many busy people.

What theological presuppositions are involved in this approach to growth in the spiritual life? It begins with a Rahnerian theological anthropology in which we see ourselves as self-transcendent creatures oriented to an inexhaustible goal which is well termed "mystery". Marcel's distinction between a problem which is essentially solvable and mystery which always exceeds our grasp is helpful in pointing out the ultimately incomprehensible character of this goal. It is by reflecting on our self-transcendence that we come to know what spirit is. We possess an inner dynamism which presses beyond all limitations and which seeks a fulfillment which exceeds all current capabilities. We are also able to step back from our world, distance ourselves from particular realities and, as Aquinas said, accomplish a return to self. Thus, the spiritual life involves spontaneity, creativity and openness. It requires a response to the call of the Mystery which does new and surprising things on our behalf.

Another premise is found in the theology of grace developed by the Greek Fathers and retrieved by Rahner and others in our own time. Grace is first of all God's gratuitous self-communication which divinizes all human beings. This uncreated grace produces in us the supernatural existential which give us a positive orientation to the Mystery. Since the Mystery has not remained remote but has drawn near in self-giving love, we can properly call it "gracious Mystery". We live and move in one graced world enveloped by God's love. Thus, the whole of life in all of its dimensions and aspects becomes the catalyst for spiritual growth.

Uncreated grace produces in all human beings a transcendental or universal revelation which modifies our consciousness and produces the call of conscience. Our positive response to this call amounts to a salvific faith. Every created reality can mediate this call. All things are potentially revelatory; but some things have a greater potential to touch the depths of our being. Thus, the spiritual life requires us to be on alert for what Peter Berger calls "the signals of transcendence".

Finally, a situational spirituality is grounded in the conviction that the experience of self is the experience of God. Genuine self-growth brings us closer to our ultimate goal. The process of self-actualization at its best expands our openness to the Mystery. In all our knowing and loving we are supported by a friendly power which is finally the source of all our progress. Thus, in the spiritual life, we are called to trust the process and to achieve a healthy self-acceptance and to mine the riches of our various situations.

II.

A second story brings out a different aspect of a spirituality of the future. It is the story of a man who comes explicitly seeking some sort of spiritual guidance. He has worked hard all his life and has risen to a high position in his corporation. He is responsible for ventures which involve large sums of money and has over 50 people working under him. He often takes work home with him. After cocktails and dinner he works for a while and then usually falls asleep while watching TV. His wife complains about their lack of communication and his children are unhappy that he doesn't take more interest in their activities. He was at one time quite active in his parish but now does not have any time for that, though he still attends Mass regularly. He used to be very athletic but now takes very little exercise and has put on too much weight. His problem now, he says, is this vague anxiety that he feels. He is getting bored with work, often feels uncomfortable in social settings, cannot sleep well at night and feels guilty over his family relationships. He has never sought counsel before and will not go to a psychiatrist. However, he is open to any advice that I have to offer. Obviously, this man's problems can be analyzed from a psychological viewpoint, but I find it helpful to set them first in a larger context suggested by the cultural analysis of Robert Bellah (cf. "Religion and the University: the Crisis of Unbelief" by Robert Bellah in *Religion and Intellectual Life* Vol. 1, No. 2, pp. 13ff). He describes a "utilitarian individualism" which characterizes our contemporary culture. It grows out of the Enlightenment ideal which celebrates the autonomy of the individual over against institutional authority and the triumph of reason over tradition. It has roots in the social thought of Hobbes and Locke who saw society as an association of contracting individuals who all had their own distinct purposes and private goals. It is fed by the rise of science and the industrial revolution and emphasizes the importance of economic self interest. These factors culminate in the "modern manager type" who specializes in finding effective means to achieve economic success. He does this without consideration of common ends, larger projects, and other more personal goals. This description fits the man in our example. He is suffering the consequences of living out an ideal which is celebrated in our culture but which leaves out much that is truly human such as commitment to the common good and a sense of sharing in an effort to build up the community of justice and love.

My intuitive reaction to this man's story was to take out a piece of paper and to write down for him a daily regimen. Work limited to 8 hours; no work can be brought home. Exercise each day: we agreed on a ½ hour workout during his lunch time. Meditate 15 minutes a day: I taught him a mantra type meditation and suggested he add a few more minutes during his busy work day. Diet must be controlled; I suggested he seek advice on the details. Sleep at least 7 hours a night; try to avoid napping after dinner. We went on to talk about his dissatisfaction with his job. I suggested he think through the possibility of bringing a more humane approach to his job. I also gave him a copy of Richard Boles *"What Color Is Your Parachute?"* as a way of beginning to reflect on the possibility of seeking other employment. We agreed that he would systematically build in time for his family. He decided to take a walk with his wife every night after dinner and to save Saturday for activities with his children. Finally, I made a strong plea that he and his wife get involved again in their parish church by joining the social justice committee and working together on projects designed to help those in need. Those of us who counsel can always point to our failures. In this case, the therapy proved to be quite successful and this man is now living a much happier and productive life.

Now we can ask what kind of theology stands behind this very directive approach. It begins again with a theological anthropology which recognizes that self-transcendent persons are always a product of previous free acts. We humans remain knowers and lovers but these spiritual activities are conditioned by our personal history. The questing impulse can be blunted and the ability to love repressed. Human development is not an automatic process. We are subject to concupiscence and are unable to integrate all aspects of our personality into our fundametal option for good. Thus, a helpful program of spiritual growth requires intelligent and systematic discipline which challenges the destructive tendencies which accumulate in the human heart.

Human beings are a product not only of their free acts but also of the society in which they live. We are conditioned by our social, economic and political situation. Our world is co-determined by both grace and sin. Evil becomes embedded in institutions. Cultural symbols and societal values are ingested and structure our imagination and influence our behavior. False consciousness is possible in which we fail to notice the contradictions built into society. It is easy for the dominant group in the culture to fail to understand the plight of those on the margins. Theology can be co-opted by the culture and become excessively private and individualistic.

Since systemic evil or social sin is so powerful, an effective spiritual program must try to raise consciousness and give individuals a systematic way of critiquing their culture from the vantage point of the Gospel.

Finally, it should be noted that God's self-communication seeks visibility. Transcendental revelation strains toward the categorical. We human beings need objectifications to express and stir up our deep relationship with the Gracious Mystery. The experince of self which is the experience of God is enriched by symbol, myth, and ritual. Scripture, creed, dogma and liturgy point to the Inexhaustible One and remind us of what we really are. Jesus Christ is the human face of the Father and the exemplar of full humanity. The "dangerous memory of Jesus" as Johannes Metz reminds us, provides us with motive and means for unmasking the contradictions and injustice in our society. A healthy spirituality needs these various objectifications in order to maintain energy and focus in the struggle against social sin.

In sum, the theological premises behind the more systematic approach to spirituality are drawn from the liberationist criticism of transcendental Thomism which is in danger of neglecting institutional and social factors. A Rahnerian theologian who wants to do spiritual direction must keep in mind Metz's criticism of his mentor. The man in the example was so taken over by the values of utilitarian individualism that he needed a very structured systematic program to free himself from these cultural constraints and to open himself to the liberating power of the Gospel.

From a theological standpoint there is no clear consensus on how to achieve a synthesis which would subsume the valid insights of liberal theology with its existential themes and openness to the culture and the legitimate concerns of liberation theology with its refocused reading of the Scriptures and its societal criticism. The two approaches stand in dialectical tension and can mutually enrich one another. A spirituality of the future which is faithful to this theological reality will necessarily be both situational and systematic.

A dialectical spirituality is ultimately rooted in the fact that we are finite creatures who are oriented to the Infinite. We have infinite longings and finite capabilities. A tension is built into the very center of our being as we are called to accept freely our dependent status. Karl Rahner well described the human person as "midpoint suspended between the world and God, between time and eternity, and this boundary line is the point of his definition and his destiny. . ." (*Spirit in the World,* p. 407). The "self" that we are then appears as a field in which a whole variety of diverse and apparently opposed tendencies contend. All spiritualities of the future must reflect this essential insight into the dialectical character of human existence.

From this perspective, we all need the courage to accept our creaturely status, the wisdom to know which side of the various dialectical pairs (for example, situational or systematic) to work on and the honesty to admit when we are in danger of becoming one-sided. This is the way toward an authentic spirituality which is properly open to the incomprehensible but gracious future which we call 'God'.

FEMINIST MOVEMENT:
THE ETHICS OF REVOLUTION

Frances M. Leap

The longest revolution which our world will know may well turn out to be the slow progress of the vision we presently call feminism.[1] The feminist vision is indeed a blueprint for revolution in our society today, but it is a dancing revolution, and one with a maintenance plan. When feminism has its way it will transform the fabric of our lives and relatedness, our definition of God, of good, of human, of love. Nor is it simply a revolution of new answers, but an earthquake of new questions, new categories, new assumptions. The possibilities of feminist movement are cosmic. But this dancing revolution is, at its heart, a moral revolution. It is upon the choreography of that daily human enterprise--ethics--that feminist movement has its most profound effects.

Discovering and embodying the meaning of the feminist vision in our lives is work which will continue indefinitely. But it is a process which must be articulated now. Change does not occur until we begin to act. Until lions write books, the great white hunters will continue to win in the stories.

I. Feminism and the Ethical Enterprise

As we examine the impact of feminism upon ethics, we must attend for a moment to the vision itself. While keenly aware of the diversity of feminist thought, the perspective of this essay is perhaps best described by the term religious feminism. This simply means that the initiative and root metaphor for understanding feminist movement lies in an experience, Presence. The word Presence is very rich in its Latin root--*praesentia*--having connotations there of efficacy, influence, power, propitiousness. Here the word is used to speak of that which cannot be defined, of experience which is more primary than reflection and cannot be recaptured completely by reflection. But the experience of Presence is definitive, efficacious, powerful, propitious. Once touched by Presence we cannot turn away and remain true to ourselves. The word, then, speaks of the divine, and of experience which is most fundamentally and transcendently human.

Primarily, feminism is movement. It is presently perceived as the movement of revolution with all the upheaval that word connotes. But long after the revolution has been won feminists will continue to move. Though at times the movement seems compelled, in truth, the movement of feminism is more similar to the power and openness of dance. Sometimes feminism is a wild tarantalla, amazing everyone, including the dancers, with its energy and effectiveness,[2] while in the same moment it is a funeral march, mourning, remembering, enshrining. It can move with the controlled dignity of classical ballet, yet shattering convention with the expressionism of interpretive dance.

Reverence and Rage

The ever dancing movement has its genesis in a two-fold source: the twin responses of reverence and rage. Feminists move in response to a Presence which is emerging and yet still painfully absent in our lives and in lives we share.[3] Reverence is conceived of the possibilities offered and embodied by this Presence. This is the primary experience of value; the value of persons and of creation in profound interrelation.[4] Rage is born as this experience of value and its possibilities, offered and embodied within the Presence, are denied, trampled, and murdered. What this Presence offers is transformation of earth as well as heaven. It is in some sense a calling back to our roots, back to the possibilities of a lost alternative, but it is also a call forward toward the embodiment of new possibilities. People have been dancing their reverence and rage about this Presence since the first glimmers of personhood began to shine in human hearts, for without this primary experience of value we cannot begin to speak of what is human and what is good.

This Presence brings the potential for mutuality in relationships among men and women, and in their relationship with creation. It offers the simplicity of process in place of the gods of technology and progress. It speaks of well-fed, well-cared for children world-wide and of an end to starvation and oppression.

Experiencing the embodiment of this Presence is an irresistible invitation to the feminist dance born of reverence. But concomitant with this is the painful realization that the Presence has not yet come in its fullness and moreover that systems and persons are actually fighting against its emergence and embodiment. An experience of rage and righteous anger is the other form of the irresistible lure into feminist movement.

Alienation is the major reality which inhibits the emergence of the Presence. Feminist movement is called this because the alienation of male from female--sexism--is the oldest and deepest form of alienation in our culture. Rosemary Radford Ruether has pointed out that sexual symbolism is foundational to the perception of order and relationship that has been built up in cultures. The psychic organization of consciousness, the dualistic views of the self and the world, the hierarchical concept of society, the relation of humanity and nature, and of God and creation--all these relationships of alienation have been modeled on sexual dualism.[5] Therefore the transforming possibilities of the Presence seem to attack the basic stereotypes of authority and identity, and are perceived as blueprint for revolution in our society of patriarchy, which is systematized alienation.

Feminist movement though is not for women only. It is based on a recovery of "the other," the female, the oppressed possibility of our history. It is therefore a call for the liberation of men too. Feminism is not simply a women's movement, nor even a human movement; it is a cosmic movement of all creation, struggling for freedom, for fullness.

The two-fold response of reverence and rage serves as the foundation of feminist ethics.[6] But more than simply changing how we make an ethical decision, feminist ethics offers a new foundation for why we engage in ethics. It does not seek to answer a question of duty or coercion -- "What must I do?" "What ought I to do?" Rather, it arises from an experience of the Presence and asks "What can I do?" "What shall I do to participate?" Feminist ethics is the daily endeavor to embody the Presence in reality. The simplicity of that statement should not deceive us, however, into thinking that feminists readily agree upon how to do that, or just what it means.

Feminist Maintenance Plan

Often revolution is perceived as a violent, bloody means to a better and peaceful end. Feminist ethics however, does not tolerate a distinction between means and ends. It recognizes that how the change is brought about is as important as the change itself. Means not only shape the ends but in a very real sense the ends and the means are one. Feminists recognize that the only way to make the vision reality, to bring the presence to fullness, is to embody the Presence in every moment. If we live as though the revolution has been won, then in some way the revolution will in reality have been won.

At the heart of the feminist maintenance plan is an experience of wholeness. The vision is not a great new idea, but a presence, an embodied reality, an encounter which transcends the categories of alienating dualism, especially the mind/body split. The unfortunate severing of mind and body has affected every area of life, and has served as fuel for the fires of misogyny. Restoring wholeness and unity to life, feminist ethics finds it necessary to overcome the dualisms and affirm negative aspects as part of whole joyful, human existence. Beverly Harrison indicated that the dimension of our western intellectual heritage most damaged by the mind/body split has been our moral theology and moral philosophy.[7] It is this dualism which allows many Christian ethicists to presume that "disinterestedness" and "detachment" are necessary preconditions for responsible moral action. "In the dominant ethical tradition, moral rationality is disembodied rationality.,"[8]

Feminist ethics cannot but reject this disembodied rationality as the means to a disembodied end. The total destruction of the village of Ben Tre during the Viet Nam war could never by "rationalized" for feminist ethics by "We had to destroy this village in order to save it," as it was for a colonel at the scene.[9] Violent means beget violent ends.

196

The wholism of feminist ethics leads to a rejection of other dualisms, notably the personal/political split. This paralyzing dichotomy has enabled traditionally "masculine" virtues to become moral norms for public and political life, while the traditionally "feminine" virtues have not ventured beyond the threshold of home and hearth. Feminist ethics would heal this split. The personal is the political. Faithfulness to the maintenance plan requires that we affirm some of the traditionally feminine virtues as public policy.

Feminism does not breed a personalistic ethic but rather an ethic of personalism. Feminists cannot afford to be personalistic in a narrow vision which fails to take account of the global proportions and interrelations of the problem. Feminist revolution critiques and subverts systems. But feminists recognize that change occurs only through persons. Intrinsic to the maintenance plan is this sweet equity. We cannot bring in contractors to engineer this revolution for us. The feminist vision is the work of feminist visionaries who labor in reconstruction of reality at every moment.

Education by Diversity

Recognizing the structural nature of the revolution has improved feminist eyesight, enabling it to recognize the disguises of patriarchal power. Imperialism, racism, militarism, classism, sexism are some of the many forms which the patriarchal chimera assumes in its work of alienation and oppression.

The feminist movement is not monolithic. Despite a shared history of sexism, women do not move with a single story. We battle the chimera on many fronts. As feminists, we value this diversity and know it to be what keeps the revolution a dance and not a goose step. But our movement must be of one spirit in our willingness to hear the cries of oppression from wherever they arise in whatever form they arise. We must be of one integrity in the struggle to transform alienation.

Feminist ethics must be at home with plurality and educated by diversity. This is especially important for white feminists of North America, for there is great danger that like white males we will make our culture normative. We must remove leisure-encrusted blinders of wealth and security to see that our vision is cosmic. The Presence tenderly embraces the struggle in many forms. The words which Domitila Barrios de Chungara, a lower class woman of Bolivia, spoke to the International Women's Tribunal of the United Nations come to mind:

> They couldn't see all those things. They couldn't see the suffering of my people, they couldn't see how our compañeros are vomiting their lungs bit by bit, in pools of blood. They didn't see how underfed our children are. And, of course, they didn't know, as we do, what it's like to

get up at four in the morning and go to bed at eleven or twelve at night, just to be able to get all the housework done, because of the lousy conditions we live in.[10]

Presence and Prophecy

Intrinsic to feminist ethics is what Mary Daly has called a "new naming in the realm of morality."[11] This means not only renaming some traditional values for what they really are, but also offering a transvaluation of value, a redefinition of value itself in light of the feminist vision. As humans we communicate our thoughts, emotions, experiences through language, yet traditional ethical systems have had no words to convey the experience of women and other alienated groups. A primary task of feminist ethics is to give voice to these experiences of over half the human race. This is very much a creation event, as we cease to define our lives through categories developed largely by white males in positions of power. As Eleanor Haney points out, any reluctance to challenge the accumulation of "inspired" traditional wisdom is quickly overcome by recalling the less than inspired consequences of this wisdom for those who are "other." The feminist vision calls us to take seriously our own experience and insight and take responsibility for acting upon them.

This process of new naming is rooted in the experience of reverence and rage. It means being attentive to the emerging Presence in our lives, and recognizing her embodiment as well as her murder. It means speaking words of comfort as well as words of anger. In this way feminist ethics will redefine Good (and this leads us to new ideas of God). Because this transvaluation draws its energy from both reverence and rage, feminists must be ready to risk not only emodiment of the Presence in their own lives, but risk the challenge to inspired tradition which has done so much to murder her Presence. Feminist ethics becomes an ethics of prophecy in this respect, "speaking for" the oppressed, the murdered possibilities of her Presence.

One of the primary examples of the new naming as prophecy is to be found in the feminist critique of self-sacrifice as the central moral virtue in Christian life.[12] Agape has been traditionally defined with a heavy emphasis on other-regard and self-sacrifice.

Feminists, decrying its oppressive use when narrowly defined as one-sided self-sacrifice, are new-naming agape as mutuality. Mutuality implies that all parties in a loving relationship display both active and receptive qualities. Feminists reject the notion of receptivity as totally passive, recognizing that it can be an active posture. Harrison protests the rejection of "mere mutuality"; believing that mutual love is love in its deepest radicality.[13]

Barbara Andolsen points out that feminist ethicists will need to imagine radically new ways of organizing social life so that work, politics, and personal life are meshed in a way which will allow and enhance the possibilities for growth and celebration of the Presence.[14] Andolsen also makes the point, much needed in the work of ethics, that in order to envision radical new structures which integrate the feminist vision, ethicists will need to learn more about concrete conditions in the public world. The false dichotomies of personal/ political, mind/body, reason/affect have served to keep women in large measure ignorant of world realities and focused in on self. Women were to worry about the private, material and feeling side of life, while the burdens of running government and international relations were reserved for the strong shoulders of men. We have come to see that ignorance and lack of control over world affairs leads to devastation at home. We have been dutifully providing a good home and good children for men who have created weapons to destroy the homes and wars to destroy the children. The political is indeed very personal. Knowledge of business, government, and national relations is an absolute necessity if the feminist vision is to be true to it's maintenance plan of revolution.

It should be abundantly clear by now that feminist ethics is certainly not "feminine" ethics. Though many of the values and norms of feminist ethics will be those traditionally associated with women, to place these values as central is to restore them to their proper places as human values equally important and necessary for men as well as women. To speak of a feminist vision is not to identify the revolution with female bodies but to say, rather, that in the struggle for human liberation it is the work and values and strength of women's historical experiences which can offer a salvific alternative to the oppressive macho-masculine path of destruction upon which our society is launched today. Feminism draws upon the strengths of humanity while recognizing that it is the strengths associated with women which have been historically devalued. Feminist ethics will draw upon what is best among the stereotypical "masculine" virtues as well. Courage, initiative, and honesty are virtues often associated with men yet without them feminist ethics would fade from the anthem for revolution of Muzak to die by.

Directions for Feminist Ethics

Ethics is a daily human activity that begins for persons even before they have left the womb. We learn about meaning and value in life and responses to the meaning; we ask what is human, what is good, what is moral? But long before we join the search and formulate questions we are already learning answers. An infant is already learning that the world is a place of warmth, comfort and smiles, or perhaps that the world is generally unresponsive unless barraged by loud and constant demand, and then rough and angry-faced when it arrives. We begin to learn from earliest days how it is that humans act and what is valuable, so that much of our ethics proceeds from an instinctual level. We are constantly involved in a moral or immoral manner, but most often without malice or benevolence aforethought. We simply embody what we have been taught or what the culture prescribes.

If 95% of our ethical activity is not consciously so, then to have any impact upon reality feminists must focus attention in two ways. The first task is to bring more of our moral ability into conscious action. Even if only in retrospect, we must drag more of our unconscious decisions into the light of conscious reflection. This means bringing feminist perspective to the moral decision-facing process, and that will concern us as the second part of this paper.

The second task is in an area often neglected by moral theory, that of character formation. If most of our ethics proceeds from our perception of the world then feminists will have their greatest impact by nurturing one another and their children upon the new possibilities and values of the feminist vision. Believing is seeing since most of what we see lies behind our eyes. Feminist eyes must be seeing what is possible.

We have long said that the primary material for feminist theology is women's experience. So too will feminist ethics develop and enflesh itself from the stories of women's stuggles, dilemmas and decisions. Our ethics will change as our perceptions change, as our stories about reality change. Character development is a social process, a two-way street between selves and society. As we offer the vision and embodiment of new values and ways of being to one another, we slowly change reality, slowly discard patterns of alienation and oppression. The major requisite here for feminist ethics is the exercise of revolutionary patience.[15] If we can see the end of our work within our own lifetime, then we are not asking big enough questions.

Because character formation is a slowly processive reality, not easily pigeon-holed and systematized, it is frequently neglected by masculine moralists in their search for systems and methods. Feminist ethics, though, must find itself more at home with the unsystematic value and importance of the story as an ethical tool. The feminine predisposition for networking, pejoratively portrayed as gossip, is an excellent example of areas where a change of value and vision is communicated. If in our networking we are not pre-occupied with requirements of patriatrchy, then we can begin to spread the stories of our own encounter with the Presence, and struggles to enflesh the vision.

As we begin to reject the social conventions of patriarchy and the damaged instincts it has instilled as moral training, feminists become acutely aware of a need to fill the gap. Women are experiencing this in an especially painful way as they emerge in what Margaret Mead has called our "prefigurative culture." We live in a world without models. Mead writes of a time when our culture was post-figurative, that is, children could look to their grandparents and parents as models for their own futures and so too their moral lives. Today we cannot even hope for a configurative culture for the prevailing models of soicety are in upheaval, barraged by sincere but devastating challenges.

Feminists have found it necessary to reject the very concept of model as traditionally understood because it has often hidden an oppressive agenda. The notion assumed that to legitimate our present experience we must have some recourse to the past, tradition equals truth. As Mary Daly has pointed out, the notion of *imitatio Christi* as used by moral theology is especially devastating to feminists today who are living and becoming in ways unimaginable to even our mothers and grandmothers, let alone Christ and his blessed mother![16] Feminists, therefore, have not been about the formation of new models, as much as the breaking of old ones. This is not to say that we do not benefit from one another's experiences, strategies, and skills; we do. But feminist "models" are instances of enspiriting courage; strong women who influence us with infectious freedom. Their important gift is the freeing of others to become unique selves; pointing beyond limitations to the potential for further liberation.

II. Feminist Movement and Moral Decision-facing

For all the iconoclasm of the feminist vision, though , there is yet a need for some method to our seeming madness. If we are indeed a blueprint for revolution then our maintenance plan must be communicable. The dancing revolution must choreograph its patterns so that others may dance along. This second part of the paper will examine some new perspectives which the feminist vision brings to the moral decision-facing process.

Whether our conversion to the vision has been the experience of rage or reverence, feminists bring with them a strong sense that the Presence is embodied in flesh or nowhere. Feminist ethics reside in the real. An ethic abstracted from life is not ethic at all. When too much attention is focused upon systems and abstract universals what is created is oftentimes a blind willingness to sacrifice people to principles. Ethical abstractions are frequently patriarchal strategy for oppression.

Feminists ethics is well aware that our world is made for good or ill through human activity. Harrison reminds us that though this freedom is often abused, the power to create a world of moral relations is a fundamental aspect of human nature itself.[17] Occasions for moral decisions though tend to be times of exceptional awareness of our moral ability, when the moment (however long) is of supreme importance. When we attempt to embody the "awe-full, awe-some truth that we have the power through *acts of love* or lovelessness literally to *create one another*. Genuine nurturance is a formidable power."[18]

Disclosure Phase

Feminists, however, are also keenly aware that "love without strategy is little more than a fleeting feeling."[19] Hence they enter the first stage of the moral decision-facing process strongly cognizant of the need for honesty and ethical homework. This first part of the moral process is the time for disclosure or exposition of the problem; defining just what we are really deciding about. The very war in which we define our problems or pose the issues will already have launched us far into the ethical enterprise, e.g. abortion defined as killing babies or removing undesirable tissue.

Traditional moral theology has usually begun the moral process with a definition of good or right or the "nature" of something in an idealistic sense. From there it has then deduced the nature of an ethical situation. Defining the problem in this way, of course, reflects the assumptions of the system, the dominant ideology of patriarchy.

Feminist ethics however takes as its starting point concrete historical experience and, in the manner of other liberation theologies, proceeds from a reflection on praxis to a more general understanding of the ethical situation. Carol Robb reminds us that "the act of defining a problem is a political act; it is an exercise of power to have accepted one's terms of a problem."[20]

For this reason feminists bring a hermeneutic of suspicion to the disclosure phase of the process. Frequently moral problems are defined in ways which do not adequately take account of the historical experience of women, and the data gathered as relevant to the problem does not accurately reflect women's reality.

The hermeneutic of suspicion also leads to the realization that where there are differences we can make distinctions. Traditional ethics will define a moral problem in ways which reflect the assumptions of patriarchy, e.g. questions concerning the ethics of lesbian lifestyles frequently define the problem in terms of heterosexual concerns and expectations.

Educated by diversity to celebrate rather than fear pluralism, feminist ethics recognizes that ethical consensus can be a disguise for oppression. The values and responsibilities accepted by the white middle class are not the same as those which must be embraced by the poor. Celebration of ethical pluralism can lead to ethical insight. The material of feminist ethics is not limited to agreement concerning a list of principles, it is rather the personal stories of unique individuals. "If vision is the warp of feminist ethics, the lives of women are its woof."[21]

Word should also be given to the hermeneutic of suspicion and its exercise upon ourselves. Even feminist women are women raised in the culture of patriarchy and trained by its distorting systems. The exorcism of the demon from our minds is more easily accomplished than tearing it from our hearts. We must exercise some suspicion in respect to our own feeling and ideas which may be originating from patriarchal poison and not clearheaded grasp of the vision. A properly exercised hermeneutic should also be there to haunt us if we succumb to complacency. Feminist ethics is a processive, moving reality. We will never have all the answers, and besides, the questions will always be changing. Conversion to the feminist vision does not mean preservation from evil.

Discernment Phase

Defining *what* we are dealing with leads to the question *what about it*, and we are launched into the second phase of moral decision-facing, the stage of discernment or evaluation. We are, of course, involved to some degree with discernment in the definition phase as we judge and value the data collected as pertinent to our dilemma. But to a more conscious degree we must now reflect upon the possible alternatives open to us in a moral dilemma. What I will do here is suggest several sources for consultation, drawn from the feminist vision, which can offer perspective in the discernment process. These sources are most often ignored by more traditional and patriarchal ethical processes.[22]

1. Imagination and Courage

The first and most important source for feminist ethics I submit is the eye open to the vision and the heart laid bare to the touch of the Presence. If the reverence/rage response to the Presence serves as the foundation of feminist ethics, it is primarily in reference to this Presence, then, that we must base our ethical discernment process. The question becomes what alternative before me will best embody the Presence in life, further the revolution.

A requisite for feminist movement is an imagination wild enough to see the possibilities inherent in a moment, and a heart courageous enough to act upon some of them. Imagination allows us to touch upon what eye hath not seen nor hath ear heard, even as it stands before us.

Imagination and courage are both discovered and nurtured in community. It is in this sense that the retreat of women to an Otherworld of Womanspace can be a valuable and wholly thing. It is in the security and challenge of sisterhood that women begin to articulate their possibilities and glimpse the vision. If we are about hearing one another into speech then we are also about imagining and encouraging the vision into reality.

It is feminist imagination and courage which expands feminist ethics beyond the narrow perimeters of what is good and what is right. Feminists are in agreement with Marcuse when he writes, "What is can never be true."[23] systems of rules and principles can encompass us and bring us gift-wrapped to damnation if we submit to the temptation of believing that in them we hold the truth. Truth is fragmentary and fleeting like a hare running amidst our lives and moral discourse. Once we have snared it, it languishes and dies of our attempts at vivisection. Feminist imagination can never rest content with what has been or what must be or ought to be, but runs ahead with the hare to what shall be.

2. Experience

Political as well as personal amnesia maintains oppression. An important source of ethical insight for feminism is simply the anamnesis of our own history, personal and collective. In consulting our own experience feminists exercise their hermeneutic of suspicion again, for we correctly suspect that patriarchal ethics has ignored and even denied the values which well from women's experience. Consulting our own experience feminists exercise their hermenuetic of suspicion again, for we correctly suspect that patriarchal ethics has ignored and even denied the values which well from women's experience. Consulting our own experience also means not trusting what the patriarchal system defines as our experiences. The myth of the vaginal orgasm is a case in point. Patriarchy defined sexual maturity for women as the ability to leave behind the "infantile" clitoral orgasm and experience the male induced vaginal orgasm.[24] It took a long time for women to trust their own experience sufficiently to finally say there is no such thing as vaginal orgasm and deny the associations of immaturity with clitoral stimulation.

Attentiveness to experience can also yield new possibilities. Knowing the courage and imagination of our fore-sisters can give new insight to contemporary dilemmas. Knowing that as a black and a woman Rosa Parks had the courage to say "I won't get up," as she sat with tired feet in the front of the bus, could inspire sisters and brothers today to act with similar courage.

3. Affect

St. Thomas was not a notable feminist thinker but he was a sensible thinker in the most basic meaning of that word; he recognized that thought proceeds from sense knowledge. *"Nihil in intellecu nisi prius in sensu."* Feminist ethics eschews patriarchal ethics as relying upon disembodied rationality.[26] This is based, in the feminist maintenance plan on its rejection of the reason/affect dualism. Feminist ethics would correct the faulty notion that we make our most moral decision when dispassionately weighing the life struggle. Moral reason is affective, caring reason. Mere technological reason is not human in moral matters. Technological reason has its place in the disclosure phase of ethics. It allows us to formulate clearly just what we are talking about but it will not, cannot tell us what to do with our dilemma. The evaluative response must rely on reason rooted in affect.

Harrison cautions us, however, that the moral question is not "what do I feel?" but rather "what do I do with what I feel?"[27] There aren't right or wrong feelings. A feminist ethics must accept affect as a primary part of our relations with reality. Our affect is not the only source of judgement in the moral discernment process, but without it our very moral ability -- the capacity to care and value -- is severed.[28]

4. Community

Moral decisions are not isolated mathematical problems. Like pebbles cast into water the ripples of a moral decision affect the entire surface. The realization that moral decisions are embodied decisions rises from the feminist consciousness of, and commitment to community. To recognize this embodiment implies an acceptance of repsonsibility for the foreseeable effects of a moral decision upon self and community. We make decisions with an eye to their impact upon reality. This does not mean that the reactions of others should have undue influence upon us. But rather that we are as clearly as possible aware of the potential effects our moral decisions will have upon reality, and can accept the consequences.

Because feminist ethics cannot accept principles as the only word in an ethical dilemma, neither can it hide from the responsibility of embodiment. Blind reliance upon principles can lead to the sacrifice of persons. Sacrifice may indeed be required of persons as a consequence of a moral decision, but feminists should at least be clear that it flows from their understanding and acceptance of responsibility for the decision and not from a disembodied rule to which they blindly adhere.

The other side of this belief in embodiment is that not only must those who make the decision bear the consequences, but also that those who bear the consequences must have the power to make decisions. This ethic of embodiment would have implications for the birth control and abortion debate in Catholic moral theology. Those who bear the consequences of raising children must have the power to decide some regulation of their birth.

Another aspect of this communitarian element to our decisions is recognition that moral action is the primary catalyst for moral change. Until we begin to express our dissatisfaction with the system of alienation and embody alternatives in our lives, social change will not be possible. Feminists must take it upon themselves to effect the dissolution of patriarchy. We must be able to say to the system:

Seem like what drives me crazy has no effect on you But I'm gonna keep at it, till it drives you crazy too.[29]

5. Mystery

Women have struggled for the gift of life against incredible odds.[30] Perhaps because of this we are in danger of becoming *reactors* to patriarchy rather than actors and builders of our own visions. We must pause in the struggle to celebrate our strength and place this strength at the center of our ethics. Feminist strength is the result of openness to mystery.

Our sense of mystery is the ability to experience the depth of life. It is a sense of the profound value of life which has kept women struggling against the incredible odds, knowing that the heart finds more than what meets the eye. Openness to mystery is two-edged. It allows us to recognize and rejoice in our power in our moral ability to create one another. But it has a darker side too, reminding us that for all our sound and fury the spiral of life and death will go on. But this is of comfort too, to know that death is but the balance of life, not a fiend to be feared but a partner with whom we must dance. In embracing mystery we embrace our own limitations in laying hold of the gift of life.

Openness to mystery is the child of reverence and rage. It is a sense that her Presence reaches us in unexpected ways, that we are cradled by a gracious parent. There will be moral dilemmas when our partner death leads the dance, when no alternative can relieve the anguish and we rage to see our vision denied. Yet as a child fighting sleep will finally abandon in the arms of a parent, so, too, will we at times, relinquish in trust and hope to the tender embrace of her redemptive Presence.

Embodiment Phase

A sadly neglected aspect of moral decision-facing has been the last stage of the proceess, that of moral decision-living. Once a decision has been made there begins a whole process of self-accepting commitment.[31] The moral strength of our decisions resides in our ability to embody them.

We may choreograph beautiful new patterns in our process of discernment but unless we are ready to make our decisions a part of the dance, the revolution will go on without us. All too often women and others suffering oppression are able to complete the disclosure and discernment stages of facing a moral dilemma, but lack the self-acceptance and self-confidence necessary to follow through. It is a problem of what Mary Daly has called existential courage. Frequently the dilemmas faced and decisions made by women and other aliens pull them into a confrontation with the destruction which is patriarchy and their own non-being is that system. Frightened by this confrontation many persons slip quietly away from their dilemmas, closing their eyes and hearts. The situation is often such for many battered women.

Intrinsic to this final stage of moral choice is an adequate notion of freedom. Feminists must be aware that the making and embodying of choice *opens* the possibilities for freedom rather than limits them. Abstractions about freedom keep us paralyzed in non-action. Unless it is embodied, real freedom does not exist. Decisions flow *from* our personhood and *form* our personhood, making real freedom the ability to become ourselves, to choose who we will become and embody the reality. Failure to face a moral dilemma or failure to live our decisions will both rob us of the freedom of becoming.

Here again there is the need for revolutionary patience. We must be able to *live* with controversy and contradiction. Our moral decisions will always be particular, partial, provisional responses because they are real; the concrete is always partial. We must be able to live in that, not bound and determined by it, but living in the process of it.

It may be well to sound a sober tone about moral decision-living. The movement of feminists is indeed perceived as revolution today. Conversion to the vision is treason to patriarchy. As other revolutionaries can witness, living the vision may come to mean dying. Beverly Harrison reminds us that

> *radical love* creates dangerous precedents and lofty expectations among human beings. Those in power believe such love to be unrealistic because those touched by the power of such love tend to develop a reluctance to accept anything less than mutuality and self-respect, anything less than human dignity, anything less than an authentic relatedness. It is for this reason that such persons become powerful threats to the status quo.[32]

The lives of Jesus, of Martin Luther King, of the four church women killed in El Salvador serve as powerful witness that the vision is serious and dangerous reality.

But it is our commitment to this reality, to the enfleshing of her presence which gives power and meaning to our lives. It is our call to build a new heaven and earth which keeps us willing to risk, even unto the final dance with our partner death, so that the power of love may become real in our world. And our ends shall not be passive acquiescence to crucifixion, but our struggle to see them stopped. So that

> swinging our great grandmothers' bones we shall not die by our own hands.[33]

NOTES

1. I use the terms feminism and feminist ethics normatively and not descriptively. I.e., I speak of what ethics should be if genuinely informed by feminist movement. Similarly, in my efforts to express what feminism at its best is struggling to be, I tend to use terms such as moral theology and traditional ethics descriptively rather than normatively, i.e., thinking of them in terms of what they are patriarchally rather than what they are struggling to become when open to feminist consciousness and sensibility.

2. Traditionally the tarantalla originated as a wildly energetic dance in which a person engaged following a poisonous spider bite, in an effort to sweat the poison out of the system. The energetic movement of feminists is often an attempt to have a similar effect upon the poisonous bite of patriarchy.

3. Eleanor Humes Haney offers a similar discussion of fidelity to the feminist vision as the key to understanding feminist ethics. See "What is Feminist Ethics? A Proposal for Continuing Discussion" *Journal of Religious Ethics* 8 (1980) 116-17.

4. For an excellent discussion of the perception of value as the foundational moral experience, see Daniel C. Maguire, *The Moral Choice* (Garden City, N.Y.: Doubleday, 1978).

5. Rosemary Radford Ruether, *New Woman New Earth* (New York: Seabury, 1975) 3.

6. See above, n. 1 for my use of the term feminist ethics.

7. Beverly Wildung Harrison, "The Power of Anger in the Work of Love," Ethics for Women and Other Strangers; *Union Seminary Quarterly Review* 36 (suppl. 1981) 49.

8. *Ibid*.

9. An example quoted by Daniel Maguire, "The Feminization of God and Ethics," *Christianity and Crisis* 42, 4 (1982) 61.

10. Domatila Barrios de Chungara, *Let Me Speak!* (trans. Victoria Ortiz; *Monthly Review;* New York, 1978) 203.

11. Mary Daly, *Beyond God the Father* (Boston: Beacon, 1973) 100.

12. Barbara Hilkert Andolsen, "The Journal of Religious Ethics" 9 (1981) 78.

13. Harrison, "Power of Anger" 52.

14. Barbara Andolsen, "Agape in Feminist Ethics" 79.

15. A phrase used by Dorothee Solle, *Revolutionary Patience* (Maryknoll, N.Y.: Orbis, 1974).

16. Daly, *Beyond God the Father,* 74

17. Harrison, "Power of Anger" 47.

18. *Ibid*. 48.

19. Robert M. Cooper, "Faith, Hope and Love: Three Books," *Cross Currents* 23 (1974) 337.

20. Carol Robb, "A Framework for Feminist Ethics," *Journal of Religious Ethics* 9 (1981) 50.

21. Haney, "Feminist Ethics" 117.

22. For a fully developed model of moral decision-making I recommend Maguire, *The Moral Choice*, as a work highly compatible with the feminist vision.

23. Herbert Marcuse, *One Dimensional Man* (Boston: Beacon, 1964) 124.

24. Rosemary Radford Ruether, *New Woman New Earth* 139.

25. Harrison, "Power of Anger" 49.

26. *Ibid*.

27 *Ibid*.

28. For further discussion on the role of affect in moral decisions see Maguire *The Moral Choice* esp. 281-305.

29. Quoted by Jacquelyn Grant during a presentation at a workshop on feminist theology, Women's Spirit Bonding. July 11-17, 1982, Grailville, Ohio.

30. Harrison, "Power of Anger" 45.

31. This third stage of the moral decision-facing process was first suggested to me by Mary Louise Young, August of 1982.

32. Harrison, "Power of Anger" 52.

33. From a poem by Marge Piercy.

COMPUTER ETHICS:
TYPES OF ISSUES BEING RAISED
Edward Stevens

Computer Ethics is finding its way into curricula as a distinct field in applied ethics. This article is aimed at teachers desiring to introduce such a course or module into their curriculum. It outlines three kinds of issues currently debated in the recent and growing body of writing about computer ethics. These are: (1) Social Impact Issues, (2) Legal and Professional Issues, and (3) Metaphysical Issues.

1. Social Impact Issues

These issues are less "computer-specific" than the other two areas. The problems raised and the principles for solution parallel problems and principles in other areas of applied ethics. Also, it is social impact issues that are most often disussed in the press and popular media. Consider the following.

Telecommuting:--Here we see cottage industry issues raised now in the form of the electronic cottage. What is the social and ethical impact of the home's becoming the workplace? Those self-employed at their home computers (lawyers, accountants, management consultants) must weigh the impact on family members and on self-development of this career style. But more acute issues of justice arise for clerical workers employed by others at home (word-processors, copy-editors, file-managers). Is there potential for abuse here similar to that inflicted on home piece-workers in the garment industry? Is low-level telecommuting a career dead end for the telecommuter cut off from informal daily contact with supervisors and colleagues? What potential human abuses cause labor unions (like the organization, 9 to 5) to frown on this workstyle?

Access to Computer Technology.--Has computer literacy become as essential to American living as have verbal literacy, television, and the automobile? People deprived of transportation, access to media, and ability to read are effectively deprived of basic human rights in American society. Can the same be said for denial of access to computer literacy? Information becomes access to power. Students in the nation's poorest school districts are four times less likely to have access to computers as students in the most affluent districts.[1] Questions, too, have been raised about women's access to this technology. Does a society organized around the computer favor the male's penchant for distancing and non-intimacy? In the light of Carol Gilligan's "women's different voice", has the computer become a new way of systemically excluding women from power?[2]

Impact on the Workplace.--Radiation danger and supervisory abuse are two workplace problem areas. Note, for example, that pregnant VDT workers have thrice the normal number of problem pregnancies. Industry is facing up to this problem, but not so, the problem of supervisory abuse of VDT and clerical workers. There is the growing practice of monitoring their work by computer--the exact amount of time spent with the terminal, the number of mistakes made, the amount of work accomplished. The human is made to march to an electronic beat. The computer becomes master rather than tool. Human dignity and freedom suffer. How balance workplace efficiency against human boredom and stress? [3]

Privacy.--Computer technology brings a new dimension and urgency to the traditional ethical concern for the right to privacy. With instantaneous speed, computer records about you can be sold, given away, traded, or stolen, can be used to make decisions about your credit, insurance, education, medical care, employment, consumer behavior, taxes, and law enforcement. A small error can grow and multiply. And all this without your knowledge or consent. In sum, the most intimate data about individuals are being amassed, are instantaneously accessible even to those with no right to the data, are bought and sold without the individual's knowledge or consent and used for purposes often harmful to the individual and beyond the intentions of the intitial data-gatherers. This is a social impact issue that ethicians and policy makers have only begun to tackle.[4] At issue, again, is whether computers will detract from or enhance human freedom and self-determination.

2. Legal and Professional Issues

This next area turns from the impact of computers on society at large to the duties of computer professionals. Here, teachers of professional ethics have two major resources. The first consists of the codes of ethics drawn up by professional associations such as the Association for Computing Machinery (ACM), The Association of Data Processing Service Organizations (ADAPSO), The American Society for Information Science (ASIS), and the Data Processing Management Association (DPMA). The second resource is a book of cases used by almost all teachers of computer ethics today, Donn B. Parker's *Ethical Conflicts in Computer Science and Technology* (Arlington, Va.: AFIPS Press, 1979).

These sources deal with ethical conflicts common to all professions (e.g., instances of professional demands clashing with personal morality). But more often they deal with issues specific to the computer professional, e.g., with "theft" of computer time. Is it licit to use your company's computers during off-hours for personal ends if there is no appreciable cost to the company? Is the computer more like air-conditioning, part of the environment, or more like the company car?

We will not attempt here a list of professional ethical concerns. Rather, we will illustrate the work that still needs to be done by focussing on just one issue, the legal and ethical question of who owns computer programs. Computers have created new types of assets, and ownership issues remain hopelessly murky. Judgements about individuals copying software for their friends or for themselves, and judgments about the applicability in the commercial world of patent, copyright, and trade secrecy laws await the resolution of these ownership issues. In the matter of software, who owns what, and why?

First, the "what". what is a software program? A program at heart is an idea for a computational solution to a problem. So once a problem is clearly formulated, the solution is expressed step by step, ususally in flowchart form. This problem-solving idea, the algorithm, is a most valuable and yet most intangible component of the asset we call computer software. Next, this algorithm is expressed or coded usually in a high level computer language like Fortran or Pascal or Cobol. This coded set of instructions is a second valuable and more tangible component of the asset under discussion. It is called the *source program*. Finally, the source program is fed into the computer and "translated" (by an operating system program called a "compiler") into low level machine language that sets the computer's switches to execute the algorithm. This is called the *object program*. It is the third component of this valuable asset called computer software.

It is easy to see the necessity here for the cooperation of ethicians, lawyers and computer professionals to determine the moral and legal rights and duties revolving around this new type of asset created by computer technology. Does the programmer have the right to exclusive control over the product of his or her labor? If the product is intangible--the algorithm, then the programmer is not deprived of the product when another appropriates it. They both share the same problem-solving idea. But the other can deprive the originator of profit. Should not the orignator of the idea be able to profit from it, as well as "own" it? Once I have your algorithm, I can write my source code and object code, and profit from your idea. Law and ethics are closely entwined here, and neither has yet come fully to grips with the reality of the kind of assett involved.

Copyright laws can be brought to bear to protect the tangible expressions of the algorithm, the source code and object code, but not the most valuable component, the underlying alogrithm itself. Trade secret agreements aim at keeping the programs out of the hands of others altogether. Licensing agreements give the buyer the use but not the ownership of software. The label on the package of the program you buy for your microcomputer pretends to sell you a license to use the program, but not ownership of it. Lawyers protest the appropriatness of such licenses, divorced, as they are, from trade secrets.[5]

Patent laws attempt to protect the right of programmers to profit from their work. But it remains to be clearly determined whether software is a patentable entity. Patent laws consider it against the common good to patent entities in the realm of nature that are and should remain the common property of all. Mathematical formulas and forms of life are such entities. We have heard during the past few years the debate over the products of DNA research: are they to be considered patentable artifacts or natural life forms? We hear now a similar debate about computer algorithms: are they patentable constructs or mathematical formulas?

This comment on the ownership issue in computer ethics illustrates the kind of work that needs to be done on those issues where law, ethics and computer science overlap. Especially, the very terms of the disussion need to be clarified. Words like "hardware", "software", and "program" are more confusing than useful for determining ethical and legal rights and duties. The human and social realities and behaviors that underlie these words need to be made explicit so that their ethical and legal consequences can be grappled with.

3. Metaphysical Issues

The issues that cut most deeply are what I have called metaphysical. They involve the meaning of human intelligence and the meaning of "human" itself. They arise out of the objectives and interpretation of Artificial Intelligence (AI) reseach.

Hardcore AI operates under the assumption that computers can, at least in principle, duplicate and even surpass human intelligence. Mathematician Alan Turing suggested the test for whether machines are intelligent. Go into a room where there are two terminals, one connected to a human and the other to a computer. If, by judging the feedback you get from each terminal, you cannot tell which is the human and which the computer, you may safely say that the computer is intelligent. This is "Turing's Test". [6] The popular program, ELIZA, that simulates a psychiatrist's responses, is an imperfect fulfillment of Turing's Test. Computer chess programs are more successful simulations. It may be objected that these programs only do what the humans programmed them to do. A truly human simulation will be a computer which is able to do *more* than you tell it to do. Heuristic programming and parallel processing are moving in this direction. The first involves giving the computer general principles rather than specific steps for problem-solving. The second involves several programs working in parallel rather than in series, and together coming up with solutions that not one of them alone could have managed. Here the computer system as a whole is qualitatively different from the sum of the parts, i.e., from the limited agency of the separate programs. And, say the hard core AI advocates, this is a way we think about living things!

Clearly hard core AI is behaviorism redivivus. What counts is what the computer does. A unitary agent, an "I", intentionality--these are all irrelevant. It is enough that computers accomplish their result. The intention to accomplish the result is irrelevant to the result. They accomplish what humans need intelligence to accomplish, and that is enough. This is Turing's test: a perfect simulation of intelligence is intelligence.

Soft core AI, on the other hand, sees lack of intentionality as a crucial failing. Intentionality is essential for assigning responsibility and motivating actions. It imputes reward and punishment to the person, not the deed. To dismiss intentionality, in this view, is to court misunderstanding of the computer itself. This is the fallacy of mystification that has so bedeviled our lives in the computer age. It attributes human qualities to the computer that it does not have, often surrendering responsibility to the computer for everything from sending an erroneous invoice, to starting a nuclear war.

The ethical import of this AI debate focusses on autonomy. Is the computer an independent agent to which humans must conform? Yes, say employers, who use computers to monitor and pace their employees. Yes, say teachers who use Computer Aided Instruction (CAI), to drill and condition their students into desired responses.

Or on the other hand, are human beings the primary agents, not the servants of computers but using computers as tools for human ends? If so, CAI will more likely see students programming computers, than the other way around.

The first view looks to a society run by technological rationality controlled by computers; the second sees society governed by human rationality and autonomy enhanced by computers.

Conclusion

The computer is a "defining technology". As did the movement of human beings from a hunting to an agricultural economy, or from guns to atomic weaponry, computer technology has redefined humanity's self-image and relationship to nature. Herein lies the deepest import of computer ethics. And the central impact of the social, legal, professional and metaphysical issues outlined above is on human autonomy. All of these issues could be reframed from these two points of view: (1) the autonomy we cede to the computer; (2) the autonomy we retain and enhance for ourselves by using the computer.

NOTES

1. See *Infoworld* 5 (No. 44) 33. On telecommuting, see "Home is Where the Job is," *Ibid.* (April 23, 1984) 30-36.

2. Dr. Margaret Hinning and Anne Jardin, *The Managerial Woman* (New York: Doubleday Anchor, 1983). Dorothy Heller and June Bower also address obstacles to women's access to computers in *Computer Confidence: A Woman's Guide* (Washington, D.C.: Acropolis Books, 1983). The latter tends to be patronizing of women, answering such burning questions as "Will It Blow Up If I Touch It?".

3. Highly recommended is Craig Brod and Wes St. John, *Technostress: The Human Cost of the Computer Revolution* (Reading, MA: Addison-Wesley, 1984) in which are discussed both computerphobia and over-identification with computer technology, as well as abuses of computers in the supervision of employees. Douglas W. Johnson, *Computer Ethics: A Guide for a New Age* (Elgin, IL: Brethren, 1984) is a useful discussion at the level of the individual and microcomputer usage.

4. See Arthur R. Miller, "Computers and Privacy," in W. Michael Hoffman and Jennifer Mills Moore, eds., *Ethics and the Management of Computer Technology* (Boston, MA: Oelgeschlager, Gunn & Hain, 1982) 93-114. This is a very useful collection of articles from the Fourth National Conference on Business Ethics at Bentley College, Waltham, MA.

5. See Roy N. Freed (Founder of the Computer law Association), "The Demands of High Tech Lawyering," *The New York Times* (Sunday, Oct. 2, 1983) F3. Dr. Deborah G. Johnson has an excellent discussion of ownership issues in her upcoming book *Computer Ethics* (due December, 1984). And of course, Donn Parker's book of cases cited in the text above is a classic for Professional Computer Ethics. Also, be aware of the *Computer Law Journal,* and alert for an upcoming issue of *Metaethics* to be devoted to Computer Ethics.

6. See J. David Boltert, *Turing's Man: Western Culture in the Computer Age* (Chapel Hill, NC: U. of North Carolina, 1984; and for a view of hard core AI, Igor Aleksander and Piers Burnett, *Reinventing Man: The Robot Becomes Reality* (New York: Holt, Rinehart and Winston, 1984). For an excellent treatment of the psychology and sociology of computers including the status of the AI debate, see Sherry Turkele, *The Second Self: Computers and the Human Spirit* (New York: Simon and Schuster, 1984).

CONTRIBUTORS

Robert C. Ayers is adjunct professor of humanities at the College of Technology, SUNY at Utica/Rome. His research has focused on F. X. Kraus and liberal Catholicism at the turn of the century.

James J. Bacik, campus minister and adjunct professor of humanities at the University of Toledo, is the author of *Apologetics and the Eclipse of Mystery* (1980). He was the writer for the editorial committee of the U.S. Bishops' 1985 pastoral on campus ministry, "Empowered by the Spirit." He is currently working on a book on great religious teachers of the 20th century.

Denise Lardner Carmody is professor and chair of the faculty of religion and director of the Warren Center for Catholic Studies at the University of Tulsa. A prolific author, her most recent works are: *The Double Cross: Ordination, Abortion and Catholic Feminism* (1986), *Caring for Marriage* (1986), and *Exploring the New Testament* (1987). She is currently engaged in a study of biblical women.

Robert J. Daly, S.J., editor of this volume, is professor and chairperson of the theology department at Boston College. His books include *The Origins of the Christian Doctrine of Sacrifice* (1978), *Christian Biblical Ethics* (1984), and *Christians and the Military: The Early Experience* (co-author, 1985). He is currently working on a study of sacrifice in Origen.

Nathan R. Kollar is professor of religious studies at St. John Fisher College, Rochester, New York. He is the author of *Songs of Suffering* (1982) and *Options in Roman Catholicism* (1983). He is presently working on the relationship of secular fundamentalism to American culture.

Catherine Mowry LaCugna is assistant professor of theology at the University of Notre Dame. She has written "The Relational God: Aquinas and Beyond" (1985), "Philosophers and Theologians on the Trinity" (1986), and "Problems with a Trinitarian Formulation" (1984-85). She is currently preparing a book on trinitarian theology.

Frances M. Leap is adjunct professor of theology at Marian College, Fond du Lac, Wisconsin. She wrote her dissertation at Marquette University on the significance of feminist theology for ethics, and is currently doing research in Christology.

Joseph T. Merkt, a theology consultant for the Office of Catholic Schools and lecturer and chaplain at Spalding University in Louisville, wrote his dissertation on theological method in Aquinas' theology of hope. A theological consultant for several publication of the N.C.E.A., he is currently involved in a research project analyzing parental religious knowledge, attitudes and practices in the Archdiocese of Louisville.

David J. O'Brien is professor of history at the College of the Holy Cross, Worcester, Massachusetts. Among his numerous works are: *American Catholics and Social Reform: The New Deal Years* (1986), *The Renewal of American Catholicism* (1972) and, with Thomas Shannon, *Renewing the Earth: Catholic Documents on Justice, Peace and Liberation* (1978). He is currently working on a biography of Isaac Hecker.

William L. Portier is associate professor of theology at Mount Saint Mary's College, Emmitsburg, Maryland. His writings include: *Isaac Hecker and the First Vatican Council* (1985) and "Isaac Hecker and 'Testem Benevolentiae': A Study in Theological Pluralism" in *Hecker Studies* (1983). He is currently working on John R. Slattery as missionary and modernist.

Margaret M. Reher is chairperson of the department of religion at Cabrini College, Radnor, Pennsylvania. She has written on Americanism in *Theological Studies* and *Dialogue*, and is currently working on a study of American Catholic intellectual life.

Edward Stevens is professor of religious studies at Regis College, Weston, Massachusetts. Among his works are: *The Morals Game* (1978), *Business Ethics* (1979), and *Making Moral Decisions* (1984). He is currently doing research on emerging issues in business ethics.

J. Milburn Thompson, an assistant professor of religious studies at St. Joseph College, West Hartford, Connecticut, is the convenor of the ethics section of the C.T.S. His articles and reviews have been published in *Emmanuel, Fellowship,* and *Choice.*

Rodger Van Allen is professor of religious studies at Villanova University. A former president of the C.T.S. (1982-84) and co-founder of *Horizons,* he is the author of *The Commonweal and American Catholicism* (1974) and the editor of *American Religious Values and the Future of America* (1978). He recently (1986) published an expansion and updating of John Cogley's *Catholic America.*

Thomas E. Wangler is associate professor of church history at Boston College. Among his numerous publications on American Catholicism are: "Birth of Americanism" (1972), and "American Catholic Expansionism" (1982). He is currently working on a history of the religious life of American Catholics.

INDEX OF PERSONS